The New Teacher

9780060427337

"Critical Issues in Education"
Under the Advisory Editorship of Louis Fischer

FOR JAMES JARRETT
AND TORSTEN LUND

THE NEW
TEACHER
Copyright © 1973 by **G. Louis Heath**

Printed in the United States of America. All rights reserved. No part of this book may be used or reproduced in any manner whatsoever without written permission except in the case of brief quotations embodied in critical articles and reviews. For information address Harper & Row, Publishers, Inc., 10 East 53rd Street, New York, N.Y. 10022.

Standard Book Number: 06-042733-7

Library of Congress
Catalog Card Number: 72-11497

The New Teacher

G. Louis Heath

Illinois State University

Harper & Row, Publishers
New York, Evanston, San Francisco, London

Contents

Editor's Introduction
Preface

1 Community Relations 1
2 Teacher Aides 20
3 Teacher Organizations 37
4 Accountability and Vouchers 59
5 Alternatives 78
6 Student Rebellion 99
7 Ecology Education 111
8 Sensitivity Education 127
9 Sex Education 143
10 Drug Education 154
11 New Media 166
12 Minorities 179

Editor's introduction

In a diverse, pluralistic culture the institutions, policies, and practices of education will be influenced by the major disagreements of the times. Education in America, a diverse nation searching to define its brand of pluralism, most certainly reflects the major conflicts of the culture.

The dominant tradition of our past attempted to keep the public schools above or away from the controversies of the times and attempted to transmit a common core of learnings. Those tranquil days are gone, perhaps forever. Today, consistent with John Gardner's phrase that "education is the servant of all our purposes," various interest groups attempt to influence and even control public education. Such groups represent political and economic diversities; racial, ethnic, and religious preferences; business interests, conservationists, internationalists, isolationists; proponents of women's liberation, sex education, and sensitivity training, to name but the best-known voices. In addition to these influences from the culture at large, developments more indigenous to schooling must also be considered. Among these are the various forces urging innovation, accountability, professionalism for teachers, and community control. They are concerned with combating institutional racism and sexism, violence in the schools, and the civil rights of teachers and students.

Teachers must become informed about these issues and conflicts if they are to function as professionals. Toward this end, a beginning must be made in teacher education programs and continued into a teacher's maturing years. The titles in this series were conceived with such a goal in mind. Each volume can stand on its own, yet the several volumes are easily relatable. This arrangement maximizes flexibility for professors who may select one or more volumes, while the student's budget is also respected.

The authors were selected on the basis of their competence as well as their ability to write for an audience of nonspecialists, be they teachers, prospective teachers, or others interested in the dominant issues in our culture that influence the schools.

Louis Fischer
Amherst, Massachusetts

Preface

The teacher and school are vested with the power to define the formal learning experiences of our society's youth. When they use that power intelligently and humanely to promote genuine learning, they have more than the power granted by law; they have authority, or power that has been legitimized.

The legitimation or justification of the legal power to determine the learning experiences of students is the responsibility of the school and the teacher. Schools fulfill this responsibility partly by acting in response to recent trends and innovations in both educational and social contexts. This book is devoted to a discussion of the most crucial frameworks in which the teacher and school must act responsibly to preserve their authority for the teacher-learning process, to insure that they are not merely wielding unjustified power. Thus this book is about the critical educational issues of the day. It is a discussion of the specific new ways educational institutions and teaching staffs must relate to contemporary learners so that they do not become anachronistic.

Rapid change in American society has had a disorienting impact on the public school teacher. Unless the teacher can deal adequately with the school environment, he may develop a severe neurosis that is not at all conducive to the continued institutionalization of the teaching role. The teacher must become new. He must become the "New Teacher," imbued with pedagogical professionalism, expertise, and relevance.

As the traditional teacher becomes the New Teacher, the entire network of authority relations and responsibilities that focus on him must be radically revised. A radical reconstitution of the teacher's role vis-à-vis the school and society is essential to the maintenance of the instructional role as a creative, vital, and ennobling influence in our society. For the teacher, renewal is tantamount to survival.

This book discusses the changing patterns of authority and responsibility that make the New Teacher necessary. It also considers and analyzes the forces and programs—some initiated by teachers, others beyond immediate control—that are operative in renewing the way the historically very traditional American teacher relates to old clienteles. We see how the New Teacher can meet the serious challenges of our time in order to redefine conventional forms of authority and produce a renaissance in the classroom.

G. Louis Heath

The New Teacher

1
Community relations

The school is an integral part of the society. Whether the school relates well or badly to the society determines a great deal of what happens to and in the schools. The social composition of both the student body and the community that controls the schools, the degree to which the school uses community resources for educational purposes, and the organization of the school substantially determine the quality of relations between school and community. A major issue in education today is how the school can share authority for the educational experience with the community. Today's teacher should be familiar with the crucial issues, history, and forms that the sharing of authority has assumed.

THE URBAN DISENCHANTMENT

The problem in the relation between school and society is focused in the inner-city. Local communities in the inner-city have become very angered at the failure of school desegregation plans and compensatory education programs. Minority group members in some cities have concluded that the white school establishment cannot or will not meet their educational needs. Some feel that conventional education is not enough—educational programs must transmit the minority culture. Some maintain that integration and compensatory education are not essential to the education of disadvantaged students. After all, why must a black kid sit next to a white kid in order to learn? Integration is surely a racist myth. And compensatory education assumes that the problem of the minority group child is that he is not white and proceeds to compensate accordingly. What is really needed, the disenchanted inner-city dwellers say, is community control of education: The community alone can provide a high-quality, relevant educational program. Token gestures like one-way busing and Headstart are not enough.[1]

The major force in ghetto life throughout the 1960s has been the thrust toward involvement. The efforts of the civil rights movement, the antipoverty program, the Urban Coalition, and foundations and universities have raised the expectations of central-city residents. They have now mobilized to compel an improvement of their condition. Nothing short of a revolution has come to the ghetto. The white backlash cannot stem it because the community control movement is part of the larger process of social change that engulfs us all.[2]

A HISTORY OF COMMUNITY CONTROL[3]

Although the community control problem was a major issue in the 1960s, control of schools is not a new problem. It began in the period after the 1890s, when city schools were governed by mammoth school boards. Members were appointed or elected on the ward level. Politicians included the schools in the patronage system. They awarded jobs and contracts as political favors. School board committees handled the governance of the schools. They discharged such responsibilities as examining applicants, choosing textbooks, and awarding printing contracts. This situation promoted widespread corruption.

Reformers began to campaign for a more rational administrative system. They advocated a small school board of community leaders, a professional superintendent, and an administrative staff directly accountable to the superintendent. This reform took place throughout the school systems of the nation between the turn of the century and 1920. Not only did the school boards become smaller but the power of the superintendent increased greatly.

The structure of city school governance remained constant between 1920 and the early 1960s. It saw the schools through the Depression, the demands of two wars, and the great enrollment fluctuations that accompanied those wars. Demographic trends after 1950 transformed the central cities into black ghettos while the suburbs became largely middle class and white. As a consequence, schools in city and suburb became more racially and socioeconomically homogeneous. The minorities in the cities increasingly demanded better service from their schools. Almost simultaneously, a militant urban teacher union movement came to power. Unfortunately, the minority demands upon the schools often constituted a criticism of the organized professionals who taught in them. This led to a tragic clash between the civil rights movement for teachers and the civil rights movement for minorities. At this point, the old model of city school governance collapsed. The minorities questioned whether schools run by middle-class white communities could meet their needs. They criticized what they regarded as the inflexibility and irrelevance of the schools. They demanded control of their schools. Thus the movement for community control of schools began.

RECENT DECENTRALIZATION HISTORY

Decentralization involves the reorganization of an entire school system into a number of semiautonomous districts.[4] It originally became attractive in New York when the city tax commission advised that the city's schools could qualify for substantially more state aid if the entire system were divided into five districts. On the basis of the report, the Board of Education endorsed decentralization. The Ford Foundation followed suit by announcing in July 1967 that it would finance planning for three decentralized demonstration districts.

The state legislature appropriated additional funds for the New York City schools contingent upon the development of a decentralization plan. The "Bundy Committee," appointed to draw up a plan, delivered a proposal that was much more far-reaching than originally anticipated. The Bundy Committee recommended thirty to sixty semiautonomous districts. Each district was to have a governing board composed of six members elected by the community and five appointed by the mayor. This direct form of citizen participation in educational decision making frightened the United Federation of Teachers. The union aggressively lobbied the state legislature to reject the Bundy report as a directive for policy. The legislature responded to teacher power and did not accept the Bundy recommendations.[5]

New York City is the foremost example of the dynamics of decentralization among the nearly thirty cities that have attempted some form of decentralization in the 1960s. It is in New York City that the struggle has been most intense, perhaps because the mistakes and problems have been so great. The problems are aggravated by the fact that although more than half the students are black or Puerto Rican, about 95 percent of the administrators and more than 90 percent of the teachers are white. The failure of highly publicized compensatory education programs and integration schemes, racial tension, insufficient resources, and bureaucratic rigidity have contributed substantially to the incapacity of the schools to educate well. The learning environment of the New York schools has been thoroughly deficient, providing the perfect backdrop for community control conflict.[6]

The decentralization of some New York schools into semiautonomous demonstration districts in 1967 was an attempt to involve the people and capitalize on the energy and concern of the community in order to reform the schools. Three demonstration districts were established: Intermediate School 201, Two Bridges, and Ocean Hill-Brownsville. The intent was to open the educational hierarchy so that information and participation could flow from the bottom up. This was the concept of a federalism that would allow community and hierarchy, citizen and professional to share in educational decision making. However, granting the local governing board broad, ill-defined powers proved disastrous. The local board in the Ocean Hill-Brownsville district began firing and transferring "racist" white (mostly Jewish) teachers and replacing them with black teachers. This practice precipitated a nationally prominent confrontation that led to charges of black anti-Semitism.

In Ocean Hill-Brownsville, the community determination of who should teach collided head-on with the professionalism of teachers and with their strong union, the United Federation of Teachers. The union argued that the local board could not hire and fire teachers at will. The local board insisted on that right. Tragically, the civil rights movement and the movement toward professional status for teachers had collided. This collision of professionalism and civil rights promises to repeat many times unless a way can be found for the two interests to work together.

THE PRESENT THREAT

Decentralization and community control seem to be a particularly serious threat to the teacher's professional prerogatives because they deny the conventional assumptions of education. The professional determination of who teaches and what should be taught and even tenure and salaries are challenged by community control advocates who claim that only the people know what is relevant and useful education. This militant affront is disconcerting at a time when much of the major struggle for teacher recognition and the right to participate in policy formulation has been won. Now, abruptly, community control threatens to collapse the movement for professionalism that teachers have worked arduously to build.[7]

The community control movement threatens the organized power of teachers. It is only through acting collectively, even to the point of striking, that they wield any political clout at all. If teacher organizations must bargain with a multiplicity of school boards, their position is considerably weakened. They will no longer be able to present a united front in order to bargain for a single, advantageous contract. They must deal with many adversaries over many issues on many fronts. Their unity will be greatly undermined. In fact, the teacher organizations regard complete decentralization and community control as equivalent to the destruction of the teacher union movement (see Chapter 3).

Teachers will not relinquish their hard-won professional rights easily. They won their power when reformers extricated education from local machine politics. Community control seems an ugly device for breaking down the professional standards they have since established to guarantee a separation of education and politics and to maintain a high quality of teaching and allow minorities access to the teaching profession, an opportunity that has not always historically been attained. Recently, however, as the historic New York City crisis exemplifies, some minority members have claimed that the standards have continued to keep them out of the educational system rather than letting them in.

COMMUNITY CONTROL AND DESEGREGATION

Although opponents of community control contend that community control impedes the efforts to desegregate our schools and society, community control advocates say this argument is not valid. Segregation has increased since 1954, but community control advocates were not yet active during most of this period. Thus there is no proof that community control is particularly injurious to desegregation.

The advocates stress that a difference exists between desegregation and integration. *Desegregation* simply means the physical proximity of different races. *Integration* means people relating to one another as equals. If integration is, in fact, the eventual societal goal, it is imperative that all minority groups first achieve a stable identity and control of their institutions. Once they have realized a significant degree of environmental control, they will be in an excellent position to relate to members of white society as equals rather than as the "socially disadvantaged," or whatever the current term may be.

The stated goal of desegregation is quality education for all. But desegregation cannot produce universal quality education unless there is universal desegregation. In view of the fact that segregation has increased since 1954, it seems reasonable to consider alternatives. The alternative now being considered is, of course, community control. The persistence of segregation and inferior education for minorities makes community control an appealing option. When everything else has failed, why not involve the inner-city community? All of the 85 percent of the ghetto children who cannot read,[8] can't be unintelligent—perhaps the problem is not with the learner but with the institution. If so, reform is not likely to come from within the institution but must be fashioned from without.

POLITICIZATION AND PARTICIPATION

The latent danger in community control is that educational standards will become political, that the curriculum will focus not on skills and values but only on values, and that teachers who do not espouse those values will not be hired or will be fired immediately. If this happens, community control of schools will offer no improvement on the present system. It will produce just as inflexible and monolithic a system as we now endure. However, the dangers that accompany the plan should not obscure the human necessity for a reform that allows people, especially the historically disenfranchised and deprived minorities, to contribute to a determination of the kind of education they will devote a substantial part of their lives to. The basic question is legitimacy, not prerogatives and professionalism.

Community representatives should participate in the selection of teachers. This process must, of course, be safeguarded by policies requiring minimum qualifications of candidates. Community involvement in selection would allow cooperation between citizen and school to be much more easily achieved. This approach would tend to prevent friction between school and community.[9]

Each school should establish a school council and charge it with several responsibilities. The council should keep parents, staff, and students informed of the activities and accomplishments of the school in order to foster greater participation in the life of the school. It should plan for the representation of the school in community organizations and at major events in the life of the community. It should hear appeals by parents, students, or faculty and deliver prompt decisions. The council should be composed of parents, school employees, and at least one student, except at the elementary school level. Each member would be elected by his respective constituency. The principal would serve as an executive officer.[10]

In a situation of maximum community control, a locality does not share decision-making powers with a central school board. The local board has the same jurisdiction and authority as any other school district board in a state. It independently carries out the responsibilities for education with which the state has charged it. Schools are not part of the city school system but function as autonomous school districts. In this capacity, they can recruit, hire, transfer, and release faculty and staff. They may also generate a lot of friction and problems in the process. Safeguards are, of course, necessary to prevent this turn of events. Although there is little danger that decentralization and community control will turn the clock back to political control and the absolute power of local boards to fire without stating cause, one very good safeguard against this is teacher organizations, which protect employee rights and working conditions. The community school boards would be legally required to adhere to school law and the due process clauses written into teacher contracts.

THE MEANING OF DECENTRALIZATION

The struggle for control of the schools, the most visible and the closest institution for community residents, perhaps constitutes the initial stage of a larger struggle of citizens to gain control of their social institutions. That this is the case tends to be substantiated by such movements as Common Cause, a grass roots organization that is attempting to influence policy decisions that vitally affect our lives. In the complex society of the United States, bureaucracies and professionals have become too insulated and isolated for the good health of a democratic society. Many decisions are not made democratically and, in some cases, nobody really knows how they got made. Our institutions, including the schools, should be increasingly accountable to the needs and desires of the people they are charged to serve.

The proponents of community control envision it as a political instrument for bringing about educational change. Community control alone is not sufficient, but it can be a first step toward more comprehensive change. If it can compel the allocation of large sums of money to the urban schools, catalyze effective integration programs, and provide a solid curriculum that prepares students successfully for jobs and college admission, then community control will have contributed vitally to the public interest. However, if it promotes only conflict and operates in a framework of financial austerity, community control will have served no useful purpose.

The participation of community members must be more than mere noise. The community must infuse its values into the school and curriculum. Community members must sit on school boards and define the objectives of the schools. If the residents want black arts and Swahili or Mexican history and Spanish, these should certainly be integral to the curriculum. The inner-city residents, having a culture different from the middle-class white, must exercise power if the schools are to respect and teach their values. They must sit on district governing boards and school advisory panels and demand that the professionals—whatever culture or color they may be—be accountable to the values and will of the community (although accountability does not mean subservience).[11]

THE CASE FOR EDUCATIONAL FEDERALISM[12]

Educational federalism is a compromise between total decision making by a centralized bureaucracy and absolute community control. In this form of governance, the community and the professional bureaucracy cooperate. Both have power and both make contributions to decisions. The inputs of the bureaucracy promote stability and professionalism while the involvement of the community stimulates responsiveness, accountability, and relevance in the educational experience.

David Selden, president of the American Federation of Teachers, is an advocate of educational federalism. He believes that the central board should operate the high schools. The central board can enforce uniform standards of educational quality, assuring that no school totally abdicates its responsibility to educate. Only the central board can effectively govern and provide for specialized high schools, something local boards do not command the resources to do. The vested interest of the society in quality education is too great, according to Selden, to allow standards to deteriorate through absolute local control. He argues that parochialism alone cannot be a sufficient foundation for an educational system.

Selden maintains that pure community control is an extremist form of educational governance. He proposes that members of city boards of education be elected both at large and at local levels. Some members would be elected by vote of the entire school district and some would be elected from subdistricts. This is the method that is presently used in the District of Columbia. This election procedure results in better representation of groups that would achieve little or no voice through purely at-large elections. Most school boards would have to be enlarged to make room for both at-large and subdistrict representatives; they should include nine to thirteen members.

The Coleman report stressed that social integration is a critical educational input.[13] Thus the establishment of separate school districts in virtually homogeneous communities would be both educationally and administratively unsound. Certain guidelines must be heeded in setting up subdistrict school jurisdictions. The local district must be sufficiently large so that different types of people reside within it. This is equivalent to providing for socioeconomic and racial integration. Adhering to these guidelines, most cities would establish local districts ranging from 100,000 to 500,000 population. A city of one million may have, for example, subdistricts of 100,000, whereas cities such as New York or Chicago may organize much larger subdistricts of about 500,000 population. However, in some cities, such as Washington, D.C., achieving integration by drawing district lines is almost impossible.

The members of the local subdistrict boards, as opposed to the central board, should all be elected directly by the residents of the community. It is important that the residents of the local subdistricts have a genuine sense of participation. This would be an improvement upon appointed local boards, currently the procedure in New York City. There are thirty district boards in New York, with seven members each. New York is the only metropolitan school system to decentralize in this way. But the appointed boards have been a failure. The authority of the boards has been very limited and the subdistrict superintendent has often effectively controlled the board. If boards were elected, they might enjoy more political power and independence.

The local boards should not have the power to levy taxes and raise their own funds. This would not be feasible or desirable. This function of government should be reserved for the central board. But it is desirable to devise a budgetary formula to allocate money to subdistricts on the basis of their educational need. The funds should be granted as a lump sum, rather than as a line by line budget, so that the subdistrict boards can exercise a considerable degree of control over fiscal policy.

The local communities should possess a substantial degree of control over the curriculum. Each school must, of course, provide a common basic curriculum that assures that all students learn fundamental skills so that they will be able to compete for jobs and college admission. However, there must be latitude to innovate and set up a cultural curriculum that makes sense to the local community. Thus, instead of the school perpetuating exclusively middle-class values, the values of the ghetto can come into creative, aesthetic, and educative play. Minority children might come to value themselves and their culture rather than suffering intense stigma. Combining relevant values and job-getting skills in the same educational package will do much to advance the status and welfare of minority groups in our society.

If decentralization and community control are to result in the reduction of alienation between school and community, school administrators must actively seek to bring community representatives into the schools as paraprofessionals, aides, or visitors. If the proportion of minority teachers on the staff is less than the percentage in the surrounding population, the minority representation should be increased. If not adjusted, it can only be regarded as racial discrimination. Any imbalance must be moderate and unavoidable if the school is to achieve credibility and the community is to believe that the school is educating their children.

The extreme form of decentralization, no less than polarization and apartheid, has no place in a democratic society. But a reasonable amount of decentralization and community control, in the context of central board authority, will increase citizen involvement in the educational process and the capacity of the schools to serve the community well.

THE SEARCH FOR A SOLUTION

Vocal minority leaders proposed decentralization and local community control as the solution to their problems. Robert Havighurst of the University of Chicago believes that these approaches contain flaws. He argues that decentralization and community control programs do not achieve their objective of giving adequate autonomy to the local schools. Even if a big-city school system decentralizes, the subunits are still quite large—as large, in fact, as some small cities. This type of decentralization probably offers little or no increase in autonomy to the local school. The structure must be scaled down considerably if residents are to realize a sense of participation and control.

Decentralization produces schools segregated principally on the basis of race, ethnicity, and social class. The capacity of the schools to work for integration is, according to Havighurst, seriously impaired. But the political interests in the various parts of a city can consolidate and strengthen their local positions. They need no longer compromise or reflect reasonably upon the issues. Each has only one relatively homogeneous constituency to worry about. This turn of events is fine in terms of short-term political advantage but, as far as solving urban educational problems, it is a total loss.

What Havighurst advocates as an alternative to decentralization and community control is a balance of power between the local and central levels of school administration. This is a federalism intended to allow both participation and stability. Havighurst stresses that "achieving a constructive alliance between localized power and decision making and area-wide power and decision making is the main task of educators in the large cities and metropolitan areas during the seventies."[14] He warns that the complex bureaucracies that characterize our post-industrial society cannot be abolished in the smoke of community control conflict without dire consequences. They must be reformed and made more accountable rather than destroyed in the foolish hope that the institutional forms of a half-century ago might somehow prove adequate.

Havighurst argues that there is considerable danger in taking power from the central administration of a school system and transferring it totally to autonomous districts within the system. This redistribution of power tends to create highly politicized community schools, often rife with corruption. Havighurst has stressed the practicability of educational federalism.[15] He advocates that substantial power should reside at the local school level and that this should be balanced with considerable power wielded by the central administration of the school system. This produces a system of checks and balances and therefore a more effective school system.

The optimum situation, according to Havighurst, would be one where a single central authority commanded substantial control over the educational system in "the natural population unit of a city and its suburbs."[16] The community school boards would share certain responsibilities with the central board. This type of sharing of authority generally requires a single metropolitan area district. However, although this form of government has been established in a few cities, it is not politically feasible in most. The most desirable, feasible alternative is a considerable degree of cooperation among city school boards. The focus here is upon coordinated policy decisions, especially in such areas as finance, plant expansion, use of mass media, special education, and adult education.

IN PURSUIT OF INTEGRATION[17]

Middle-class parents attach a great deal of value to the schools. Their selection of a place to live is heavily dependent on their perception of the quality of the schools in the neighborhood. Many choose basically according to the types of families from which the students in the schools come. They want their children's classmates to reinforce the behavior and values they are teaching at home. Thus the parents avoid schools where the students come from the part of society where crime, juvenile delinquency, and premarital sex rates are high, the English is not correct, and personal relations are less verbal and more physical. They regard this sort of behavior as the "lower-class" way of life, in the sense that a higher percentage of poor and nonwhite exhibit the behavior than middle-class whites. But the percentage of the minority poor who are criminalistic, sexually promiscuous, and violent is a small percentage of the total. Nevertheless, middle-class parents feel strongly they need middle-class schools and neighborhoods to reinforce their middle-class home life.

Middle-class citizens have other motives in their pursuit of homogeneity. They are concerned about taxes and believe that controlling the social composition of the neighborhood and school will keep the local property tax rates down. They want a low crime rate and predictable public behavior. They feel that the entry of low-income families into the community will depress the market value of their homes. And, of course, by keeping low-status human beings out, they hope to protect, if not enhance, their prestige.

Neighborhood integration is necessary for genuinely integrated schools. Busing, open enrollment plans, and similar devices should only be temporary means of integrating schools. Our social policy should be to disperse low-income housing throughout our cities, suburbs, and towns. Decentralization and community control could then not result in *de facto* segregation. Federal funds should be used to subsidize low- and moderate-income families in the areas where housing is too expensive for depressed incomes. In areas where low-income households are deliberately introduced, property value guarantees should be given to homeowners. Something like an FHA guarantee of existing values could eliminate anxiety over possible losses in property values and thereby facilitate residential integration. Educational assistance should also be given to offset rising property taxes. These guarantees would remove the economic arguments against integration.

A number of specific programs are highly practical for achieving residential and educational integration. The government could enforce a regulation requiring that suburbs receiving federal aid must build low- and moderate-income housing. Rent subsidies and public housing rent allowances to families could be used to stimulate the construction of new low- and moderate-income housing units in the suburbs. Such programs could remove the financial penalty of accepting low-income residents into a community. Zoning restrictions that exclude low-income citizens should also be contested in the courts. The government and reform-minded groups could undertake research into the benefits of residential integration for school and community. The results could be widely publicized in order to inform public opinion.

SCHOOL AND COMMUNITY

There are aspects to community relations other than power and participation, community control and decentralization, and desegregation and integration. The way the school uses the resources of the community is the other important consideration. The *Parkway program* in Philadelphia uses the city as a classroom. The *educational park* brings all the children of a community together under one roof to learn in an environment supersaturated with information. And community and national *educational planning* is badly needed to coordinate our learning resources and programs effectively so that we might teach each individual well.

THE CITY AS CLASSROOM[18]

The new teacher relies on the resources of the city to expand the walls of the classroom. The city, offering a diversity the school cannot provide, becomes the classroom. Students learn by experiencing the museums, libraries, symphonies, and theaters of the metropolis. They learn by talking with community figures from all walks of life. There are many great teachers in the city that can help the classroom teacher discharge the school's responsibility to produce a graduate sensitized to and knowledgeable about many aspects of the complex urban environment. The school need only grant students and teachers the freedom to learn together in the city.

When we speak of the city as classroom we are talking about options. American youth suffer a public school system that largely will not let them grow up and learn in different ways. Hence the society is burdened with many alienated dropouts and misfits. If we open up the city to our young through learning-by-doing, work-study, and other direct forms of learning, many young people who had previously learned nothing imprisoned (their literal view) behind four walls could now learn. A teen-ager who spends an entire weekend working on his car but is totally inert in class is often not unable to meet a teacher's challenge but just plain bored. He could learn more, faster, elsewhere. If he could participate in a work-study program, for example, that places him part-time in an auto repair shop, he might make more sense of his education. He could learn something that he really wants to learn, and that—a simple but neglected truth—is much of what education should be. Letting students be in the city is not as dangerous and silly as the puritans and bureaucrats (who long ago gave up living and learning) would lead us to believe. We must act upon the principle of freedom or lose an increasing number of our youth.

Philadelphia's Parkway School takes advantage of freedom and the life of the city. The city is, in fact, the curriculum. The students cover the entire territory of the city, visiting factories, government offices, and museums, talking to professionals, artists, craftsmen, and teachers, and inquiring into any question they think important. Formal instruction in basic skills such as reading and arithmetic takes place in storefronts and rented apartments throughout the city. There are no grades or arbitrary rules.

The Parkway program has distinctive features that supply instructive guidelines. The tutorial group, consisting of fifteen students and two teachers, is the program's basic unit. It convenes for two hours four days a week. During the meetings, each student plans his schedule, receives personal counseling, and gets any remedial instruction in basic skills he may need. The group is responsible for a comprehensive written evaluation of both students' and teachers' work. The stress is on evaluating each participant on the basis of his contribution to the total educational experience.

Students are selected for the Parkway program by lottery. The objective is to avoid measurement and biased, standardized tests. For example, 130 names were drawn from among 10,000 applicants at one drawing. The randomness insures that the program will serve a racial and socioeconomic cross section of the city. This is an educational outcome that no other school has been able to achieve without resorting to elaborate, expensive schemes.

Committees consisting of parents from the community, teachers and students from the program, university students, and visiting teachers select faculty members. Each candidate is interviewed. Those who survive are subjected to a unique examination. They are required, as a group, to decide how they will fill the limited number of openings. The committee observes the teachers making their decisions and selects according to their observations.

The tutorial groups solicit the cooperation of community institutions in the development of courses and projects. Each group has been able to offer at least thirty courses and projects. The courses include Multi-Media Journalism, Film-Making, Kite-Flying, Vagabond Sketching, Psychology and Personal Problems, creative writing workshops, and courses in ten languages. The catalog describing all Parkway-sponsored educational endeavors lists ninety cooperating institutions.

The Parkway program operates as a participatory democracy. Weekly town meetings are the main form of governance. Students discuss policy questions ranging from program expansion and regulations to routine matters such as the processing of applications. This version of total participatory government, although inefficient, provides students a sense of community that is essential to sustaining the positive learning environment that the Parkway program needs for success and survival.

The Parkway experiment defies conventional evaluation. It recognizes that learning is often not neat and sequential, that it cannot be easily packaged for consumption in certain places (schools) at specified times (classes). Although converting all high schools into Parkways would be neither educationally desirable nor logistically feasible, it is a move in the right direction, a move toward sharing authority for learning with the entire community and relying heavily on all relevant, available resources. The program offers an alternative for the many students who find nothing behind four walls. It is certainly a reasonable model for educational reform.

EDUCATIONAL PARKS

The educational park is a multiple-school campus. Some serve grades ranging from kindergarten through college; others serve only elementary, junior high, or high school student populations. The physical plant varies from city to city but the Syracuse, New York, plan is typical.[19] In Syracuse, each campus will contain eight separate classroom buildings for about 500 pupils each, a library, language and science laboratories, remedial centers, multipurpose buildings for special education, gymnasiums, and a central building housing an auditorium, a kitchen, and art and music facilities. Each site will accommodate 4,000 to 4,300 students. Parks in more sparsely populated areas may accommodate only 1,500, whereas parks in the larger cities may enroll as many as 35,000. The park offers a great number of courses and programs, a rich diversity of learning materials, modern facilities, and a highly qualified, specialized professional staff.

The educational park is a very effective institution for merging school and community. The park serves everybody. The objective is lifelong learning. Hence an educational park is really a people's park. The park raises the general level of community culture and learning and promotes a spirit of solidarity. It revitalizes the community it serves because it is part of the community.

It is not enough to replace schools in each neighborhood as the need arises. This is not the way to achieve integration and financial savings. Neighborhood schools draw upon a homogeneous population. But parks can generally integrate learners of different socioeconomic and racial backgrounds, grades K through 12, due to the larger areas and populations they serve. The parks have created new attendance areas out of small, inefficient neighborhood schools, thereby assuring demographic stability. They are relatively unaffected by individual changes in neighborhoods caused by such forces as urban renewal projects and shifting populations. They replace unattractive neighborhood schools with buildings and programs that appeal to families rather than driving those who can afford to leave to the suburbs. Greater plant size and multiple, intensive usage of facilities cause the per capita cost for the park's superior program to be comparable to costs in the conventional school. Economists call this "economy of scale"; that is, one can purchase more and better education because more students are involved, keeping per capita cost down.

Marshall McLuhan claims that the information level outside the school is so much higher than that inside that students regard the school as an interrupter of their education. For example, the average high school graduate has completed 11,000 hours of school but he has seen more than 15,000 hours of television.[20] It is therefore very significant that the educational parks are providing an innovative, technologically sophisticated curriculum. The use of television, videotape cassettes, and other recent technology helps break down the barrier between learning outside and inside schools. Organizing learning differently will also help. For example, team teaching and a nongraded curriculum are standard. Teachers specialize in subject matter disciplines. Everything possible and reasonable is done to force the information level up in order to enrich the curriculum and allow the learner a significant number of choices. The learner may then find the educational park an appealing way to learn.

COMMUNITY PLANNING

What the city and nation need is educational planning. We have in every metropolis and, to a lesser extent, every town enormous resources that can sustain an immensely successful educational venture. We need only coordinate those resources toward our educational objectives. The resources outside the school include television, preschool and adult programs, industrial training programs, and much more. We should establish metropolitan education commissions to coordinate a community's diverse educational resources. The commission should initially inventory the available educational resources. The list would include theaters, museums, concert halls, public projects, churches, and unoccupied commercial buildings. Following the inventory, the commission should prepare a master plan for the city, specifying the resources and programs available for the lifelong education of every individual. Such a plan would provide an excellent view of the proper and most useful role of the schools in relation to the entire range of possible educational experiences in the community. Since the young do the bulk of formal learning, the plan would naturally focus on their needs.[21]

The master plan might include the following elements:

1. There should be established a single experimental school, centrally located in the city, to accommodate students who want an unconventional education. We have discussed the Parkway School in Philadelphia. Other examples of this type of program include the John

Dewey High School in Brooklyn, the downtown Loop High School in Chicago, and the John Adams High School in Portland, Oregon.

2. Faculty members should be periodically shifted among schools. This diversifies the student's educational experience, increases faculty racial integration, and insures that all students learn, at least part of the time, from the best teachers.

3. Students should be allowed to divide their attendance among two or more schools. Thus they can select schools on the basis of their own interests and abilities. For example, an enthusiastic and talented science student can attend a high school particularly strong in science. Students specializing in vocational subjects such as electronics, auto mechanics, and practical nursing might split their time between vocational and academic schools.

4. An open attendance rule should be established. Inner-city students should be free to enroll in integrated or middle-class schools where teachers, facilities, and the learning climate are generally superior. Counselors should advise the ghetto students of their options, encouraging students to capitalize on them.

5. Educational parks, which we have discussed, should be constructed to draw students from the full spectrum of socioeconomic, racial, and ethnic backgrounds. The park would accommodate a socially representative student body so that the school could legitimately be termed a comprehensive one.[22]

The search for both integration and diversity, both defensible professional standards and community control, and innovation as opposed to convention, are policy challenges on a grand scale. Protecting educational excellence while reforming the school and society is no mean feat. Difficult as the problems may seem, however, a way must be found to bring both citizen and professional to the conference table to deliberate and decide how the great educational issues of the day will be handled. There is no other way to preserve decent community relations.

NOTES

[1] See Sol Gordon, "The Bankruptcy of Compensatory Education," *Education and Urban Society* (August 1970), 360–370.

[2] See Luvern L. Cunningham, "Community Involvement in Change," *Educational Leadership*, 27 (January 1970), 303–366.

[3] Robert J. Havighurst, "The Reorganization of Education in Metropolitan Areas," *Phi Delta Kappan*, 52 (February 1971), 354–358.

⁴See Delbert K. Clear, "Decentralization: Issues and Comments," *The Clearing House*, 44 (January 1970), 259–267.

⁵See Marilyn Gittell and Alan G. Hevesi, (eds.), *The Politics of Urban Education*, New York, Praeger, 1969. All the material pertaining to the New York community control controversy is drawn from this source.

⁶*Ibid*.

⁷*Ibid*.

⁸Mario D. Fantini, "Participation, Decentralization, Community Control, and Quality Education," *Teachers College Record*, 71, no. 1 (September 1969), 96.

⁹See Larry Cuban, "Teacher and Community," *Harvard Educational Review*, 39, no. 2 (Spring, 1969), 253–272. For a collection of *Harvard Educational Review* articles on community relations, see Reprint Series No. 3, *Community and the Schools* (June 1969), especially Charles V. Hamilton, "Race and Education: A Search for Legitimacy" and Robert H. Salisbury, "Schools and Politics in the Big City."

¹⁰S. M. Brownell, "Desirable Characteristics of Decentralized School Systems," *Phi Delta Kappan*, 52 (January 1971), 286–288.

¹¹See Thomas Green, "Schools and Communities: A Look Forward," *Harvard Educational Review*, 39, no. 2 (Spring 1969).

¹²David Selden, "School Decentralization: A Positive Approach," *Teachers College Record*, 71, no. 1 (September 1969), 85–92. The section entitled The Case For Educational Federalism is drawn heavily from this source.

¹³James S. Coleman, *et al.*, *Equality of Educational Opportunity* (Washington, D.C., U.S. Office of Education, 1966). The sections A History of Community Control and The Search For A Solution are drawn substantially from this source.

¹⁴Havighurst, *op. cit.*, p. 356.

¹⁵*Ibid*.

¹⁶*Ibid.*, p. 354.

¹⁷Anthony Downs, "Residential Segregation: Its Effects on Education," *Civil Rights Digest*, 3 (Fall 1970), 2–8. This section In Pursuit Of Integration is based on the Downs article.

¹⁸Henry S. Resnik, "High School With No Walls," *Think*, 35 (November-December 1969), 33–36. The section The City As Classroom is drawn substantially from the Resnik article.

¹⁹Wayne Jennings, "Educational Parks: Tomorrow's Schools," *Audiovisual Instruction*, 15, no. 8 (October 1970), 42–44.

²⁰Alvin C. Eurich, "Recommendations for Changing the Urban School," *The Bulletin of the National Association of Secondary School Principals*, 55, no. 351 (January 1971), 189.

²¹*Ibid.*, pp. 190–191.

²²"Big-City Schools, Present and Future," *The Bulletin of the National Association of Secondary School Principals*, 55, no. 351 (January 1971), pp. 94–104.

2
Teacher aides

The new teacher has realized the advantage and virtual necessity of sharing authority for clerical, monitorial and custodial non-professional duties in order to free himself as fully as possible for professional teaching commitments. This is a redefinition of authority that changes the nature of the teacher's job. The routine, bureaucratic details that must be attended to divert too much of the teacher's time and effort from the education of students.

As much as 30 percent of the teacher's time is devoted to activities that do not require the attention of such a highly trained person.[1] By allowing aides—paraprofessionals, who are specialists with two or more years of advanced training, and subprofessionals, personnel with limited training, such as trained technicians, teacher aides, and housewives—to assist, the teacher will be able to function more as a professional than as a part-time clerk and monitor, part-time teacher. He will be able to devote considerable time and energy to the development of sound instructional strategies and the diagnosis of pupil learning progress.

FINANCING AIDES

The budgetary squeeze has prevented many school districts from hiring additional personnel to assist teachers. Some districts have managed to finance teacher aide programs with local funds and operate others through contributions from Parent-Teacher Associations and civic groups. A few colleges of education and school districts have cooperated to develop pilot aide programs.

A number of federally funded model programs, especially those concerned with the socially and educationally disadvantaged child, provided the original stimulus for the use of educational aides. Programs such as Head Start fostered experimental teacher aide programs. The major single source of federal funding for teacher aide programs has been Title I of the 1965 Elementary and Secondary Education Act. The Education Professions Development Act of 1967 formally recognizes the need for the development of auxiliary personnel in both secondary and elementary schools and also provides money.

AIDES AND
THE COMMUNITY

The aide can not only help the teacher become more effective, she can diversify and enrich the educational experience. This is particularly the case when the aide is culturally different and older. Then cross-cultural and cross-aged learning occurs; one example would be a Chicano senior citizen serving in an all-white classroom. The end product of the greater efficiency and diversity obtained through the use of aides is more teacher professionalism and increased classroom pluralism.

What types of people can help the teacher? The list can be as long as there are categories of people in the community, but the following groups are most important:

- Intern teachers
- Professionals from the community
- Volunteers from community organizations and clubs
- Student assistants
- Hired clerical, monitorial, and custodial assistants
- Hired library and classroom teacher aides[2]

The support staff for teachers will, at least in the early stages of development, include two principal divisions. The lower level divisions will consist of subprofessional personnel with limited training. Paraprofessional specialists with two or more years of advanced training will compose the upper level. A hierarchy of positions will exist within each division, providing opportunities for advancement and specialization.

The subprofessional staff will perform both monitorial and clerical tasks for the teacher. The monitorial tasks involve the control of students outside the classroom. Clerical tasks are routine secretarial and record-keeping duties. The titles that have been suggested for those performing these functions are "staff aide" for the monitorial employees and "clerical aide" for the clerical employees.

The staff aides will handle the bulk of pupil control tasks which absorb much of a teacher's time. They will monitor traffic in the corridors, outdoors, on field trips, at assemblies, and in the cafeteria. They will be available to handle emergencies and problems that arise and that require the counsel, management, and understanding of an adult.

The clerical aides will serve basically as secretaries. They will type, keep records, duplicate materials, inventory, and handle the many other duties that must be performed for a school to operate successfully. The teacher, relieved of such responsibilities, will have substantially more time for professional endeavors.

The major source of subprofessional aides should be the community, especially for the ghetto schools. Not only does this policy provide employment opportunities, which are most important for poor minority people in the inner-city, it also opens up lines of communication between school and community. The possibility that careful selection of subprofessional aides will help the school understand the community and the community believe in the school should not be overlooked.

Aides can become a powerful force for merging school and community. Their knowledge of the values and culture of the community will help make the school sensitive and responsive to the community's educational needs. They will be able to interpret the programs and policies of the school to the community. They may bring teachers and administrators into informal contact with parents and residents so that deeper understanding will be realized. The aides will certainly be able to influence curriculum and teaching strategies, making them more appropriate to different types of learners. Fitting the school to the student rather than the student to the school will do much to make the school a genuine part of the community. Subprofessional personnel can contribute much toward achieving this goal.[3]

Aide roles provide the means through which the community can influence the educational system. The aide can communicate to the school what the community really wants, thereby terminating the virtually total reliance on what professionals think the community needs. Thus aides are part of the consumer control movement: people getting what they want rather than what professionals think they should get. Aides are becoming involved in determining new forms of instruction and defining new educational goals. As they become more usual in the school, their influence will increase. By 1977 there will be 1½ million teacher aides in the United States.[4] This means that the impact of aides on the substance and focus of our educational system will be considerable.

About ¼ million persons who have no teaching credentials are now working in the schools. Their involvement in educational programs requires that the teacher learn how to work with paraprofessionals and subprofessionals. Recent research indicates that the teacher's most important training deficiency is the lack of sufficient skill in working effectively with aides.[5] The NEA and AFT and their state affiliates have acknowledged this deficiency by publishing literature on aides and sponsoring workshops, seminars, and in-service programs. The teacher aide movement promises to be no short-term fad but a permanent innovation that everyone who relates to the schools must somehow adapt to.

SELECTION CRITERIA

Since staff and clerical aides do not need lengthy training to do their jobs successfully, high school graduation or the equivalent should constitute sufficient formal educational qualification. The schools should give careful consideration to a candidate's special abilities, experience, and maturity, particularly her capacity to work congenially and advantageously with students. The applicant should, of course, be able to express herself clearly and be free of serious physical and emotional problems.

The selection of aides can become a major project. The methods used to advertise jobs and interview candidates will determine how burdensome and unwieldy the task becomes. The Pennsbury school district in Fallingston, Pennsylvania, handled the application procedure rather efficiently.[6] It sent letters home to parents with each of more than 7,000 elementary school pupils in the district. The letters described the aide's job, specifying duties, working hours, working conditions, and pay. Interested parents and residents were asked to return a tear-off coupon, reporting name, address, telephone number, and the school where they wished to work.

Of these parents, 650 returned the coupon and indicated a willingness to work. A follow-up letter was mailed to the interested parties, announcing qualifications for the job as follows:

- A genuine interest in elementary school children
- Previous experience in youth work
- Previous experience as an aide or teacher
- A desire to work daily to insure program continuity
- A desire to work any time during the day and report daily at the same time

This letter brought 260 replies. Principals and representatives of the district personnel office conducted evening interviews at the elementary schools. Each school decided whether to offer jobs during the interview sessions. When possible, the recently recruited aides reported to work the next day. Each school also selected a number of substitute aides.

Most aides the district employed were housewives whose children were grown or at least no longer of preschool age. They wanted to use to advantage their educational background and spare time. Salary was not a serious consideration. The beginning wage rate was $1.75 per hour for a 1½- to 4-hour day.

The Pennsbury school district's approach to hiring aides can serve as a model for other districts. The basic idea is to screen the initially large number of applicants and conduct personal interviews with the much smaller number of parents who satisfy minimum requirements. This procedure saves a great deal of time and prevents many mistakes.

PRE-SERVICE PROGRAMS

The school districts must offer a well-organized pre-service training program that thoroughly prepares new employees before they begin work. The pre-service session should last three to four weeks, preferably immediately before the opening of school. Although each pre-service program will, of course, be geared to the special needs of a particular district, every program will probably include the following elements:

1. An orientation to the school district, providing information on organization and specific programs.

2. A consideration of the subprofessional and paraprofessional's roles in the school authority system, including a detailed definition of the duties of the subprofessional and paraprofessional and their conditions of employment, promotion, and retention.
3. A short course on child growth and development stressing the child's problems as he develops emotionally and intellectually. The course should present the school district's policy regarding the treatment of children.[7]

In-service programs should also be available to the subprofessional and paraprofessional staff. These programs should be structured to meet the unique needs of the school district, its staff, and the community. They can be effective instruments for making the school an integral part of the community life. They can give the aide staff a chance to learn new skills and advance to higher occupational classification and salary.

PARAPROFESSIONALS IN TECHNOLOGY AND INSTRUCTION

Many schools have begun to use talking typewriters, teaching machines, computer programing, videotape production and playback equipment, information retrieval centers utilizing data bank equipment and microfilm material, and learning laboratories equipped with console-controlled equipment. The school's adoption of such technology has created a need for paraprofessionals in educational technology. The teacher can use paraprofessionals trained in educational technology to help with equipment and much more. The paraprofessionals can perform such functions as retrieving information for classroom use, assisting in the production of programs, and testing student progress and recording evaluations. They can also apply their technical skills to streamline administrative practices in the schools. The total effect of the presence of paraprofessionals trained in educational technology will be to free teachers and administrators to solve pressing educational and administrative problems.

Another type of paraprofessional, the instructional aide, will assist teachers in nontechnological activities. Instructional aides will perform such tasks as demonstrating experiments, tutoring small groups of students, and helping students with term paper projects. Such tasks are integral to teaching and have been considered professional duties to date. Thus the use of instructional aides will modify the teacher's duties.[8]

TRAINING AND RECRUITMENT

Most paraprofessionals in educational technology and instruction will be trained, for the present, in junior colleges and private technical schools. These institutions are now more nearly prepared to train students to meet the technological and instructional needs of schools than are colleges and universities. However, the four-year institutions, especially colleges of education, will undoubtedly establish sophisticated programs, especially for the preparation of instructional aides. Aides will eventually require as much education to attain to the highest level of advancement as teachers now require to begin teaching.

The minimum requirement to qualify as an aide will probably be an associate degree in educational technology or instruction. Junior colleges can capitalize on the recent use of aides by establishing programs to satisfy projected needs. Junior colleges now offer programs for the training of systems analysts and computer programers. They can easily make a transition to the preparation of specialists in education, and some have already done so. Their teacher aide programs require courses such as Educational Psychology and Introduction to Education in addition to work in the major field. The best programs place the student in local schools as an intern under the guidance of the school's professional staff and college supervisors. This work-study approach seems to be extremely important in preparing the aide to serve effectively in the schools at the outset of her first employment.[9]

THE IMPACT OF AIDES

The efforts of aides definitely have a telling effect upon pupil performance. Every research study undertaken demonstrates that the aide in the classroom does help to educate children. For example, the Metropolitan Reading Readiness Test was given at five-month intervals to 234 children in Minneapolis. The major finding was that kindergarten pupils tutored by an aide achieved significantly greater progress than untutored pupils in reading readiness, number readiness, and total readiness. Classes tutored by instructional aides gained an average fifteen points compared to only ten points for classes unassisted by aides.

Indiana University's Psychology Department found that children tutored by aides made great gains in reading performance. The aides instructed first-grade children fifteen minutes daily, Monday through Friday, in fifty projects located in twelve states. Before beginning their assignments, the aides took twenty-one hours of programed instruction in pre-service sessions. A questionnaire research in Wayne County, Michigan, revealed that school administrators and teachers felt that paraprofessionals contributed substantially to the educational system. In Greeley, Colorado, teachers believed that measured increases in pupil performance in an ESEA Title III program could be traced to aides' efforts.[10]

Mobilization for Youth sponsors STAR, Supplementary Teaching Assistance in Reading, which uses aides to train parents to read to their children. The program aides teach Puerto Rican parents one hour each week. The first-grade Puerto Rican children whose parents have been tutored by aides score higher in nine different reading tests than matched children to whom professionals have given two hours of instruction weekly. The results demonstrate that parents can provide the highly effective, individualized, and intensive instruction that their children need.

Even very young aides have a positive impact on pupil performance. The New York City Board of Education reported extraordinary results using young aides in a model antipoverty program, Mobilization for Youth. Over a five-month period, low-achieving older children tutored younger children with reading difficulties. The children in tutored groups gained 6.0 months in reading achievement, whereas a control group improved only 3.5 months. The tutors themselves gained a remarkable 2.4 years compared to 7.0 months for their control group counterparts. The Mobilization for Youth data demonstrate that truly significant learning results can be achieved through the use of young aides. The National Commission on Resources for Youth operates Youth-Tutor-Youth Centers in Philadelphia, Newark, and Washington, D.C. Their results also substantiate that youth can serve as effective aides.

Permitting students to become teachers as early as possible releases the learning potential in learners' interpersonal relations. Students who have recently learned required material stand in an excellent position to understand and tutor the student approaching a topic for the first time. The teacher can divide classes, teaching each student different subject matter. Students can then be paired to allow one to teach the other. The Education Professions Development Act encourages this type of student-to-student learning. A number of state departments of education also encourage it.[11]

THE BERKELEY EXPERIENCE

The Berkeley Unified School District in California initiated a teacher aide program that has produced a significant change in the attitudes of everyone involved.[12] Ninety aides from low-income families are now working in the program. The original decision to employ aides constituted a formal recognition of the fact that low-income parents often feel isolated from and ignored by the schools. The Berkeley faculty and administrators believed that the educational and human condition of the school system would improve if they could become acquainted with their pupils' parents.

Parents and faculty have reassessed one another through the Berkeley aide program. Low-income parents learned that the school—middle-class white fortress that it is—is not as hostile as it appears from a distance, that the school can serve their child's needs. Teachers learned that low-income parents are valuable and, in fact, pleasant colleagues once initial rapport has been established. Everyone found that they could work together toward mutually agreeable objectives. The aide program made educational problems more easily soluble and cultural differences less forbidding. The community and school succeeded in educating the low-income child where the school alone had failed.

The selection criteria for aides did not include formal educational achievement. The aides were chosen basically according to their interest in and ability to relate to children. The emphasis was heavily upon personal commitment and facility in human relations. Other major factors were financial need and enrollment of at least one of the aide's children in the school where she served but not in the particular classroom that was her assignment.

Only teachers who volunteered to cooperate with the program were assigned aides. The teachers and aides collaborated in a week of orientation prior to the parents' involvement in the classroom. The essential purpose of the orientation was to sensitize the professional to the parents' feelings, fears, and interests and facilitate their first days as paid school employees.

The teachers felt that the aide program offered them a way to know parents, and thus get closer to the community. They reported that this had been impossible to achieve on personal initiative. Volunteer contacts had proved largely strained and artificial. The teachers claimed that only through the aide program did they really begin to know parents and develop stable understandings. A substantial growth of interracial appreciation, respect, and trust ensued.

The parent aides' early fears and timidity diminished rapidly. Their cynicism about the school's teaching methods and management of children receded when they saw that they made a difference in the school. Teachers and administrators' stereotypes and fears were diminished when they worked daily with aides. What was happening was a revolution of changing attitudes, a humanistic reformation that was making real education and dialogue possible.

Teacher, administrator, and aide eventually became open and frank with one another. The aides expressed their real feelings about the curriculum and student discipline. They criticized honestly, recommending reforms. Through forthright dialogue, the aides became confident of their own methods of handling children. They witnessed the viability of their own culture and life style as a part of the school program. This feeling of belonging was perhaps the most valuable result of the program. Morale in the school and community improved immeasurably. By sharing authority with parent aides, the school had improved not only the educational program but also the quality of human relations.

AIDES AND
SOCIAL CONCERNS

The school board in Simsbury, Connecticut, voted in September 1966 to participate in Project Concern, a busing plan that transported 265 children from the Hartford central city to five suburban schools.[13] Simsbury hosted twenty-five ghetto pupils, aged five to ten. Since the children were bused too far from their Hartford homes to receive parental help in case of an emergency, thirty-three Simsbury mothers volunteered to serve as "foster parents" in case of accident or sickness. However, few emergencies occurred and the foster mothers devoted most of their time to improving race relations between suburb and inner-city. They often invited the Hartford children to dinner and drove them home in the evenings. Many mothers hosted the children as overnight guests.

It was not long before the Hartford children joined the Simsbury Cub Scouts, Boy Scouts, Brownies, and Girl Scouts. They attended numerous school and community events. The pupils became considerably more than superficially involved in Simsbury's community life. In fact, some began spending part of their summer vacations in Simsbury. The net result of parental aide activity in Simsbury has been improved human relations between two normally polarized and geographically separate communities, the ghetto and suburb. If aides can play a role throughout the nation in bringing these two mutually distrustful communities together, they will have contributed to both a multiracial educational experience and the salvation of a society.

DIFFERENTIATED STAFFING

A differentiated school staff is organized on several levels of responsibility and salary.[14] A completely differentiated staff includes classroom teachers, special service personnel, subject specialists, and a considerable number of subprofessionals such as classroom aides and teaching interns.

Differentiation provides a career ladder for teachers to climb. Teachers are assigned according to their educational attainment, previous performance, and capacity to perform required duties. They receive different salaries for different assignments. Their salary schedule exceeds the schedules of schools without differentiated staffing, basically for the reason that personnel with substantially lower salaries than teachers perform much of the routine work. Incentives for moving up definitely exist. Thus the best teachers can remain in teaching rather than pursuing an administrative promotion in order to advance their careers. Differentiated staffing abolishes the demoralizing state of affairs where there is only "beginning teacher" and "ending teacher."

THE TEMPLE CITY MODEL[15]

Dr. Dwight Allen, dean of the University of Massachusetts School of Education, developed one of the first differentiated staffing models. He presented it to the California Board of Education in 1966, and it was first tried experimentally in Temple City, California.

Allen's model is hierarchical: from organizational top to bottom are master teachers, senior teachers, staff teachers, associate teachers, and three categories of paraprofessionals—laboratory assistants, resource center assistants, and teacher aides. Duties and salary vary by position. However, only the staff teacher and associate teacher can attain to tenure.

The teaching function is differentiated at Temple City as follows, moving from the top of the school organization down:

1. *Master teacher.* Her major commitment is to district-wide application of research to curriculum design, but she spends at least some time in the classroom.
2. *Senior teacher.* The senior teacher instructs students, but she also

spends substantial time developing in-service training programs and instructional strategies, consulting with associate teachers, and establishing resource banks for new instructional units, especially those involving the use of media.

3. *Staff teacher.* She is an experienced teacher who handles specialized duties such as small group instruction and tutorial sessions. She develops new forms of teaching and curricula and tests these innovations before they are formally adopted.

4. *Associate teacher.* Usually a beginning teacher who devotes most of her time to classroom teaching. She is constantly evaluated by her supervisor, who is a higher ranking teacher.

There are two differentiated staffing models that are significantly different from the Temple City model. Lloyd J. Trump's hierarchical model provides for staff specialists, teaching specialists, general aides, and community consultants. The Head Start model, an outgrowth of the federal Head Start program, has only two major levels: a "lead teacher," possessing no effective authority, and assistant teachers, who are numerous and do most of the teaching. The only real difference between the two strata is that the "lead teacher" is paid more.

THE FLORIDA EFFORT

Differentiated staffing has been most extensively implemented in Florida.[16] In 1968 the legislature directed the state department of education to "develop and operate model projects of flexible staff organization, in selected elementary and secondary schools, based on differentiated levels of responsibility and compensation for services performed." The state department conducted a feasibility study and initiated pilot projects in Leon, Dade, and Sarasota counties.

The Florida model is more differentiated than Allen's Temple City model. From the bottom up are teacher aides, educational technicians, assistant teachers, associate teachers, staff teachers, senior teachers, teaching curriculum specialists, and the teaching research specialist, who functions much as a principal.

COMPLEX DIFFERENTIATION

School differentiation can become quite complex. The thirty-nine school districts in Wayne County, Michigan, which includes Detroit, make extensive use of aides.[17] The districts employ more than 6,000 aides as a supportive staff for the county's 28,000 teachers. Research funded under Title III of the Elementary and Secondary Education Act identified twenty-six positions in which the county uses aides. No one school district uses aides in all twenty-six positions, but several approach that number. The Wayne County program demonstrates to what degree staffing can become differentiated.

The positions that Wayne County has developed are useful as a model for other school systems:

1. *Classroom aide.* She does monitorial and clerical tasks for the classroom teacher.
2. *Audiovisual technician.* She maintains, operates, inventories, and stores AV equipment.
3. *School counselor's aide.* She performs monitorial and clerical tasks for guidance counselors.
4. *School cafeteria aide.* She is responsible for maintaining order in the cafeteria during lunch periods.
5. *General school aide.* She performs any duties assigned by the principal, assistant principal, or a teacher.
6. *School-community aide.* She informs parents of school programs and services and advises teachers and administrators of parent and community needs.
7. *School hospitality aide.* She welcomes parents and visitors to the school and takes them to conferences. She is responsible for refreshments.
8. *Departmental aide.* She performs assigned tasks, such as record keeping and typing, in a specific department.
9. *Library aide.* She assists the librarian in such tasks as shelving, filing, and clipping.
10. *Testing service aide.* She administers and scores standardized tests and records results.
11. *Teacher clerical aide.* She does clerical tasks for the classroom teacher, such as duplicating, filing, and record keeping.
12. *School security aide.* She is assigned by the principal to security duties at lavatories, parking lots, corridors, and doors, particularly during periods of heavy traffic. She is also responsible for banking school receipts.
13. *After-school program aide.* She supervises after-school events such as rallies and club meetings, working under teacher supervision.
14. *Resource center assistant.* She assists in the operation and maintenance of a program learning laboratory or resource center.

15. *Special talent aide.* She assists teachers of music, arts, or crafts. She is selected on the basis of demonstrated talent in such areas as sculpture, painting, or music.
16. *Crisis center assistant.* She works with emotionally maladjusted children who have been removed from regularly scheduled classes. A teacher, school psychologist, or counselor supervises her work. She may help the children with emotional problems or even assist with their homework.
17. *Special skills aide.* She aids teachers by using special skills in foreign languages, homemaking, or shop.
18. *Playground or recreation aide.* She assists teachers with physical education activities in such capacities as referee and umpire and by leading exercises.
19. *Reading improvement aide.* She helps the reading specialist with basic and remedial instruction, tutoring children and assisting them in the use of such instructional material as drill cards and reading lessons.
20. *Special education aide.* She supports the special education teacher's instruction with drills, reviews, and demonstrations.
21. *Speech correction aide.* She helps the speech correction teachers with drill exercises in the formation of sounds and diagnostic work, often operating equipment for the teacher.
22. *Attendance officer aide.* She assists the attendance officer by performing such tasks as contacting parents and keeping up-to-date records.
23. *Bus attendance aide.* She supervises the loading and unloading of school buses.
24. *High school theme reader.* She reads essays for particular errors specified by the teacher.
25. *School health clinic aide.* She works under the supervision of the school nurse to help operate the health clinic. She performs such duties as typing, assisting with examinations, and ordering supplies. With proper authorization, she takes sick or injured children to their homes or the hospital.
26. *Laboratory technician.* She helps instructors in language and science labs by operating and servicing equipment and ordering necessary supplies.

THE CALIFORNIA INSTRUCTIONAL AIDE ACT

The California Instructional Aide Act of 1968 authorizes school districts to hire instructional aides to assist teachers.[18] The objective is to improve the quality of instruction by freeing teachers from routine. The act provides a legal basis for schools to employ noncertificated personnel to help with the instruction of students. The law had previously restricted teacher aides to nonteaching duties. The 1968 law specifies: "Any school district may employ Instructional Aides to assist classroom teachers . . . in the supervision of students and in instructional tasks which, in the judgment of the certificated personnel to which the Instructional Aide is assigned, may be performed by a person not licensed as a classroom teacher."[19]

There are, of course, very real dangers in the unregulated use of teacher aides. The California State Council of Education's Teacher Education Committee was concerned that aides would be used as a cheap supply of teachers. The Council demanded that the bill preclude the utilization of aides to enlarge class size. As a result of the Council's request, Section 13599.2 provides: "Instructional Aides shall not be utilized to increase the number of pupils in relation to the number of classroom teachers in any school district, or in the state."[20] The act provides no legal basis for the replacement of teachers with aides.

Although aides may not replace teachers, they may complete the professional training for certification. The Instructional Aide Act provides aides an opportunity to undertake the preparation for becoming a teacher. This allows those previously financially unable, or perhaps simply lacking motivation, to attain to professional status. The daily involvement of aides in the schools can do much to bring into teaching people who would not otherwise have contemplated entering the profession. The low-income person finds it particularly advantageous to earn an income as an aide while satisfying professional certification requirements. The aide programs provide incentives for economically depressed persons to become teachers. Their representation is badly needed in the many schools whose staffs are virtually totally middle class.

The California law allows aides to assist teachers in supervising and instructing pupils. However, teachers are not required to accept the help of aides. The policy governing the use of aides is negotiable in each school district. Guidelines can be established to meet local needs and conditions and the preferences of teachers, administrators, and community. The California law certainly does not constitute an inflexible, statewide standard; it merely legalizes the use of aides for schools that elect to employ them.

THE PAYOFF

When professionals share authority for the formal educational experience with subprofessionals and paraprofessionals, what does it accomplish? There are basically two benefits. The first is a genuine career advancement system, where there are differences in duties, salary, and status. Incentives are built into the system for teachers to continue their learning and improve the educational experiences of their pupils. One might classify this result as motivational.

The second benefit is an improvement in the quality of instruction, owing basically to the fact that differentiated staffing enables individualized instruction. The support of paraprofessionals and subprofessionals allows teachers to spend most of their time and effort in personal and professional involvement with pupils. Thus pupils can progress at their own rate rather than trying to keep up with curriculum and teacher. They can assert their cultural and emotional differences, thereby growing to genuine maturity rather than being molded to a single pattern.

The individualization of instruction possible in a differentiated staffing context promotes both individual progress and authentic cultural pluralism. Differentiated staffing can be the instrument for capitalizing educationally on the differences among learners and cultures. If it accomplishes this, it will be well worth the money and effort.

NOTES

[1] Jody L. Stevens, "Of Immediate Concern: Better Teacher Utilization," *The Clearing House*, 43, no. 8 (April 1969), 504.

[2] *Ibid.*, p. 505.

[3] Frank P. Bazelli, "Organization and Training of Paraprofessionals," *The Clearing House*, 44, no. 4 (December 1969), 206.

[4] Frank Riessman and Alan Gartner, "New Careers And Pupil Learning," *CTA Journal* 65, no. 2 (March 1969), 9.

[5] *Ibid.*, p. 6.

[6] John E. Keefe, "Paraprofessionals: Get Them When You Need Them," *School Management*, 13, no. 2 (February 1969), 46–52.

[7] Bazelli, *op. cit.*, pp. 207–208.

[8] Bazelli, *op. cit.*, p. 208.

[9] Bazelli, *op. cit.*, pp. 208–209.

[10] Riessman, *op. cit.*, p. 7.

[11] *Ibid.*

[12] Harold J. Maves, "The Community Enters the Classroom," *CTA Journal*, 65, no. 2 (March 1969), 26–28.

[13]Leonard G. Lanza, "Paraprofessionals: School Aides Bridge A Social Gap," *School Management*, 13, no. 2 (February 1969), 46–52.

[14]"Differentiated Staffing," *Nation's Schools*, 85, no. 6 (June 1970), 43.

[15]*Ibid.*

[16]*Ibid.*, p. 44.

[17]Arnold Glovinsky and Joseph P. Johns, "Paraprofessionals: 26 ways to use them," *School Management*, 13, no. 2 (February 1969), 46, 48–49.

[18]California's Instructional Aide Act . . . and What It Can Mean to the Profession," *CTA Journal*, 65, no. 2 (March 1969), 5, 57–59.

[19]*Ibid.*, p. 5.

[20]*Ibid.*, p. 5.

3
Teacher organizations

Teachers have joined together to take advantage of their collective power. In a world of complex educational bureaucracies and increased demands upon the schools, the old individual authority relation of teacher to administrator, parent, and community has proved inadequate. Some means of presenting a united front to the public and school administrators was needed. Professional associations and unions have been the teachers' responses to the new forces impinging upon them; through such associations teachers protect and enhance their working conditions and salary levels.

Several forces have influenced teachers and caused them to seek a new authority relation with administrators, parents, and community. It is very important to understand them in order to grasp the full significance of the teacher's new role in American society.

SOCIAL AND ECONOMIC FORCES[1]

American society is changing. The country is becoming a nation of cities. In the city, human relations are impersonal, mobility is great and a sense of community is lacking, and many problems plague the schools. Teachers seldom teach where they grew up or even live in the communities where they teach. They face new problems and demands in the city that make teaching there less satisfying. Serious discipline problems and the challenge of educating inner-city youth deprived by our society are central concerns. The city presents, in short, a number of alienating situations teachers must contend with.

All but the small, rural schools have become complex bureaucracies. Where once a sense of common purpose and identity existed between administrator and teacher, now there is a labor-management schism. As the schools grew larger, the task of administering became more cumbersome and specialized, and in the process, the mutual interests of teachers and administrators were eroded. No longer did some individuals both teach and administer. As the burdens imposed on the school increase and as the school grows to factory scale in the city, teachers are being removed further and further from the centers of decision making. Teachers, historically always ready to substitute job satisfaction and middle-class pretensions for financial rewards, have become dissatisfied with their lack of participation. Experiencing an uncomfortable diminishment of job satisfaction and a denial of significant involvement in determining the conditions of their work, they began to think of salaries and fringe benefits to compensate for their loss of psychic income. Regarding themselves as professionals, yet treated as employees in the big school bureaucracies, they painfully confronted their substantial lack of power and evaporating job satisfaction.

The issue of economic injustice has become very important as teachers have contended with factors that have made old authority relations less satisfying. Teachers have been sensitized to the statistical fact that they earn considerably less than most other occupational groups with comparable education and, in some cases, less than unskilled workers.

The social composition of the teaching force is changing. A large number of young males and working-class and minority people have been attracted to teaching. They are a new breed of teacher. They are not at all tolerant of paternalistic administrators and inadequate support for educational programs. Their heavy entry into the teaching force has begun to change the monolithically conservative social composition of the teaching force.

The role of the public employee is changing. There has been an increasing recognition that the old no-strike laws do not actually solve labor relations problems between schools and teachers. Throughout the nation, pressure has increased for legislation granting public employees organization and bargaining rights. Teachers are supporting this movement.

Nonviolent revolution has had a great impact upon teachers. The black civil rights movement legitimized direct action in American society, involving other minority groups in the cause of human rights. Teachers learned new values from this great movement; they were inextricably caught up in the revolution of rising expectations. They began to view themselves as an oppressed social and economic group. However, in the attempt to act individually or locally upon their new perceptions and sense of deprivation, teachers experienced widespread frustration. This was the antecedent to their present militancy.

UNREALISTIC DEMANDS

Americans have always embraced a great faith in the capacity of schools to solve social problems. Their faith in education has sometimes led them to accept the tenet that education is a panacea. This considerable reverence—which has only recently faltered—has led citizens to place unrealistic demands on the schools. As demands have been increasingly imposed, teachers have experienced a growing estrangement. Traditionally, the schools have been able to meet the challenges. They Americanized a nation of immigrants, providing citizenship training and teaching skills to develop a high-quality labor force. But today the demands have escalated into teaching sex education and the dangers of alcohol and drug abuse, teaching science for winning the space race, and the compulsory education of students who are poorly prepared to learn.

Parents in the inner-city, recently aware that the schools have failed their children, have demanded that the schools serve more effectively (see Chapter 1). Many teachers, poorly prepared to teach in the inner-city, have found it difficult to live with, much less act upon, ghetto parents' demands. In the suburbs, anxious and status-conscious parents demand that teachers teach well enough to get their child into Berkeley or Harvard. The teacher, no possessor of Godlike faculties, is somewhat overwhelmed by all the exorbitant demands. Compared to other college graduates, his academic achievement is average. He manages on a limited income and his job security depends on careful cooperation with the school bureaucracy. Yet somehow he is expected to work miracles. The intense feeling of being overburdened with unrealistic responsibilities (and underpaid for them) has psychologically done much to free the teacher to organize and express his desire for professional salaries and working conditions. The American credo that education is a cure-all has finally outstripped the human capacity of teachers to sustain that faith.

RISING EXPECTATIONS

Following the shock of the Soviet launching of Sputnik I in 1957, politicians and the public began to inquire closely into the state of the educational establishment. How had the Soviets orbited a satellite before us? The very idea of the Soviet Union challenging us so abruptly shattered our national composure. The finger of accusation was pointed at the school, especially the high school. The critics said we were losing the "space race" because the American comprehensive high school was deficient, especially in science education. James B. Conant, eminent chemist and president of Harvard, summarized the criticism levied at the schools in his *The American High School Today*. He offered proposals for reform in the same volume. Major weeklies—*Look, Newsweek, Time, Saturday Review*—opened their pages to the dialogue. Articles with titles such as "Why Ivan Can Read And Johnny Can't" elaborated on the failure of the American schools and the alleged superiority of the Soviet schools. This national dialogue constrained educators to a self-conscious and painful inspection of the schools.

The consensus that politicians, the public, and educators arrived at was that the schools were, in fact, deficient. Moreover, they agreed that the schools were certainly an instrument of national defense; that we should do our best to educate quality chemists, biologists, physicists, and foreign language experts to assure our national pre-eminence. Thus the critical examination of the schools, verging on scapegoating, produced a national commitment to the schools. Congress passed the National Defense Education Act in 1958 to fund, among other things, the training of science and language teachers and the development of curricula in science and foreign language.

Out of the flurry of criticism, suggestion, and legislation, teachers emerged sensitized to their importance in the national structure of priorities. They were enamored with the idea that education was recognized as the nation's major "growth industry." This new status brought them rapidly into the revolution of rising expectations. Perceiving their significance, teachers began to expect rewards commensurate with their contribution. But the shock came shortly. Teachers, long paternalized and unorganized and easily flattered with rhetoric on holidays and election days, found that expectations were not fulfilled automatically; indeed, it was the economic and political power of organized groups that won higher salaries and improved working conditions. Thus the powerless American pedagogue, highly alienated and thoroughly frustrated by his inability to make good his rising expectations, was finally ready for politics.

SEEKING A ROLE MODEL

The teacher sought a role model for his political behavior. Medical doctors, a group that had benefited from strong organization and group solidarity (The American Medical Association is effectively a union), could not be emulated because doctors are an elite professional group, generally practicing privately. Teachers, in contrast, form a mass profession of public employees. Other public employees that have effectively organized have been dependably loyal in the maze of local machine politics. Policemen, firemen, and sanitation workers have presented a united front at election time in support of candidates who will return favors in the form of pay increases and improved working conditions. Teachers have regarded this type of political involvement as a betrayal of professional standards of conduct. Thus doctors and municipal employees are inadequate or unacceptable political models for teachers.

It finally became apparent to teachers that the union model was their only alternative. Teachers had historically received the open support of organized labor but they did not reciprocate by joining unions. However, as the revolution of rising expectations begun in the early 1950s increasingly influenced teachers, it became clear that the desire for professional salaries and working conditions could be achieved only by building a powerful organization. Teachers were then ready to join the ranks of the labor movement.

To achieve their demands, teachers have worked through the American Federation of Teachers (AFT) and the National Education Association (NEA). The AFT, founded in 1916, is a nationwide union of classroom teachers, affiliated with the AFL-CIO. It has more than 250,000 members in over 900 locals in the United States and abroad. It serves only the interests of teachers, excluding administrators from membership, although a union local may voluntarily grant principals membership. The AFT stresses that it is the only organization devoted solely to the interests of teachers.

The NEA is a professional association open to all educators, including administrators. It has a membership of over 1 million, about 85 percent of whom are classroom teachers.[2] The NEA believes that all educators must work together for better schools and the enhancement of the professional status of teachers. It has traditionally regarded a discussion of teachers' salaries and working conditions as "unprofessional," advocating that the "education profession" avoid entangling alliances with "special interest" groups, especially labor unions. Lately, however, it has grown considerably militant in response to the realities of the marketplace. It now provides the power of a labor union to its members while still radiating the public image of an exclusively professional association. In reality, the AFT and NEA operate similarly. Neither is a union in the full sense of the term, despite the AFT's affiliation with the AFL-CIO, but both, although particularly the AFT, can function as unions in crises.

SOME TEACHER UNION HISTORY[3]

The United Federation of Teachers (UFT), a local affiliate of the AFT in New York City, was elected bargaining agent for 44,000 New York City public school teachers in 1961. The UFT won almost three times as many votes as the NEA affiliate, the Teachers Bargaining Organization. The most important event of the election was that the labor movement, for the first time, actively supported a teacher organization with money and manpower. Shortly after the UFT won election as bargaining agent, the AFT returned the favor to organized labor by joining the Industrial Union Department of the AFL-CIO, the major contributor to the UFT. The IUD has since been very active in organizing public school teachers for collective bargaining. It realizes that if it can organize teachers nationally now, it might be able to organize a sizable portion of the growing number of white-collar and professional workers later. The UFT enjoyed, for this reason, lavish union aid in its campaign to win election as bargaining representative for New York City's teachers.

Following its impressive victory, the UFT immediately started negotiations with the New York City Board of Education. When negotiations collapsed in April 1962, the UFT called a strike that resulted in 20,000 teachers being absent from their classrooms. The strike lasted only one day. A salary agreement was soon reached as politicians pressed for a solution. The end-product of negotiations was a detailed forty-page agreement that specifically defined teacher rights, privileges, responsibilities, and salary levels.

The collective bargaining agreement negotiated by the UFT and the school board in 1962 encouraged teacher organizations across the nation to step up their efforts. American Federation of Teachers' affiliates in other cities mobilized to secure bargaining rights. National Education Association affiliates did the same to avoid the attrition of their membership. In fact, NEA affiliates even began to take the initiative in some cases, obviously reasoning that if they did not represent the teachers, the AFT would. The NEA thus began to compete seriously with the AFT. To do so successfully, it had to become militant and participate in what amounted to collective bargaining. The NEA prefers the term "professional negotiations" in order to distinguish its efforts from those of the labor movement. But its organizational efforts are similar to those of unions, as are the AFT's; that is, initiate work stoppage when all other channels have been exhausted. What has happened is that the competition between the NEA and AFT has been almost as great a source of bargaining activity as the dissatisfaction with working conditions and salaries.

The struggle between the NEA and AFT continues unabated. The AFT has proven more successful in the urban areas. As indicated, job satisfaction has diminished greatly there. The more militant, overtly union tactics of the AFT have appealed to urban teachers who have grown increasingly alienated from their jobs. One analyst has explained the popularity of the AFT in the cities by the fact that urban teachers "face working conditions and a social milieu similar to those of lower level employees of mass industry."[4] The NEA has maintained strength in rural areas where the traditional middle-class behavior of teachers has remained somewhat workable. However, since the nation is increasingly metropolitan, the NEA must organize in the cities as successfully as the AFT or it will eventually lose substantial membership and prestige. To date, the NEA has been considerably successful in co-opting and emulating AFT strategies and programs in the cities. In fact, in New York state, where teacher unions are especially strong, the NEA and AFT have become aware that through their intense competition they have actually been fighting a common battle. Consequently, they have merged. NEA-AFT mergers have been transacted in a number of other states, involving communities such as Gibraltar, Michigan, and New Orleans, Louisiana. Delegates at the NEA's 1972 annual convention in Atlantic City, New

Jersey, acted upon the new consciousness by voting for a national NEA-AFT merger. There is now, however, a stalemate over the question of affiliation with the AFL-CIO, the AFT's parent union in the labor movement. The NEA wants disaffiliation; the AFT does not.

THE CHANGING PATTERN OF POWER[5]

The concept of sovereignty has changed substantially as authority patterns in the society have changed and public employees have asserted a right to organize. The traditional concept of sovereignty was that governments and their subdivisions enjoyed absolute power to legislate and enforce the laws within the framework of constitutional authority. The government established the terms and conditions of employment for teachers and other employees unilaterally. Under this form of authority, collective negotiations could only be an illegal sharing of power. To allow teachers to participate in decisions constituted an abdication of government responsibility.

The theoretical and practical foundations of the traditional sovereignty position have collapsed. New state laws and administrative decisions have officially altered the old form of sovereignty. Now state laws frequently require local school boards to consult with employee organizations or negotiate conditions of employment with them. Consequently, unilateral decision making has given way to codetermination of policy. School boards and teacher organizations share power in most contemporary educational contexts.

The Wagner Act of 1935 requires employers in the private sector to negotiate on wages, hours, and conditions of employment. The definition of what constituted "wages" and "hours" was quite clear. Defining "conditions of employment" was much more difficult. Labor board and court interpretations through the years have increased the issues that can be negotiated. Today, private employees can raise such considerations as an employer's prerogative to unilaterally subcontract work to outside firms. The unmistakable trend has been to expand the scope of bargaining.[6]

The procedures developed for labor-management relations in the private sector have, however, limited application to the situation of public school teachers. Employees in the private sector enjoy an almost unlimited right to strike. In contrast, teachers have not yet won the legal right to strike except in Hawaii, Alaska, Vermont, Michigan, and Pennsylvania, where there are no legal penalties for strikes. The private employer can make binding commitments and implement them. Many school boards, however, are not authorized to make such commitments. Much depends upon the appropriation of sufficient funds to meet teachers' demands for higher salaries and improved working conditions. Negotiations must proceed under the assumption of adequate funding, lately a rather untenable assumption. Finally, some conditions of teacher employment have been politically established through legislation, which is much less often the case in private industry. It is apparent that teachers, as public employees, must be covered by a separate statute that provides for the unique aspects of their public service.[7]

No uniform guidelines for negotiations in public education exist at this time. Each state negotiates in its own way. The Minnesota law states that the school board is obligated to discuss "conditions of professional service, as well as educational and professional policies, relationships, grievance procedures, and other matters as apply to teachers."[8] A New Jersey study commission on public employee relations advised the governor and the legislature that "issues subject to mutual resolution are those relating to wages, salaries, working conditions, and other terms of employment. The scope of collective negotiations should not exceed the legal jurisdiction of appointing authorities of public employees or recommend legal policy."[9] The commission recommended that "The broadest latitude for collective negotiations should be available to the public employers and employees," excluding the right to strike and lockout.[10] California law specifies that school employers "shall meet and confer" with employee representatives concerning issues relating to employment conditions and employer-employee relations, including but not restricted to wages, hours, and other terms and conditions of employment and regarding the "definition of educational objectives, the determination of the content of courses and curricula, the selection of textbooks, and other aspects of the instructional program to the extent that such matters are within the discretion of the public school employers or governing board under the law."[11] Other states limit negotiations to employment conditions and salaries.

The right of teachers to organize in order to advance their interests as professionals has been well established. State constitutions and the First and Fourteenth amendments provide the legal basis for the right. The two amendments guarantee the rights of assembly, association, and petitioning the government for redress of grievances. Many states have actively supported the right of public employees to organize, although a few states and municipalities have attempted to prevent public employees from joining labor organizations. Nevertheless, the right of teachers to organize in their own interest is an undeniable reality. This right does not include the right to strike. That remains illegal, except in Hawaii, Alaska, Vermont,

Michigan, and Pennsylvania, the only states that do not penalize teacher strikes.

THE PROCESS OF COLLECTIVE NEGOTIATION

Collective negotiation is a constructive relationship for the solution of problems based on the mutual interests of the parties involved. It is more than a bilateral arrangement; it is multilateral. The bargaining parties—school boards and teacher organizations—are responsive not only to each other but also to their constituencies, other interest groups, and public opinion. As long as this responsiveness prevails in a dispute, collective negotiation can continue and a solution is possible.

RECOGNITION

Lacking an organization to bargain for him, each teacher stands as an individual before the school board. He must live with the unilateral decisions of administrators. He is no better than a petty civil servant. To preclude this unenviable state of affairs, an organization must represent the teachers before the school board, effectively compelling the board to share authority with teachers. The school board must recognize a teacher organization as the authorized representative of the professional staff in order for productive negotiations to occur. It possesses the authority to negotiate with teacher organizations and implement collective bargaining agreements. If it realizes that teachers who participate in decision making will perform at higher levels of productivity and contribute substantially to the betterment of the educational program, it will find it in its enlightened self-interest to recognize and bargain with teacher organizations.[12]

The NEA and AFT have adopted a policy of exclusive recognition. This means that the teacher organization that enjoys majority support from the professional staff should be granted exclusive negotiation rights. An election determines which organization has majority support. Administrators and school boards have also decided to support exclusive recognition. In 1966, the American Association of School Administrators accepted exclusive recognition. Its revised policy states that all professional staff members should belong to a single organization that will be accorded exclusive recognition.[13] In 1967, the National School Boards Association also expressed approval of exclusive recognition.[14]

The policy that only one organization should represent teachers is often opposed as undemocratic. But compare this to political life, where a congressman represents all members of a voting district. Critics have the right to disagree, but there is still only one representative per district. There is, therefore, nothing revolutionary about one organization representing teachers in each school district or whatever geographical area constitutes the negotiating unit.

To understand the need for a single representative, one has only to consider the alternatives. The alternatives are proportional representation and the recognition of more than one organization. In a system of proportional representation, a negotiating committee is composed of representatives from each teacher organization in proportion to the number of members each organization has in the school district. The committee represents all teachers before the school board. This system does not promote effective representation. When representatives from several organizations sit on a committee, each member tends to compete with the others to gain popularity from his constituency and win new members. Representatives of minority organizations have nothing much to lose through intransigence and unreasonableness. In fact, they may hope to enhance their position through hard-line tactics. The majority organization's representative must meet the minority's challenge. He may occasionally seek to do so by acting equally intransigent and unreasonable. This state of affairs does not at all contribute to productive negotiations. Each representative will attempt to win as much credit as possible for any bargaining gains. Even without the rivalry, it is certain that the representatives will reflect their organizations' differing philosophies in the discussions. This makes the solidarity that helps win benefits hard to come by.

The recognition of more than one organization as bargaining agent presents serious problems, too. If negotiations are to amount to anything worthwhile in a multiple recognition situation, several representatives rather than just one must agree with the school board's position. Thus, instead of reaching one agreement, several must be negotiated. The bargaining strength of teachers is considerably weakened. The board can take advantage of the divisiveness by pitting one organization against another so that they waste their time quarreling rather than working together for an agreement benefiting all teachers. The solution is, of course, exclusive recognition. The teacher organization must inform the school board that an agreement reached through collective negotiations with its exclusive representative is, in fact, an agreement with the entire teaching staff.

The school board determines the composition of its own negotiating panel. It may appoint the superintendent as chief negotiator or it may designate a school board member to do the job. It can also select a third party, often a person skilled in conducting collective negotiations, to assume the responsibility for negotiating on behalf of the board. The school board often employs lawyers to advise during the bargaining.[15]

The school board and the teacher organization are required to bargain in good faith. By good-faith bargaining, we mean that both parties are obligated to meet at reasonable times, submit counterproposals, and commit the negotiated agreement to writing. State law varies on the subject. Most states with legislation on the subject require that bargaining be in good faith and that the agreement be in writing. The critical consideration is that *both* parties are obligated to negotiate in good faith. Bargaining cannot be a one-way street.

THE SCOPE OF NEGOTIATIONS

The scope of collective bargaining is considerably broader in public education than in private industry. In the private sector, the stress is on job security and economic reward. But the public school teacher is also interested, although usually secondarily, in educational policy, involving such matters as curriculum, faculty self-governance, and extracurricular duties. The NEA has, in fact, stated that bargaining must include all matters that concern the quality of the educational system. The AFT has proclaimed that no issue is outside the purview of negotiations. Some school boards have overreacted to the NEA and AFT's policy guidelines by attempting to severely restrict the scope of negotiations for fear they will relinquish their decision-making power. But most school boards, especially in the cities, have been willing, at least under the threat of a walkout, to talk over the whole range of pressing issues.[16]

The excessive limitation of issues discussed in negotiations makes the process less productive. School boards, accustomed to unilateral decision making, often find the sharing of power an unpleasant experience. They are inclined to negotiate a minimum of policy matters to diminish the effect of collective bargaining. They also claim that many policy concerns are actually administrative prerogatives that cannot be negotiated. This is a very negative, uncreative approach to negotiations. The school boards must think less of their prerogatives and more of effective problem solving that will eventuate in teacher job satisfaction and quality education.

The ultimate purpose of negotiation is problem solving so that the schools can have satisfactory human relations and a quality educational program. It is important that employer and employee representatives maintain a flexible outlook in their discussions. They should not severely limit the list of negotiable items before talking with one another. This causes the discussions to be strained and artificial. The employer should recognize that by discussing issues, he is not abdicating his authority over policy. And the employee representatives should refrain from being excessively demanding or belligerent.

The attitudes of those involved in professional negotiations are crucial. If the school board or teacher organization takes a hard line, there is much polarization and conflict. The resulting emotional climate is not conducive to agreement. There is considerable work stoppage, legal action, political maneuvering, and outright deviousness. However, when all parties express the attitude that they have a responsibility to solve pressing problems that affect the welfare of students, parents, and the community, as well as themselves, professional negotiations are much more likely to result in a workable agreement.

NEGOTIATION IMPASSE[17]

Negotiations between the school board and teacher representatives occasionally break down. Further bargaining, at this point, appears hopeless. A neutral third party must be brought in to act as catalyst or arbitrator. Four impasse procedures are available:

1. *Mediation.* A neutral third party assists the negotiators in settling their dispute with counsel and suggestions. This process is voluntary and the decision is not binding.
2. *Fact finding.* A third party conducts a formal hearing to investigate the dispute. Each disputant presents his case. Upon completion of the hearing, the fact finder issues a public report that usually contains recommendations. The justification for this procedure is that the public will tend to accept the fact finder's report and exert pressure on both parties to reach an agreement.
3. *Binding arbitration.* Both school board and teacher representatives submit their dispute to an impartial third party whose decision is final. Both parties must accept the arbitrator's judgment. In this procedure, the preliminary method of investigating the dispute is similar to the fact-finding process.

4. *Advisory (non-binding) arbitration.* This procedure is similar to binding arbitration, except the arbitrator's judgment is not final. The investigation is similar to that in fact finding.

Several states have established impasse procedures administered by the state departments of education or the state labor relations boards. These agencies can provide experts in employee-management relations for any one of the four impasse procedures. State laws or local agreements between school boards and teacher organizations determine which state agency will handle an appeal.

ADMINISTERING THE AGREEMENT

The most important aspect of collective negotiations is the routine administration of the agreement, commonly referred to as the grievance procedure. Through this procedure, employees and employer can meet to interpret what was written into their agreement. The employer is required to hear employee appeals at successively higher levels of the administrative hierarchy until the dispute is resolved. The grievance can be something on the order of a violation of school policy or a contract violation. If no settlement results, the dispute is usually submitted to an impartial third party for arbitration.

The grievance procedure can be quite legalistic or clinical. If both parties insist upon rigid adherence to the letter of the law, the procedure is legalistic. This situation is highly formalized and promotes conflict. The disputants frequently resort to an attorney and legal methods of resolving problems. In the clinical procedure, both parties abide by the intent of the agreement. Misinterpretation and disputes occur, but the parties are more flexible and reasonable in their approach to the resolution of conflict. This method is very sophisticated; it demands accommodation and cooperation.[18]

THE STRIKE[19]

If all else fails, the strike emerges as a legitimate, but not legal, alternative. The First and Fourteenth amendments seem to support unionization and ultimately striking by public employees, but the law does not. Present trends promise that there will be some modification of this legal position. Now, however, although we may feel that a strike is needed, we cannot consider a strike a legal method of bringing change.

Two proposals are frequently heard in favor of legalization. In one proposal, a strike would be legal if the school board rejected the fact finder's recommendation. If this became law, the fact finder would be under pressure to produce a report the school board could accept. After all, the fact finder knows that rejection could lead to a lawful strike. Since his goal is to resolve the conflict as directly as possible, he will be inclined to favor the school board in order to preclude (or at least diminish) the possibility of prolonged dispute.

The second proposal is to deny injunctive relief where it can be demonstrated that the school board did not act in good faith to resolve the dispute. In this case, the strike should be lawful. If a clear and present danger to the public health or safety exists or if the teacher organization has not resorted fully to all available statutory impasse procedures, an injunction should be issued, but it should be no broader than necessary. It should prohibit only the teacher actions that are a demonstrated threat to public health or safety and it should specify the teacher organization's violations. The injunction should be lifted when the threat to the public safety or health has been removed or the teacher organizations have ceased the violations in question. This second proposal, denying injunctive relief under certain conditions, would discourage impasse and promote forthright negotiations.[20]

School quality may deteriorate when teachers cannot withdraw their services. If teachers could legally strike, school administrators and elected officials would have to make hard political decisions. If they allowed problems to fester, they would no longer have a teaching staff. Thus the threat of the strike would preclude administrators and public officials from abdicating their responsibility for quality schools for the sake of political convenience. They would have to provide the necessary resources for education or witness the collapse of the educational system. The threat of the legal strike would introduce some very real incentives to solve problems in educational settings. Although illegal now, the strike is still a practical reality. Teachers have been striking and will continue to strike, in the last resort, to win demands.

A considerable amount of altruism attaches to teacher strikes. The statistics demonstrate that a good percentage of strikes seek the improvement of the educational system as well as better salaries and fringe benefits. David Selden, president of the AFT, believes "it is often more harmful to the children for teachers not to strike than it would be to close down the schools for a while."[21] In response to criticism of teachers during the April 1962 strike in New York City,

Charles Cogen, then UFT president, argued, "It is better for a child to lose a few days or weeks of schooling than go through life handicapped by years of inferior education."[22] As a result of the one-day strike, the school budget was increased by $13 million in order to expand direct services to students. School board members and administrators should be very pleased that teachers care enough to close the schools down.

Teachers possess intimate knowledge of the learning and emotional needs of their students. If their expertise cannot play a role in developing a school policy that will meet those needs, they can only experience intense frustration. Recently, teachers have begun to act directly upon their frustration by striking. Their activism has promoted quality education.

SOME ALTERNATIVES

The strike is the teachers' final weapon in the pursuit of their demands. Teachers do not strike each time they have grievances. To do so would be unproductive as well as illegal. A method short of the strike, which the NEA in particular likes to use, is the sanction. The sanction does not require a work stoppage. It serves as a warning signal that unless substandard conditions improve, the school system may be impaired. The sanction tactic may assume several forms:

- Informing the citizens of a school district that adverse conditions exist in the school system.
- Advising business and industry to avoid the district because of substandard conditions.
- Censuring a school system for specific or general deficiencies.
- Advising teachers to refuse to apply for or accept appointments in a school district offering unprofessional working conditions and depressed salaries.[23]

American Federation of Teachers president David Selden specifies four alternatives to teacher work stoppage,[24] which he feels, however, are less effective than the strike. The alternatives are (1) living with present conditions, (2) persistent friction between teachers and school authorities, (3) political involvement, and (4) arbitration. The first alternative is, of course, no solution. The second only promotes low staff morale and political firings. The third produces little in most situations because the available political candidates who can possibly win do not support effective solutions. As to the final avenue, arbitration, neither party to a dispute will bargain in good faith if it knows the dispute will ultimately be decided by an arbitrator. The disputants will simply present their most adamant arguments and let the arbitrator compromise between the two extremes. Nobody expresses reasonable views or yields on any points. The arbitration sessions become a form of theatrics.

Selden believes that the strike emerges, in a consideration of alternatives, as the avenue most likely to provide a viable solution to educational grievances. When teaching conditions are substandard, it is actually professionally incumbent on teachers to strike. If they cannot withdraw their services when the conditions under which they work are unprofessional, they certainly cannot claim professional status. And if they are not professionals, they will certainly play no significant role in solving educational problems.[25]

CONTRACTS

The majority of collective bargaining agreements have focused on salaries, sick leave policies, grievance procedures, and other conditions of work. Clauses concerning professional matters such as curriculum, in-service programs, class size, and instruction are generally of secondary concern, but they often appear.

The typical collective negotiation agreement consists basically of clauses specifying the teachers' working conditions and benefits. The working conditions and benefits most frequently covered include length and frequency of faculty meetings, length of the school day, extracurricular duties, teacher lounges, parking, severance pay, health and medical insurance, and tuition reimbursement for teachers taking courses. Clauses concerning teacher promotion, reassignment, and transfer are included in most contracts. Many contracts guarantee teachers the right to see their files.

The following items recur most frequently in collective bargaining agreements:

- Budget preparation
- In-service training programs
- Salaries and fringe benefits
- Assignment
- Tenure
- Merit pay
- Teacher recruitment

- Curriculum preparation
- Class size
- Teacher transfer
- Extracurricular responsibilities
- Daily schedule
- Evaluation[26]

Despite this impressive array of issues that teachers have been successful in negotiating, the NEA has not yet achieved its objective of negotiating with school boards all concerns that affect the quality of the educational program, nor has the AFT achieved its objective of negotiating any issue that affects teachers' working conditions.

THE IMPACT OF COLLECTIVE NEGOTIATIONS

Collective negotiations seem to be here to stay. It is appropriate, therefore, to consider their long-term effect. Charles S. Benson, Associate Professor of Education at Berkeley, has concluded that negotiations will (1) force teacher salaries up, (2) work to renew the inner-cities, and (3) revitalize the role of the public school teacher in the society.[27] These positive effects, should they be substantially forthcoming in the long term, seem more than sufficient justification for teachers' participation in collective bargaining. Only through professional involvement in policy will teachers be able to contribute their expertise and commitment to the solution of problems. Only through participation in the determination of working conditions and salary levels can teachers appropriately be called professionals.

Teachers have mobilized a considerable amount of collective power through their organizations. One must contrast this with the facts that teacher organizations function in an area devoid of traditional market constraints and that teachers perform a critical public service. Teachers must use their power responsibly in this context or they will inflict substantial harm on the public schools. To date, this responsibility has usually been evident. But since an adequate set of laws and procedures for settling public labor-management disputes has not yet been developed, teachers must be particularly aware that it is morally incumbent on them to act responsibly.

Collective bargaining may have resulted in larger school budgets and, in many cases, higher tax rates than would have prevailed had teachers not organized. A considerable portion of the larger budgets has been used to increase salaries in response to teacher demands. In some cases, bargaining may have caused school boards to transfer resources from educational programs in order to increase teacher benefits. Since budgets increase due to inflation, rising enrollments, and "normal" salary increases, it is difficult to determine to what extent bargaining has contributed to the reallocation of resources away from educational programs and student services. Although higher salaries help schools recruit and retain highly qualified teachers, the effects of dropping or scaling down programs to meet higher salary levels cannot be dismissed. Surveying all the evidence, it seems certain that teacher bargaining has directly caused substantial increases in public school budgets and significant modifications in educational programs. Teachers, acting in concert, have compelled the community to supply substantially more resources than it would otherwise have provided.

Teacher demands now exceed the capacity of the schools to meet them. The limitations of the local property tax base makes this so. What teachers regard as optimum class size, adequate materials, and livable incomes cannot be sustained by the present sources of revenue. Benson stresses the need for federal funding of the schools. This approach would raise constitutional questions and probably require a constitutional change.[28] The constitution now charges the states with the responsibility for education. Federal responsibility or partnership could infuse new sources of funds into the schools. If tax reform were also forthcoming, there would certainly be much new money available. For example, millions of dollars worth of oil products go untaxed annually due to the oil depletion allowance. Oil companies employ the graduates of schools to manufacture their profitable products, but they pay little to support the schools. If Congress reformed this and numerous other major loopholes, much, if not all, the money schools now desperately needed would be available. Without reform, the schools, especially in the central cities, will continue to wage a losing battle against rising costs and retrenchment of resources. And teacher demands will continue to be met at the expense of educational programs.

SHUTTING THE COUNTRY DOWN

Teacher organizations are, of course, excellent instruments for realizing teacher demands. But they also contain within them a great potential for moral good. Teachers can apply their power to compel humane policies for the national good. Whether on economic, social, or international issues, teachers should collectively express their opinions.

When our institutions are working undemocratically during crises, teachers might link up with other unionized income earners to threaten a national strike. For example, teachers might shut down the learning activities of the nation when the government attempts to embark upon an illegal, undeclared war. This would compel consultation and a realistic consideration of alternatives and consequences before another step is taken. Teachers shutting down the classroom—or, with the help of others who work for a living, teachers shutting down the economy—is an extreme action. It should be a behavior reserved for the last resort. But when the affairs of government have gone so awry that they threaten the future of the youth we educate, then teachers have the supreme moral obligation to close ranks and defy the institutions that are threatening, without justification and consent, the lives of innocent learners and the welfare of our country.

A NEW WORLD

A new world exists in the American schools today. The traditional pattern of authority between teacher, school, and community has collapsed. The teacher confronts demands in the schools that his training and experience have not prepared him to meet. To make this world endurable, even satisfying, the teacher has turned to the resources of his group. By acting as a group, teachers are redefining authority patterns in the changing schools and providing for their own social and economic security.[29] The teachers' inclination to act collectively will intensify as the demands placed upon them and the schools increase. This will be true not only in the city, for the factors alienating teachers are also beginning to tell in the suburbs and, to a lesser extent, in rural America.

A notable paradox characterizes the teacher union movement. Teachers, feeling keenly the forces depressing job satisfaction, demand and fight for better salaries and working conditions. But on each occasion that they win more benefits, their group solidarity—or alienation and isolation from the community—increases. Their victory is an organized effort at the economic expense of the community. They have confronted most untraditionally a public that would prefer to paternalize them. Thus by winning benefits, teachers become further alienated. And it is, of course, low psychic satisfaction that impelled teachers to seek benefits initially. With this sort of mechanism operative, no end to teacher militancy and demands is in sight.

NOTES

[1] The sections Social and Economic Forces, Unrealistic Demands, Rising Expectations, and Seeking A Role Model are based on James Cass and Max Birnbaum, "What Makes Teachers Militant," *Saturday Review*, 51 (20 January 1968), 54–56.

[2] The statistics about the AFT and NEA are drawn from *In Search of Excellence*, (Washington, D.C., American Federation of Teachers, 1971) and *NEA Handbook* (Washington, D.C., National Educational Association, 1971).

[3] See Miriam Wasserman, *The School Fix, NYC, USA* (New York, Outerbridge and Dienstfrey, 1970), Part II, pp. 185–390.

[4] Fred W. Smith, "Teachers Unions v. Professional Associations," *School & Society* (December 1962), 439.

[5] This section, The Changing Pattern Of Power, is based on Thomas P. Gilroy, *Educator's Guide to Collective Negotiations* (Columbus, Ohio, Charles E. Merrill Publishing Co., 1969), pp. 15–32.

[6] *Ibid.*, p. 21.

[7] "Special Feature On Professional Negotiation Legislation," *Today's Education*, 57, no. 7 (October 1968), 50–60.

[8] Gilroy, *op. cit.*, pp. 21–22.

[9] Public and School Employees' Grievance Procedure Study Commission, Final Report to the Governor and Legislature, State of New Jersey, January, 1968, p. 1.

[10] *Ibid.*

[11] Robert E. Doherty and Walter E. Oberer, *Teachers, School Boards, and Collective Bargaining: A Changing of the Guard* (Ithaca, N.Y., Cornell University Press, 1967), p. 91.

[12] Gilroy, *op. cit.*, pp. 62–63.

[13] Gilroy, *op. cit.*, pp. 72–73.

[14] *Ibid.*

[15] Gilroy, *op. cit.*, p. 64.

[16] Gilroy, *op. cit.*, pp. 63–67.

[17] See the several references to negotiation impasse procedures in Gilroy, *op. cit.*

[18] Gilroy, *op. cit.*, pp. 64–65.

[19] "Special Feature on Professional Negotiation—Part 2," *Today's Education*, 58, no. 1 (January 1969), p. 59.

[20] *Ibid.*

[21] David Selden, "Needed: More Teacher Strikes," *Saturday Review*, 48 (15 May 1965), 75.

[22] *Ibid.*

[23]"Special Feature On Professional Negotiation Legislation," *Today's Education*, 57, no. 7 (October 1968), 50–60.

[24] Selden, *op. cit.*

[25]*Ibid.*

[26]Gilroy, *op. cit.*, p. 72.

[27]Charles S. Benson, "Economic Problem of Education Associated with Collective Negotiation," *The Changing Employment Relationship in Public Schools* (Ithaca, N.Y., New York State School of Industrial and Labor Relations, Cornell University, 1966), p. 2.

[28]Charles S. Benson, *The Cheerful Prospect* (Boston, Houghton Mifflin, 1965).

[29]For extended reading in the area of teacher organizations, see Myron Lieberman, *The Future of Public Education* (Chicago, The University of Chicago Press, 1960); Ronald G. Corwin, *Militant Professionalism* (New York, Appleton-Century-Crofts, 1970); Robert Dreeben, *The Profession of Teaching* (Glenview, Ill., Scott, Foresman, and Company, 1969); Stanley Elam, Myron Lieberman, and Michael Moskow, eds., *Readings on Collective Negotiations in Public Education* (Chicago, Rand-McNally, 1967); Martin Mayer, *The Teachers' Strike: New York, 1968* (New York, Harper and Row, 1969); Edward B. Shils and C. Taylor Whittier, *Teachers, Administrators and Collective Bargaining* (New York, Thomas Y. Crowell, 1968); Marvin J. Levine, "The Issues In Teacher Strikes," *The Journal of General Education*, 22, no. 1 (April 1970), 1–18; James Cass, "Politics and Education in the Sunshine State," *Saturday Review*, 51 (20 April 1968), 63–65.

4
Accountability and vouchers

Two recent developments in authority and education are *accountability* and *vouchers*. The desire of parents, students, and the community to influence the type and quality of education is the source of the new developments. It is very important that the prospective teacher and administrator understand these two trends and the full implications of each. Both accountability and vouchers are innovations that can radically change the traditional authority relation of teachers with school boards, parents, and administrators. They can therefore greatly change the nature of the teacher's job and the satisfactions and frustrations that flow from teaching.

DEFINITIONS

Accountability simply means that the educator and school are responsible for the learner demonstrating measurable achievement following the educational experience. The demand for accountability is basically the call to make educational authority justify the experiences it has devised for learners according to an evaluation of those experiences. To do this, it is essential that educators clearly state their objectives first and compare their results to the objectives later.

Vouchers are equal shares of public educational money granted directly to parent and student who decide where the learner should attend school and what sort of program he should pursue. Vouchers provide learner and parent an individualized means to make educational institutions and professionals responsive to learner needs and aspirations. Voucher recipients can close schools that do not meet real learning needs simply by choosing not to spend their grants at inferior schools. They will choose the more successful schools or found their own independent schools. The important point about the trends toward accountability and vouchers is that both require the school and teacher to share authority with students and parents.

ACCOUNTABILITY

Schools should be accountable for educational outcomes; they should insure that children do, in fact, learn. The implementation of this principle requires proof of results rather than mere assignment of educational value to inputs. The Coleman Report of 1966,[1] perhaps more than any other source, precipitated the movement toward accountability. The Coleman study found that those variables—books, equipment, curriculum materials, libraries, teacher-pupil ratio, and so on—that educators have traditionally believed crucial to the learning process were not actually critical. The crucial factors occurred in human interaction contexts, within authority relations among people. The student's home environment, the social composition of the student body, and the quality of teachers (quality being contingent upon the relationship of teacher to learner) were the critical determinants of educational motivation and achievement. Thus the old authoritative pronouncements about "quality education" and the *pro forma* appeals to legislatures were seriously challenged. Such major education journals as *Phi Delta Kappan, School & Society, Harvard Educational Review,* and *Teachers College Record* published a dialogue concerning the Coleman Report (formally entitled *Equality of Educational Opportunity*) that disseminated widely the research findings that had effectively precipitated a crisis in educational authority.

Coleman advised educators in no uncertain terms that they must evaluate the results of educational treatments rather than assume the value of their instructional programs. This was the initial call for accountability, although the term was not in vogue in 1966. The sanctity of professional expertise disappeared in the public debate over the Coleman data. A new authority relation with old constituents—parents, legislators, school boards, and teacher organizations—began to emerge to fill the vacuum.

Parents, especially in the context of community control controversies, became aware that their children might not be failing as much as the schools were. They wanted to know why the child read several grades below grade level and could not do simple arithmetic. Their vociferous demands, beginning with the Ocean Hill-Brownsville community control controversy in New York, challenged the conventional prerogative of schools to assume the value of what they were doing. They demanded that the schools be held responsible to the community to demonstrate that the students actually were learning. The confrontation that has ensued over the accountability issue, especially in the inner-cities, is a difficult one that will continue and intensify until the schools can become more effective and prove their increased effectiveness, especially in basic skills such as reading and arithmetic, the fundamental building blocks for any future success. Parents everywhere have been applying greater political pressure on the neighborhood schools, thereby producing a challenge to teacher authority.

As money became scarce and dissent and disruption became widespread on high school campuses, legislators and school boards saw the political and financial advantage of demanding accountability. They wanted a cost-effectiveness responsiveness in high schools that would guarantee greater increments of learning for their expenditures. They pointed to the miserable failure of the education of minority children and the uncertain results of federal compensatory education projects. They were effectively informing the schools and the professionals that ran them that they must justify their programs if they were to continue to enjoy funding. Thus politicians were utilizing the power of the purse to compel educational professionals to explain what they were doing. This was accountability with a vengeance.

Teacher organizations responded to this challenge to their professionalism. They recognized the need for an evaluation of what happened in the classroom but insisted that, if they were to be held responsible for the outcomes, they should participate in the evaluation. The alternative, as they saw it, was to lose the professional status that they had worked so arduously to establish. Both the National Education Association (NEA) and American Federation of Teachers (AFT) have been very apprehensive about accountability. They were particularly concerned about being charged with the responsibility for results in education over which they exercised no control.

Teacher organizations used the section of the Coleman Report that accountability advocates ignored. That is, a student's achievement is determined by many factors other than the skill and effort of the teacher. The Coleman data, they stressed, show that a great deal of pupil performance is caused by influences outside the schools such as the learner's socioeconomic status and home environment, over which educators exercise no control, and factors in the school such as peer groups, which the teacher influences minimally at best. Moreover, of the share of pupil performance attributable to the school, only a part is due to teaching. Such factors as school management and resource availability partially determine achievement. Thus the teacher organizations claimed that if they were to be held responsible, the teacher's impact on learning would have to be separated from all the other influences and they, as professionals, must participate in the evaluation process.

Teachers are moving toward professional self-governance (see Chapter 3, Teacher Organizations). Only if they achieve full professional status can they legitimately be held accountable. Professionalism means, among other things, that teachers would participate in determining their working conditions. If they do succeed in establishing the conditions under which they teach, and if they fail—that is, their students achieve below expectation—then, and only then, can teachers be held accountable for the failure of students to learn. If conditions are imposed on teachers (especially if it is their professional opinion that conditions such as class size and curriculum are not conducive to optimum learning), there is no feasible way that accountability can have meaning. A former president of the National Education Association has noted:

It is pure myth that a classroom teacher can ever be held accountable, with justice, under existing conditions. The classroom teacher has either too little control or no control over the factors which might render accountability either feasible or fair.[2]

Given this state of affairs, accountability could become merely a means to ferret out unpopular teachers and dismiss them.

The enforcement of accountability would become increasingly justifiable if teachers wielded more authority over the very foundations of the educational process. The NEA has, as a beginning, listed four areas over which the profession should exercise more authority:

1. Establishing and administering standards of professional conduct and ethics for all educators.
2. Accrediting teacher training institutions.
3. Issuing, suspending, revoking, or reinstating legal licenses for educators.
4. Administering in-service and continuing programs for teachers.[3]

If the teaching profession controlled, or substantially participated in, these critical decisions and programs, there would exist at least a partial rationale for holding teachers accountable for educational outcomes.

If teachers collectively are to be accountable for their performance, they must certainly participate in determining who becomes a teacher. This means involvement in the establishment of standards for teacher certification, preferably through professional legal boards. Legislators must delegate the responsibility for teacher certification standards to teachers if they honestly expect to demand accountability. If power were shared in this way, no valid argument could be levied against holding teachers responsible for the results of their teaching. Only when teachers share authority for the educational process can they be taken to task for the problems. Practitioner accountability could then be assured.

Certification boards composed of teachers could update requirements to meet new demands. For example, the great need for qualified professionals in the inner-city certainly warrants a requirement focused upon disadvantaged youth and the particular problems the beginning teacher encounters. Teaching professionals could acknowledge such a need and provide for it in state requirements. In this way, in the larger legal sense, teachers would be accountable for their performance because they would have established the very standards that determine who enters the profession. One should note, however, that state departments of education and colleges of education are presently not at all inclined to relinquish or share authority for teacher accreditation standards that would be logically consistent with establishing classroom teacher accountability.

TWO TYPES OF ACCOUNTABILITY

There are two types of accountability. The first, the justification of resources allocated to instructional programs according to the results produced, we have discussed. Here educators might attempt to be accountable by showing how much more (if any) learning occurs when the teacher-pupil ratio is decreased, when teachers with advanced degrees are employed, or when more money is spent. This is an efficiency or cost-effectiveness approach.

The second type of accountability focuses on consumer choice. It is hoped that by increasing consumer choice in education, competition will also increase. And, of course, the argument continues, increased competition means increased consumer control and accountability. *The voucher system, also discussed in this chapter, best illustrates this approach. If learner and parent have access to an equal financial resource (voucher) for education and can spend it as they wish, the schools will have to become more responsive. They must produce learning results or face the loss of their students.* The beneficial impact that free-market choice can have on schools is the rationale for the second type of accountability. An economist, Milton Friedman, of the University of Chicago, originated this version of accountability.

In both forms of accountability, authority is shared. In one instance, the mechanism is a cost-effectiveness calculation by funding agencies; in the second, the mechanism is consumer selection. If the schools do not begin to do a better job of relating costs to educational outcomes and satisfying consumer demand, the implementation of these two types of accountability could eventuate in a serious decline in the size of the public school establishment.

The second approach to accountability requires an information system in order to be effective. Without adequate data to inform consumer choice, the idea of making educational authority responsive through this form of accountability is void. The parent and learner must have a sufficient basis for judging school effectiveness. The mere existence of effective educational alternatives does not guarantee accountability. Each consumer must have full information about each school if he is to be able to choose on the basis of the demonstrated educational superiority or uniqueness of a school.

PERFORMANCE CONTRACTING

One component of the movement toward educational accountability has been performance contracting. In performance contracting, authority for the educational experience is shared with organizations outside the school system: A school district contracts with an outside agency (generally a private firm, but sometimes a nonprofit organization) to implement a well-defined instructional program leading to specified, measurable educational outcomes. The fee paid to the contractor depends on how well he achieves the contracted objectives; that is, how well he has shared authority for instruction with the schools. Performance contracting obviously provides very immediate incentives for effective instruction. This becomes apparent when one considers an accountability contract.

In November 1969 the Open Court Publishing Company advertised that it would sell materials for a reading program under an accountability contract.[4] The firm was entitled to keep the full price paid for their books and other materials if a class advanced one grade level within the nine-month school year. However, for each month the class as a whole failed to attain full grade level, the publisher would reimburse the school 10 percent of the price. The measure of achievement could be any of the nationally recognized reading tests. The guarantee would apply not to individual learners but to the class average. In order to qualify for a rebate, a school would have to demonstrate that every student in a class had completed the workbook exercises and a minimum of twelve "composition cycles." Thus a contractor is only fully paid when performance satisfies mutually agreeable criteria.

There is a standard way that public schools share their authority for instruction with outside agencies in a performance contracting agreement. A public authority allocates money to a local education agency to contract with private enterprise to attain specified goals within a defined time period at a particular cost. For example, money might be targeted for dropout prevention among disadvantaged youth. This educational problem would be analyzed and the achievement objectives specified. The local education agency formulates a request for a proposal and sends it to possible contractors who are known to be competent in the learning area concerned. The request for a proposal does not dictate how the job must be accomplished, but it does specify the performance, financial, legal, and administrative guidelines for the contract. The request requires that a bidder guarantee specific outcomes for specific costs. It also offers incentives to the contractor to bring each child up to specified levels of performance. The bidder then proposes a level of guarantee, time, and costs into his bid according to the degree of confidence he has in his ability to do the job.

The trend toward public schools delegating responsibility for education raises crucial legal issues. By law, local education agencies command a very limited power to contract. If they exceed their authority, any contract automatically becomes void. Generally, schools may contract with outside organizations to furnish a service only if they are *not required* to perform the task. This guideline apparently excludes much of the present school curriculum for contracting purposes. However, the decisive factor seems to be that a school cannot contract to employ private individuals over a lengthy period when public employees are available to perform the same job.[5] A limited contract, wherein a private firm provides educational services for a relatively short time and then turns over the operation to the public school, thereby helping the schools innovate, seems to satisfy legal requirements. As a rule of thumb, the local school cannot totally relinquish the policy-making prerogatives and continuing educational functions with which the state has charged it without abdicating its responsibility, even if only in a limited area of instruction.[6]

Educators must be aware of certain hazards in contracting in order to retain authority over school policy. First, they must be certain to invite only bids for clearly specified programs. If the request for a proposal is too vague, the successful bidder may eventually usurp the school's authority over the program, effectively changing school policy. This is legally indefensible. It is imperative that schools' requests for bids be specified very carefully to preserve public school autonomy. Second, the school staff must command sufficient expertise to supervise the work of the private company. If it does not, the private firm will automatically be in control of school policy for the contracted program. A school that is uncertain of its capacity to oversee contractors could hire outside management assistance, which would, of course, be sharing authority even further. Or the school could consult with other schools that employ experts in the area under contract. Third, the schools must reject the appealing opportunity to contract the learning of their most troublesome, underachieving students. The underfinanced, overburdened school might find such a state of affairs very attractive. But, to reiterate, indefinitely contracting out learning is a complete abdication of the responsibility with which the state charges a school. In short, school administrators, businesslike and entrepreneurial as many of them are inclined to be, must keep in mind that they can only share authority with private enterprise through performance contracting—they cannot divest themselves of that authority.

The ultimate significance of accountability and contracting is that they establish precedents for a new relation between funding agencies and schools. Funding agencies may demand further evidence of performance from schools as the time for final payment arrives. Consumers of educational services also may make such demands; for example, taxpayers may insist that certain learning levels be attained in the school's educational programs before the schools can be paid for their services. Thus consumers of instructional programs will enjoy an unprecedented sovereignty. They will have inverted, through contracts and accountability, the traditional authority relation of school to community. That is, the school has been in the community, but not of or by it. If performance contracting and accountability were universally in force, the school would have to be responsive to learner, parental, and community need and aspiration, or it would perish.

Psychologist Kenneth B. Clark has called for "a system of accountability . . . to insure that each teacher is responsible to his principal or assistant principal for the reading achievement of the children in his class."[7] The principal would answer in turn to a superior, and so on, until the entire educational hierarchy up to the superintendent of schools is accounted for. In Clark's scheme, the performance of school personnel is measured primarily not by direct observations of their work but rather by their "performance . . . as this is reflected in the academic performance of their students." Clark's proposal is articulated in the cause of minority students, often largely untutored by their neighborhood schools in even the most basic skills. It recognizes that the school should be accountable first for the teaching of skills, particularly arithmetic and reading. Without basic skills, no learner can advance to more complex forms of learning. The failure of ghetto schools to teach even rudimentary skills to large numbers of learners deprives those students of opportunity. It is only socially equitable that schools be held most accountable for the most essential competencies.

What Clark has proposed is a "charter of accountability."[8] A charter of accountability is an agreement between two individuals or groups—one superordinate to the other—following negotiations. All the charters taken together cover the entire school system. Each unit head is accountable for the outcomes specified in the charter that he has drawn up and that he and his superior sign. At the top, the charters combine into a system-wide charter that requires accountability of the board of education and the superintendent of schools. This constitutes a system-wide sharing of authority among educational professionals. It exacts accountability from everyone.

VOUCHERS

The most promising financial mechanism for making schools accountable is the voucher program. The financing of schools is generally carried out by funding separate schools and, within the schools, separate functions. The voucher system inverts this system by collecting taxes centrally and distributing equal shares to parents. Parents and students spend their equal educational grant as they wish. Within a defined region, they may choose the school and program of study they prefer. If too many apply for a particular school, a lottery is necessary. Losers attend the school of their second choice, unless a lottery is required there also, in which case an applicant may have to move further down his list of priorities. Some schools may be sufficiently substandard and unpopular that they cannot attract enough of a clientele to remain open at all.

Thus the voucher recipients exercise the power of discriminating consumers in the open marketplace. They compel the schools to be responsive, or accountable, to the learner's educational needs. School administrators must look to the clientele rather than a central bureaucracy for funds. This means that financially independent consumers of education have a great deal to say about what their educational system is like. One can expect that the school and community would come closer together, diminishing much of the antagonism that now exists in some communities (see Chapter 1, Community Relations).

HOW VOUCHERS WORK

An Educational Voucher Agency (EVA) would be established to administer the voucher program. The governing board could be elected or appointed. In either case, an equitable representation of minority students must be included. The EVA might administer an existing educational district or a new jurisdiction. A jurisdictional alteration would depend upon the need for choices for voucher recipients. For example, a district with few alternatives between private and public schools, and as few between different types of curricula, might need to expand to make the voucher system meaningful. In some rural areas, in fact, the voucher system may not be at all viable due to a lack of educational choices. The EVA would receive the total amount of federal, state, and local education funds to which children in its jurisdiction are entitled. It would distribute this money to particular schools only in return for vouchers, the certificates that parents and students cash at the school of their choice. The EVA would also pay parents for their children's transportation expenses to the school of their choice.

When learners enroll in a school, they should bring their vouchers, which the school will cash. Schools must be required to accept each student's voucher as full payment for his education. Without this provision, the voucher system would be ineffectual; wealthier families would bid beyond the value of the vouchers for seats in prestigious, quality schools and poor students would often be compelled to attend schools that can accommodate neither their choices nor their talents.

Only the uniform equivalence of voucher and educational costs will eliminate deprivation as a causal variable in the determination of which school a student will attend.

In order to become an "approved voucher school," one eligible to cash vouchers, a school must satisfy certain criteria. The major criteria would be the following:

1. The school must accept each voucher as full payment for a child's education, levying no additional fees.
2. The school must accept any applicant as long as it has vacancies.
3. If there is a surplus of applicants, the school must fill at least half the seats by random selection and the other half so that minorities are represented in proportion to their percentages in the district.
4. The school must keep records of money received and disbursed. This would allow both parents and voucher administrators to ascertain whether money was being spent according to voucher program regulations. This fiscal accountability is very important if the voucher program is to effectively promote the sharing of authority among parents, administrators, teachers, and learners.

EQUALIZATION OF EDUCATIONAL RESOURCES

Patricia Sexton's research demonstrates that income is the foremost predictor of educational achievement.[9] If her research is valid, it may be that in order to give everyone an opportunity to achieve to the limits of his aspirations and abilities, an equal part of public educational monies must be allocated to all, with the requirement that the grant serve as full payment for the learner's choice of educational experiences. The equal grants, the educational vouchers, thus become excellent means of breaking the unjust link between income and educational opportunity. The way to provide for social justice is to fund individuals' educational programs rather than the curricula of schools. Hence a learner could not be relegated, due to race, socioeconomic background, or geographical location, to a school where considerably fewer resources are available than at other more favored schools. The learner would be legally entitled to an equal share of public money and schools would be forbidden to price the total educational program beyond the voucher's value.

The individual's access to an equal share of public money for education should be the subject of a constitutional guarantee. Every student should enjoy a legally defensible claim to an equal share of public educational monies. The existing laws barring discrimination, the constitutional guarantees (especially the Fourteenth Amendment), and a firm set of voucher regulations providing for equality of educational opportunity must be strictly enforced to insure the ongoing viability of an education voucher scheme.

SOME CAVEATS

Granting each learner an equal education voucher to spend as he wishes might well reinforce the preponderant public view that education is chiefly a private benefit. The policy that each learner spends public money for his own education could be converted, in the crucible of political pressure, to the practice that each learner spends his own money, either on a pay-as-you-go basis or a deferred payment plan. Citizens and politicians might begin to lament the fact that they are directly subsidizing individuals' aspirations for success. Thus the funding of schools through direct grants to parents and learners may be thoroughly emasculated.

The voucher program will introduce incentives for the growth and development of private schools. Of course, the possibility exists that educational hucksters will move significantly into the market in pursuit of easy profits. In the absence of adequate safeguards, profiteers could enjoy a field day in a market governed by vouchers. They might attempt to exploit vouchers in the same way that hucksters profitably exploited the GI Bill by founding electronics, watchmaking, and key punch "schools." The majority of the victims of such fly-by-night enterprises were former servicemen from low socioeconomic backgrounds who were seeking quick educational cures for career frustrations. The naive would certainly be the foremost target of unprincipled entrepreneurs endeavoring to take advantage of a voucher program. But regulations forcing each new school to meet high-level minimum accreditation criteria could prevent any such widespread charlatanry.

Regulation would keep the quality of the entire educational market based upon vouchers at such a high level of quality that no parent could really completely err in behalf of his child. Thus Gresham's Law—hucksterism and inferior schooling driving out high-quality education—could not apply. All schools, public and private, would be very much subject to an assessment of whether they taught the minimum skills required by the state. They would be ineligible to cash vouchers if they discriminated against any group in their admissions. Learners' cumulative choices not to spend their vouchers at a particular school would close that school. Thus, if adequate information were available to the consumer, both hucksterism in the private sphere and failure to educate in the public schools would result in consumers terminating noncompetitive educational services.

DESTRUCTION OF THE PUBLIC SCHOOLS

A frequent objection to vouchers is that they would destroy the public schools. Few pause to consider that a radical reconstruction of traditional authority patterns in the schools may be desirable, especially for the socioeconomically disadvantaged. For example, only 15 percent of inner-city students can read.[10] The reformation of the present monolithic public system is particularly advantageous to such groups. The majority also benefits because vouchers promote social mixing (according to the Coleman Report, an important determinant of achievement and motivation) and, of course, a multicultural educational experience. When each learner has an equal claim on public school money, and each school must satisfy the admission criteria we have discussed, integration of all sorts—racial, ethnic, and class—will ensue.

As with any serious attempt to change the public schools, the voucher plan would encounter the intolerant attitudes that have prevented or impeded significant change in the past. The attitudes supporting racial segregation in housing will be particularly difficult to overcome. A mere change in the form of financing education is not sufficient. It can only provide the means for beneficial change if people desire positive change. No social system operates in a moral vacuum, and vouchers are certainly not without a value context. They are, in fact, a threat to the racial and class attitudes of our society. A regulated voucher system would promote contact between the children of parents who live in fear of people who think, look, and spend differently than they do. The imposition of a full-scale voucher program, a new type of educational authority, on the residentially segregated neighborhood schools would certainly generate considerable conflict, at least initially. But American society and American schools desperately need the cathartic shock that would flow from the change.

MEANS TO RACIAL INTEGRATION

A system of vouchers, regulated to preclude discrimination, offers the possibility of considerable racial integration. Most poor nonwhites are residentially segregated in neighborhoods where they attend inferior schools. Since they must attend the school closest to their home (except the relative few who are affected by busing and other educational reforms), they enjoy no real choice. Thus the neighborhood school has a captive clientele; its authority is illegitimate. Since virtually everyone in the ghetto school jurisdiction is poor or nonwhite, each learner who attends is of a similar background. This homogeneity produces, according to the 1966 Coleman Report, a learning environment that is not conducive to high achievement and motivation. It certainly does not promote the national ideal that people of different backgrounds should attend school under the same roof.

Vouchers could collapse the authority of the neighborhood schools and produce an enriched, democratic learning environment. Since many nonwhites who are bound into inferior schools want quality education, they will use their equal educational resource to escape the segregated, ghetto school and attend integrated, generally higher-quality schools. Thus vouchers should eventually destroy inferior schools in and out of the ghetto; this is one of the main purposes of the reform. If, however, only the most talented, highly motivated students in the worst schools used vouchers to escape poor learning environments, the quality of the substandard schools would be depressed even further. If this occurred on a massive scale, it could be the undoing of vouchers as a tool of social reconstruction. If vouchers are to work at all, the government must vigorously advise the poor of the voucher opportunity and give assistance to them so that they may capitalize on the opportunity.

Regulation is definitely needed if the voucher system is to result in integration. The Jencks Commission report predicts that an absence of regulation would produce the most serious reversal yet for the education of disadvantaged children.[11] However, one should note that no school board presently needs vouchers to guarantee segregation; it need only maintain the neighborhood school system. Bigoted parents who wish to avoid citizens of different backgrounds can move to a comfortably segregated neighborhood. No governmental agency is likely to prevent this conventional practice, except perhaps in the South. With vouchers, as with any reform, the program is only as good as the motives of the people responsible for the program.

Voucher program builders must establish just regulations that reflect egalitarian motives and they must enforce them. For example, a school board in the neighborhood school context can eliminate segregation if it so wishes, but the task is much more difficult than it would be under the voucher system. An EVA committed to integration can easily devise regulations to implement its intent. Furthermore, the legal precedents suggest that the federal courts will be more strict in applying the Fourteenth Amendment to voucher systems than to neighborhood schools. The courts have repeatedly rejected voucher systems designed to maintain segregation. But they have certainly shown no general inclination to abolish the neighborhood school. Outside the South, therefore, adherents of integration can probably more easily achieve their goal through voucher systems than they can within existing school structures.

The black parent's access to integrated schools will certainly increase under a regulated voucher system. Black parents could apply to any school in the system, and the percentage of blacks admitted must at least equal the proportion who applied. This stipulation accords most black parents a far better opportunity to send their children to integrated schools than is now the case.

DIVERSITY AND PLURALISM

A voucher system could stimulate diversity and choice within the public system. If schools and students were matched on the basis of interest rather than residence, a much more pluralistic educational environment would result. Real choices among very different types of schools would be possible. The more popular public schools would attract more applicants. Since the additional students would bring extra funds, the popular schools would have incentives to accommodate them. Unpopular schools would attract few students and so would have to reform or close.

The voucher system promises to collapse the virtual monopoly of public education over the learning process. Since individuals would receive educational revenues directly, they could spend their money at established private schools or found their own unique private institutions. The creation of alternatives would liberate educational systems by allowing independent, private schools to experiment with unpopular and innovative forms of education. Thus diversity would become more than mere unsubstantiated rhetoric.

A voucher system would abolish the present situation in which only the affluent and those with access to church-affiliated schools can escape the public schools. A family now generally must accept whatever education is provided by the district in which it lives. The considerable variations in property taxes and spending levels among districts create the unfair disparities. In a voucher system, all parents and students receive an equal grant that is sufficient for them to escape the local neighborhood school. Imposed socioeconomic, ethnic, and racial segregation would thus become much less prevalent. Vouchers would guarantee the emergence of geographically decentralized schools and educational communities formulated on shared values.

One problem in building a complete system of educational alternatives is the relationship of church, state, and school. A voucher system that allows church-affiliated schools to participate would raise serious constitutional questions. The constitutionality of the indirect public funding of religious schools on a comprehensive scale would eventually have to be decided by the courts. But, in principle, if parent and student are to enjoy significant alternatives, it seems essential to include religious schools in a voucher program. A voucher program can, however, certainly work in the absence of the church school. The judiciary, state legislatures, or local educational voucher authorities could limit participation to nonsectarian schools. In fact, some state constitutions require that this be the case. The federal constitution may also require an exclusion of church-affiliated schools, but the language of the First Amendment and legal precedent are not clear on this issue.

The First Amendment prohibition against an "establishment of religion" seems to forbid payments to church schools, but the "free exercise of religion" clause seems to require that the state treat church schools in the same fashion as private schools. The Supreme Court has never delivered an opinion on such a case; for example, it has not ruled on Medicare payments to Catholic hospitals or GI Bill payments to Lutheran colleges. Both of these payments constitute indirect aid to churches in the form of vouchers. They are allowable only in the absence of a definitive Supreme Court decision. The Supreme Court ruled on 28 June 1971 that states cannot give direct aid to private schools for secular instruction, holding that this would lead to "excessive entanglement" of Church and State.[12] What it would rule on indirect aid through vouchers seems another matter. It has upheld indirect subsidies that assumed a technical form of aid to private school *students* as opposed to private *schools*. The court upheld laws in 1967 and 1968 that provided for the busing of private school pupils and the loans of secular textbooks at public expense. However, until a separate judgment or interpretation is forthcoming, the issue of indirect aid must continue to be resolved through policy decisions.

The available data indicate that church-affiliated schools have educated their children no worse than the public schools. Thus there seems to be no educational argument for denying the church-affiliated schools the public funds granted to other schools. The diversity that vouchers promise should not be destroyed by religious intolerance. There is no defensible religious or pedagogical case—perhaps not even a constitutional one—for denying the choice of parents who opt for religious schools just as no parent should be precluded from selecting a humanist or military school. The only criteria that all schools along the continuum of diversity should satisfy are the minimum state educational standards and the voucher regulations. Although the First Amendment establishes a separation between church and state, direct grants to *individual consumers* of education—private, public, religious, military, or whatever—do not seem to be in violation of the spirit and substance of the amendment.

THE CALIFORNIA PRECEDENT[13]

The California Supreme Court ruled on 30 August 1971 in *Serrano v. Priest* that financing education through local property taxes violates the U. S. Constitution. The decision stated that the present method of financing discriminates against the poor, that it violates the "equal protection" clause of the Fourteenth Amendment. For example, a wealthy district like Beverly Hills spends $1,231.72 per child whereas poorer Pasadena spends only $840.19 per child. This happens because the assessed value per child in Beverly Hills is $50,885 whereas the figure for Pasadena is only $13,706. Thus Beverly Hills is able to offer a superior educational program at a lower tax rate. Similarly, the Ravenswood Elementary School District in East Palo Alto, California, has a tax rate of $4.55 per $100 assessed valuation but raises only $1,100 per child. The Hillsborough Elementary School District in San Mateo has a tax rate of only $3.02 yet raises $1,300 per child.

The California court said it reached its decision because of the unique role of education in American society. Education is "a major determinant of an individual's chances for economic and social success in our competitive society." It is "a unique influence on a child's development as a citizen and his participation in political and community life." Therefore, the court concluded:

To allot more educational dollars to the children of one school district than to those of another merely because of the fortuitous presence of more valuable real estate is to make the quality of a child's education dependent upon the location of private commercial and industrial establishments.

The greatest significance of this decision is that it attacks the financing of public education through voter-approved local taxes on real estate in all fifty states. The supreme courts in Texas, Minnesota, and New Jersey have, in fact, also recently ruled unconstitutional the local property tax as a means of financing the schools. The prospect is that other states will follow suit rapidly.

California has not yet devised a new financing plan. But the new scheme must tax every California citizen at the same rate regardless of residence. The legislature must then distribute the funds on an equal basis to every child enrolled in school. The decision thus may lead to vouchers or equal allocations per child.

A uniform state-wide property tax will probably be the new method of gathering school revenue. Sales tax and general fund money or a state income tax tied exclusively to the schools can also, of course, be used or even substituted for the property tax. Although it is politically impracticable, now legislatures should close loopholes and increase corporation taxes. The corporations do, after all, benefit handsomely by employing the best graduates of the schools to realize profits. They should pay more and what they pay should be divided equally among all children in the form of vouchers.

VOUCHERS AS AN INSTRUMENT OF PLURALISM

The American aspiration has been to be a homogeneous society; that is, all the various disparate groups—racial, ethnic, and socioeconomic—would fade into the "melting pot" society so that they become in the most important respects indistinguishable from the whole. The entire thrust of the society has been scientific, toward an objective, centralized, bureaucratic state. However, the assertion of identity on the part of many subcultural groups, including blacks, Chicanos, Italians, Irish, Puerto Ricans, and women, indicates that the "melting pot" never really melted, that the society is actually a rich composite of a large number of cultures and identities.

This diversity is not served well by a monolithic school system but would be by one offering choices among several different types of schools. Vouchers can grant individuals within the subcultures financial independence, allowing several types of schools to grow to meet the needs of a complex society. Hence a Chicano may elect to attend a school with an outstanding Chicano studies program that he might have missed out on entirely had he been compelled to attend the school nearest his home. Or a group of Chicanos might pool their vouchers to establish their own private schools, perhaps focused on

Chicano life and culture while meeting the state's minimum competency standards. In this way, vouchers would provide the foundation for education devoted to the learning of required skills and committed to an educational program that accommodates a particular identity.

Through vouchers, the diverse subcultural groups of America could effectively collapse the authority of the single-standard public school. They could construct a system of alternatives that would provide each subculture an opportunity for an education that satisfies its own needs. In such a milieu, authority would not be destroyed but shared with each group that has a stake in a meaningful educational experience.

NOTES

[1] James S. Coleman et al., *Equality of Educational Opportunity* (Washington, D.C., U.S. Office of Education, 1966).

[2] Helen Bain, "Self-Governance Must Come First, Then Accountability," *Phi Delta Kappan*, 51, no. 8 (April 1970), 413.

[3] D. D. Darland, "The Profession's Quest For Responsibility and Accountability," *Phi Delta Kappan*, 51, no. 1 (September 1970), 43.

[4] Press release, Open Court Publishing Company, LaSalle, Ill., 21 November 1969.

[5] Reed Martin and Charles Blaschke, "Contracting for Educational Reform," *Phi Delta Kappan*, 52, no. 7 (March 1971), 405.

[6] Carl F. Stover, "The Government Contract System as a Problem in Public Policy," Menlo Park, Calif., Stanford Research Institute, 1963.

[7] Kenneth B. Clark, "Answer for 'Disadvantaged' Is Effective Teaching," *The New York Times* 12 January 1970.

[8] Leon Lessinger, *Every Kid a Winner* (New York, Simon and Schuster, 1970), p. 107.

[9] Patricia Cayo Sexton, *Education and Income*, 2nd ed. (New York, Viking Press, 1965).

[10] Mario D. Fantini, "Participation, Decentralization, Community Control, and Quality Education," *Teachers College Record*, 71, no. 1 (September 1969), 96.

[11] Center for the Study of Public Policy, *Financing Education by Grants to Parents: A Preliminary Report* (Cambridge, Mass., The Center, 56 Boylston St., March 1970).

[12] *San Francisco Chronicle*, 29 June 1971, pp. 1, 20.

[13] Robert Bartlett, "School Financing Method Unlawful," *San Francisco Chronicle*, 31 August 1971, pp. 1, 20; Ron Moskowitz, "Search Begins For School Financing," *San Francisco Chronicle*, 1 September 1971, pp. 1, 18.

5
Alternatives

Learning outcomes in the public schools have been dismal. Mario Fantini has reported that 85 percent of inner-city students cannot read.[1] Many suburban youth are bored and achieving below grade level. Such results are due partly to a lack of diversity and options. When there is only one standard and one curriculum, and many students do not fit, it is no surprise that many also do not learn. Diversity and options imply learner freedom. Without the freedom to inquire and make mistakes on one's own terms, it is not possible to learn. Teachers can inculcate facts and values, but this requires mere memorization by and indoctrination of students. Students must enjoy freedom in order to learn. They must have alternatives.

Hundreds of alternative schools have been established. Many have been very short-lived. The average life span is only eighteen months.[2] Although the failure rate is very high, the impulse to create an effective alternative to the public schools seems sincere and persistent. The fact that the search for different forms of education is so widespread and intense signifies that perhaps the public schools should share their authority for educational experiences with alternative schools.

THE FREE SCHOOLS

The free school is a school that an independent group, often representing a subculture distinctly different from the mainstream, establishes in order to offer an alternative to the public school system. Frequently the sponsors of free schools regard the public schools as rife with inequality and inhumanity, stressing performance to the detriment of self-development, and providing an inflexible, routine environment rather than a creative, fluid one. They want a humanistic alternative and they feel the free school is the answer.

The free school's objective is to allow the student sufficient freedom to learn through discovery, whether alone or with a teacher. The ethos of the free school is founded upon a great faith in the student to learn well in a creative, free environment. The assumptions are definitely Rousseauian; recent psychological research and theory, particularly that of Piaget and Bruner, tend to demonstrate that Rousseau may be correct, that those previously untutored may learn best if left largely to themselves. This is the hope of the free school proponents.

The free school operates on a financial shoestring. It is generally located in a dilapidated building. An abandoned store seems to be a favorite. (Hence the term "storefront" has become virtually synonymous with "free school.") Many of the teachers are volunteers, working for a pittance or for nothing at all. A considerable number of free schools do not last through their first year, failing due to lack of resources, but at least an equal number of new alternative schools take their place. The free school seems to be catching on despite the hardships.

THE BEGINNING OF A MOVEMENT

The free school movement began in Boston after years of tension and argument between the city's black community and the Boston School Committee. The New School for Children, established in 1965, marked the beginning of a movement. Three more free elementary schools have been founded in Boston since 1965. One of them is an experimental school financed by the state and the others are sponsored by neighborhood groups. A teacher who qualifies for certification under Massachusetts standards and a "community teacher," a parent from the community who assists the teacher, staff each classroom. The community teachers do a great deal of teaching by enriching pupils with their personal experiences and community and cultural knowledge, and attending to learners' individual needs. In each school, parents are centrally involved in major decisions. The financial situation of the four schools is marginal, but all have managed, in some degree, to successfully educate their students where the public schools have failed. They have provided a workable alternative.[3]

STREET ACADEMIES

Perhaps New York City's free schools provide the most useful alternative model for high school students. The free schools, or "street academies," operating mostly on contributions from private corporations, have been educating public school dropouts, and they have been succeeding. The students are learning how to read and write and do basic math. And all of this has been taking place with much less expenditure per student than in the public schools and with far less in the way of buildings and equipment.

Street workers operate out of the academies to recruit students. If they find a student whom they believe has college potential, they arrange for him to attend Harlem Preparatory School. Harlem Prep, housed in a former Harlem supermarket, is a college preparatory school that serves 400 students. The graduates have been entering college and staying. Only four of 205 Harlem Prep graduates who have gone on to college have dropped out.[4]

ALTERNATIVES WITHIN

Most alternatives to public education have been established outside the public system, but some have been established within. Only progressive, forward-looking schools have proved confident enough to try alternatives within their own walls. The Berkeley, California, public school system is one of the most outstanding examples.

A number of alternatives exist within the Berkeley system, but the most notable is Herbert Kohl's program, "Other Ways."[5] Other Ways is an attempt to meet the needs of students who find little or nothing worthwhile in the conventional public school. It capitalizes on individual learning styles by providing an unstructured setting and different types of learning experiences.

Other Ways operates as a nonprofit corporation that contracts with the Berkeley public school system to educate 75 junior and senior high students. The program uses the resources of the Berkeley community as its curriculum. It sends the students where the learning is at, whether in machine shops, art studios, restaurants, or junior colleges. The students learn by experiencing: for them, learning is living and doing. For example, a number of Other Ways students learn how to make pots at potters' studios and repair clocks in a jeweler's shop. They attend classes at a junior college to take advantage of course offerings not available in the Other Ways program; they use the computers at the University of California at Berkeley; they learn jujitsu and karate at a Berkeley studio. The students are relatively free agents in the community. They use their freedom responsibly to do that which informs their interests and enlarges their personal growth.

The Other Ways program pays workers in the community who teach these students. Kohl wants the students to learn from adults in real work and life situations. A lawyer has much to teach students that cannot be learned in a classroom. A mechanic can give a young man or woman authentic raw data about his occupation so the student can make an intelligent career choice. A nurse can show a teenage girl or boy much about health care in one day at a hospital. On-the-spot learning is the Other Ways version of relevance and administrators of this program are willing to distribute an entire staff salary for this learning in the community.

Other Ways does not rely entirely on the community. It conducts its own courses. The faculty announces what it wants to teach at the outset of each year and the students make public what they want to learn. Teachers and learners are then matched in courses. If there is no learner demand for a faculty member's interest, that teacher's option does not become a course alternative. And if the faculty cannot teach what the students want, Other Ways attempts to find those who can. Some of the Other Ways classes are:

1. *Human Behavior.* This is a discussion class that offers an opportunity to explore personal and social problems. Sex, racism, drugs, violence, and parents are among the legitimate subjects. Students and teachers encounter one another on an equal basis and the sessions are open ended.
2. *The Unconscious and Decision Making.* This class considers unconscious processes such as dreaming. It devotes particular attention to unconscious influences on individual decisions in daily life, especially major decisions such as marriage and career. Students explore creativity in arts and science and read works in psychology and sociology that help them understand the unconscious.
3. *Urban Suvival.* This Other Ways course teaches the student how to survive in the city. The course focuses on such matters as job hunting, municipal government, law enforcement, rent strikes and food-purchasing cooperatives.
4. *Wilderness Survival.* Students study such survival techniques as

purifying water, building shelters, and trapping animals. They travel to a wilderness area each week to practice their techniques.

Other courses include Science and Looking; Boat Building and Navigation; Photography; Guerilla Theater; Systems, the Scientist and the Person; Media; and Abstract Mathematical Concepts and the Mathematician as a Creator.[6]

OPEN EDUCATION

Open education is a form of elementary school education that is highly informal, unstructured, and individualized. The open classroom has been used widely in the British infant schools, where children are enrolled at age five to seven, since World War II. About 70 percent of Britain's public infant schools and almost 50 percent of the junior schools (enrolling children up to age twelve) have adopted the "open" form of education. Open education has recently begun to have a substantial impact on the American classroom scene.

Open education, in both British and American classrooms, shares certain elements:

1. The classrooms contain a rich diversity of learning resources including books, media such as opaque and film-loop projectors, and disc and tape recorders, as well as many types of objects such as rocks, pattern blocks, liquid containers, thermometers, and meter sticks.
2. The children can move about the classroom as they wish, choosing their own activities and talking with other pupils. A classroom often includes a cross section of grade levels.
3. The teachers devote most of their time to working with individual children or small groups.
4. The classrooms are organized into separate "learning areas" rather than regimented into conventional rows of desks and chairs.[7]

The British open school reformers' observations of children's learning behavior—that is, that each child learns differently—was later corroborated by experimental psychologists, especially Piaget. Piaget and others have established scientifically that children have different learning styles and learning rates, that they learn best that which interests them, and that they learn well from each other. Hence the freedom, the group learning, and the apparent chaos in the classroom are grounded in child psychology as we know it best today.

Open classrooms do not look like classrooms. They are more like workshops divided into "learning areas" or "interest areas," usually including art, language, science, reading, and math areas. The atmosphere is relaxed. There are private study and activity areas for the children, partitioned off by pegboard room dividers or cardboard tri-walls. Each private nook is furnished with a desk, chair, and rug. Out-of-the-way rooms are used for activities that are best done apart from the crowd. Ceramics, pottery-making, carpentry, typography, photography, sculpture, weaving, and cooking are among the independent activities. Rooms housing these activities are open to all who may be interested in them.

The open classroom curriculum is flexible and interdisciplinary. Pupils might learn drawing, spelling, reading, and writing when they work on a carpentry project. They might learn math, science, and biology by preparing an aquarium display for a regional science fair. In a model legislature, they might learn democratic principles, basic psychological truths, and the techniques of controlling anger and frustration. Learning by experiencing across subject matter barriers—that is the open classroom.

Children of different ages work together in the open classroom. This practice enables pupils to learn from each other, thus increasing the teaching (and learning) that occurs. The older pupils serve as learning and motivational models for the younger ones. They may teach simply by learning their advanced reading, writing, and math in the company of younger learners. The learning that happens in the cross-aged group reinforces the open classroom teacher's instructional objectives.[8]

THE OPEN ENVIRONMENT

The child is free to choose his own learning experiences in the open classroom. Whatever choices he makes, an abundance of materials enables him to explore and discover. In the language arts section, there are tape recorders, typewriters, word games, and much more. The math section includes balance scales, rulers, stopwatches, Cuisenaire rods, counting games, and workbooks. With a wealth of materials available, the child is constantly initiating projects in response to the environment. The materials in the open environment teach the child much. He chooses to learn with those that engage his interest.

Some open classroom environments depend on commercial materials. A few American private open schools, modeled on the British infant schools, use commercial materials almost exclusively. Other schools rely heavily on natural and homemade items. The Open Door project administered by Lillian Weber in New York City schools improvises solely with noncommercial materials.

The Educational Development Center (EDC) in Newton, Massachusetts, provides national leadership for the open classroom movement. Such EDC leaders as Rosemary Williams, former director of the Westfield Infant School in Britain, are active nationally in organizing open classrooms. They advise and consult, direct workshops, and furnish curriculum materials and free publications.[9]

The EDC has published a pamphlet that suggests inexpensive or free equipment and materials for the open classroom. The EDC guide emphasizes that the most difficult task for the teacher is to use the new materials in innovative ways in order to break away from conventional routines. The teacher must be able to invent new learning uses for new learning resources.[10]

THE OPEN CLASSROOM TEACHER

The teacher in the open classroom serves as a catalyst and guide for each child's learning experiences. She provides materials, encouragement, and assistance, working with individuals or small groups as the demand arises. She facilitates rather than dictates the child's learning activities. She enlarges freedom so that the child may inquire as independently as possible. She stimulates the child to learn how to learn, to become familiar with basic tools of inquiry, rather than learning content that becomes quickly dated. Her goal is to help develop self-motivating, self-renewing thinkers who will persist in their curiosity and continue to learn throughout life.

In order to function successfully in an open classroom, most conventional teachers must radically reeducate themselves as to how learning occurs and what their job is like. They must abandon the old self-evident truths and established routines. They must learn that educational objectives are not the same for all children; that one does not preplan every minute of the school day; and that one need not block out a child's curriculum by subject matter areas.[11] Thus the open classroom truly demands a new teacher, one sensitized to differences and competent to put them to good pedagogical use.

The open classroom means more work for the teacher. It is more difficult to guide and assist learners than to lecture at them. Personal involvement with each child requires more time and effort. For example, teachers must keep detailed records of each child's learning activities. The open classroom is certainly no easy way out for the teacher.

The uninformed visitor may regard the best open classroom as excessively permissive. But the teachers have established well-defined behavior codes that they enforce despite the apparent lack of order. The child in the open classroom may do as he wishes as long as he does not interefere with other children's work. He enjoys complete learner freedom unless he violates this rule.

The ingredients that make the open classroom successful are mutual trust and respect. The teacher assumes the child can, wants to, and will learn. The child responds by meeting these positive expectations. Once learner or teacher exploits the freedom, the value of the open classroom is lost.

THE THEORETICAL FOUNDATION

The research of Jean Piaget, Swiss child psychologist, provides the most substantial theoretical foundation for open education. Piaget finds that children learn at different speeds, through recurrent real-life experiences, and by interacting with one another. They must experience the world directly, on a "concrete level." They must hear, touch, smell, and see, building their reservoir of total experiences until they can understand abstract concepts. Thus good pedagogy demands that the educator present the child with situations that he experiences directly. He must encourage the child to manipulate objects, ask his own questions and seek his own answers, experiment and witness the results, and compare his experiences with other children's. Through such direct experiencing, the child prepares himself for abstract conceptualization, a sophisticated form of thinking that requires him to draw upon and interpret his direct experiences.

The open education enthusiasts argue that the conventional classroom actually inhibits learning and intellectual development. They claim that the regimentation of children in rows of desks, the heavy reliance on lecturing and books, and the use of large-group instruction kill the freedom so necessary for direct experience and inquiry. They advise educators to *let the children be* in the classroom.[12]

CRITICISMS AND REBUTTALS

Critics of the open classroom argue that only a program that effectively teaches basic skills such as reading and arithmetic can survive. Parents and taxpayers will not tolerate a humanistic, open-ended program if it fails in teaching the skills necessary for success in higher education and the job market. But the open classroom advocates point to the evidence that indicates their children progress normally in reading and arithmetic skills as measured by standardized tests. The open classroom children also demonstrate a greater desire to write and read and their average math comprehension scores are higher. These results are especially significant when one considers that the conventional classroom concentrates almost solely on arithmetic and reading skills the first two years, whereas the open classroom uses them as just another activity.

The critics also argue that open education does not prepare pupils realistically for life, that the child's capacity to compete successfully in a harsh world is impaired. They want to see the child attend a conventional school, where he can prepare for life's hardships, rather than be pampered in an open school. The open classroom advocates' rejoinder to all this is that their approach cultivates the independence and self-confidence that will enable their pupils to function well in any situation. In any case, it is impossible to educate learners for specific roles in a society undergoing constant and rapid change.[13] It is far better to educate the learner for change.

OPEN EDUCATION OPTIONS

There are a number of ways to organize open education. The Philadelphia Public School system is exemplary in its use of the following major open education options:[14]

1. *Learning Centers.* The nine Philadelphia Public School Learning Centers are rooms where children can freely use selected materials and equipment such as tape recorders, opaque and film-loop projectors, typewriters, adding machines, and microscopes. Other available materials include thermometers, sand, water, pebbles, rocks, soils, building blocks, meter sticks, scales, balances, art supplies, games, and books. The pupil experiments and builds, using the materials, and poses problems and attempts to solve them. He may collaborate with teachers and other pupils in any project he undertakes. He may wish, for example, to use the scales and balances to determine the volume displacement of water by different types of rocks. In this case, he would be functioning as a scientist, which is the goal of providing a diversity of discovery opportunities.

2. *Math Laboratories.* The Philadelphia Public Schools operate more than fifty Math Laboratories enrolling learners, grades K to 12. The emphasis is on the discovery approach to mathematical learning. The materials available include Dienes Logical Blocks, mnemonic devices, teacher-made resources, geoboards, Cuisenaire rods, and Pattern Blocks.

3. *Instructional Materials Centers.* IMC's have been established in virtually every Philadelphia public school. They are designed to stimulate independent study and research. Learners enjoy ready access to filmstrips, films, tape and disc recordings, books, charts, and pictures. Discovery learning is possible because all materials are easily available. The teacher serves only to guide the child in the enriched environment.

4. *Intensive Learning Center.* The Philadelphia Public Schools operate one Intensive Learning Center for grades K to 6. One part of the program, the Inquiry House, is based on open education principles. The staff includes a teacher with six years' experience in the British Infant Schools. She and the other teachers create all the materials for the center. Pupils use the materials experimentally to learn.

5. *The John Hancock School Program.* The Hancock School (K to 6) operates open classrooms, but with a difference. One problem of open education has been the suspicious, cynical, or intolerant attitude of the public. The Hancock School has solved the problem by involving parents. Sixty-five parents devote at least one morning or afternoon weekly to working with children in an open classroom. The parents participate initially in an in-service training program to learn the proper use of textual materials and instructional aids. They work individually with pupils needing special attention. In serving, parents become familiar with open education. They generally become more appreciative of the program and often constitute a source of community support that helps open education survive in the public schools.

6. *The Reading Skills Center Program.* Reading Skills Centers are located in many Philadelphia public schools. Each center initially analyzes children's reading needs. In subsequent visits to the center, each child is free to use equipment and materials as he wishes to eliminate deficiencies. He proceeds at his own pace and records his own progress. Teachers counsel each learner regarding his progress and remedially tutor individuals or small groups. The unique needs of each pupil are immediately cared for at the pupil's request. The reliance on pupil self-direction and cooperation has virtually eliminated discipline problems and promoted an educational environment highly conducive to reading advancement.

VOCATIONAL COUNSELING AND WORK-STUDY[15]

The conventional public school provides no effective program for those who will not go on to college. It does not furnish adequate training for those who wish to meet the demands of the skilled labor market. If ever there was a needed alternative, it certainly is a realistic training program for those who wish to begin vocational careers immediately following high school. Such a program would prevent from dropping out many students who now find nothing in the school to engage their interests and talents. It would also greatly diminish the widespread disruptive behavior and outright rebellion that plagues many of our metropolitan schools.

Cleveland's Kennard Junior High School established the Vocational Information Program (VIP), a vocational counseling and work-study program, and found that it worked. VIP provides instructive guidelines. The program's students, or VIP's, enjoy an opportunity to study the major vocations and train to become skilled technologists, tradesmen, and craftsmen. Retired industrialist Stephen T. Rose initiated the partnership of school and industry that made this possible.

In December 1965 Rose presented to the Cleveland School Board a plan for acquainting young inner-city blacks with major skilled vocations. The school board approved and in February 1966, Rose began his program with ten boys from Kennard Junior High's ninth grade. He arranged for the group to have some type of informational input from business and industry for one hour two mornings weekly. The inputs included guest lecturers, the showing of technical films, and monthly field trips to such enterprises as a tool shop, a printing plant, a commercial art studio, a graphic arts shop, and a research laboratory.

In 1966, VIP added a new group of fifteen Kennard ninth-graders to the program and continued with the original ten who entered the tenth grade at East Technical High School. A new phase of the program also began. Students were placed in after-school, holiday, and summer jobs. Each student's vocational interest was matched with a particular job. This aspect of VIP was called the Junior Internship. Interns have worked in a variety of jobs including landscaping, building maintenance, clerking, and direct mail advertising. Not only have they learned valuable skills, but they have learned what they really like.

The VIP program has proved successful. Thus far 150 students have completed the two-year program. They report that VIP has helped them make career decisions and raise their sights. For example, a student who thought he might want to become a garage mechanic now plans to be an industrial engineer. Another wants to become a consulting engineer rather than a draftsman.

Business and industry have applauded the program. Many firms have offered VIP students jobs. They regard completion of the program as an assurance of training excellence and high-level certification.

A NEW SEMIRESIDENTIAL SCHOOL[16]

The System Development Corporation in Santa Monica, California, has designed a new semiresidential school, an experimental school for the urban poor. All grade levels, K through 12, will be enrolled on one campus. The school will employ an ombudsman to hear community and student grievances. It will, in fact, attempt to involve students, parents, and residents maximally in school decisions. It will remain open fifteen hours daily, insuring intensive use of its facilities by the entire community. It will provide each student a private study and activity room.

The school hires every student as a member of the school work force. Each student works part of every day in addition to his study. He does work that fits his abilities and he is paid according to how much he works and the difficulty of his job. This policy does not mean that the school pays the student to attend. On the contrary, the school pays him for the performance of functions essential to the operation of the institution. There is no "made work." The student can choose any of the available jobs. The academic standout can select boiler room repair. The shop major can opt for assisting the principal.

FAMILY DEVELOPMENT CENTER[17]

Luvern Cunningham, Dean of the College of Education at Ohio State University, has developed a Family Development Center model as a means of removing some of the deficiencies of ghetto education. The purpose of the Family Development Center is to create a rich educational environment where adults and children can learn together. The basic social units are families representing all races and socioeconomic strata, including particularly the unemployed and the poor and black.

The total environment would effectively constitute a learning laboratory. Anybody with anything to impart to the educational process, especially faculty and their families, would teach, and everybody would certainly learn. This living-and-learning approach means that the curriculum would be informal and individualized. Whatever resources of the city are available—theaters, museums, art centers, universities—could easily be incorporated into the curriculum. Classes could be held anywhere that enhanced learning objectives mutually agreed upon by families and individual learners. Anybody could attend.

Unemployed heads of households would be among those selected for the Family Development Center. The center would seek to upgrade the skill and educational levels of these people so that they could secure employment. During their participation in the program, they would live on welfare payments until they were able to qualify for part-time employment. At this point, the previously unemployed students' involvement at the center would begin to revolve around a work-study approach. Once the unemployed had advanced to an adequate educational level for their own protection as consumers and citizens and were properly trained for employment, they would leave the center.

The Family Development Center staff would include medical and psychiatric specialists, social workers, and psychologists, and, of course, all of their families. Social workers would attend to welfare and employment problems. They could prove particularly helpful in assisting families in moving to and from the center. The medical and psychiatric specialists would care for psychological and physical needs.

Families would be required to remain in residence at least one year. Some would find it necessary to stay longer. A family could enroll in the center's program at a number of specified times throughout the year. The staff would assist the families completing their work and study programs to find housing and jobs. Minority graduates would be located only in those areas where open housing agreements are enforced.

The Family Development Center is an excellent educational model because it promises to solve pressing social problems. It aims at removing the educational deficiencies of both adults and children and disrupting the educational and poverty cycle. The adults could thus become breadwinners and the children would enjoy improved opportunities. Through learning together, children and parents would become more cohesive families and the quality of human relations in the entire society would eventually be improved.

THE JOHN DEWEY HIGH MODEL[18]

The John Dewey High School in New York City, an experimental high school, opened its doors in September, 1969. Its goal is to meet the diverse needs of a heterogeneous metropolitan population. It has organized its resources to provide as much individualized instruction as possible. The Dewey High program constitutes a serious attempt to establish an alternative that can meet the individual needs of learners as well as the educational needs of the city. The administration, organization, and curriculum design at Dewey High are exemplary for schools seeking creative ways to change.

Dewey High operates in full awareness that students learn at different rates and that each student learns at different rates at different times. The teachers act upon this awareness by adjusting the instructional program to the students' different learning speeds. Teachers work with students individually and in small groups, giving continuous feedback on progress. The school and faculty work in several ways to individualize instruction.

The traditional Carnegie Unit system and the annual or semi-annual reorganization have been abolished at John Dewey. There are five seven-week regular "phases" and two seven-week summer "phases." The curriculum is organized by logical, sequential units of learning that can be incorporated into the seven-week phases. Thus, if a student fails a phase or finds it not all he thought it would be, he loses only seven weeks as opposed to the conventional half-year.

Student schedules are divided into fourteen to sixteen twenty-minute periods, or "modules," daily. Each student is scheduled, however, for twenty-two modules so that he will have additional time for such pursuits as independent study and counseling. Through modularization, the John Dewey High teachers are able to meet the individual student's learning needs. They can use the flexibility of modules to adapt the curriculum to each student's unique learning style. Moreover, the module system recognizes that some material is best learned in short sessions, whereas other subject matter requires more time. For example, a biology lab is best handled in four or five modules whereas one module is sufficient for a typing drill.

The seven-week phases and the modules would not be possible

without a computer. The computer installation at Brooklyn College schedules each student's daily modules. It furnishes each student a printout of his schedule before the beginning of a new phase. No two students have yet to receive printouts with exactly the same schedule. This fact leads one to believe that the Dewey program is truly "individualized," that the term is more than rhetoric.

The Dewey High students build their own learning schedules. They select the courses in consultation with teachers and counselors. They must select one hundred phases from a list of requirements, forty from available electives, and write a senior paper on a topic of their choice in order to qualify for graduation. The student has considerable freedom in his selection since a wide range of offerings exist. Students may even decide to graduate in as little as two years or as many as six, depending on their interests and abilities.

As much as one-third of a student's time may be devoted to independent study. Students who take advantage of an independent study option utilize six major resource centers (one each for social studies, English, mathematics, science, business education, and foreign language). Teachers are stationed at each resource center to help students with their independent activities. Independent study students can also use the school's art studio, music center, homework preparation areas, and speech laboratories.

There are no grades at John Dewey. The emphasis is on satisfying competency requirements of a learning task and then moving on to a new phase. A student must achieve mastery of one learning unit before he can advance to the next part of the sequentially designed curriculum. The teacher gives students who do not achieve "mastery" or "mastery with conditions" a "prescription" identifying deficiencies that must be removed. A copy of the prescription is given the students' parents, the administration, the guidance counselor, and the teacher who will instruct the student during the following phase. A student never "fails"; he merely repeats unsatisfactory work or undertakes options to complete course requirements. The benefit of the doubt is given the student on all occasions. The assumption is that the student will use his freedom responsibly and capitalize educationally upon the alternatives open to him.

ABOLISHING COMPULSORY EDUCATION[19]

Another possible alternative is zero formal education. Perhaps a structured, institutionalized educational experience is not conducive to optimum learning for some. Radical educational critic Ivan Illich has even argued that we must abolish formal education entirely, a process he calls "deschooling society."

Compulsory education could be abolished. The fact that education is compulsory does not guarantee that a student will learn. The evidence shows that a high percentage of students, especially in the ghetto, are performing far below grade level if they bother to show up at school at all. Sitting in a classroom does not necessarily equal education, and the threat of expulsion or suspension does not even begin to intimidate the many who wanted no part of the school in the first place or soon found nothing in it.

What the students need is the right to choose their own type of education, which for many will mean a nonschool alternative. Chapter 4, Accountability and Vouchers, discusses how a voucher system can support significant educational options. The opportunity for alternatives would reinvigorate the educational process wherever and whenever the learner chose to pursue it.

COMMUNITY EXPERIENCE[20]

Both Paul Goodman and Ivan Illich argue that we should deinstitutionalize education. We should require every learner to venture forth into the community and construct his own educational experiences through the choices he makes. Goodman, in contrast to Illich, favors some schooling as absolutely necessary, preferably under conditions of maximum freedom.

For every learner, we could mix basic formal schooling and direct experience in the community. One way to achieve this mix is to release the student for a semester or year's foray into the real world. The student would have to deal with situations that he would not encounter in the formal curriculum. He would grow through the diversity of his encounters and become wise in practical affairs that the bookish public school will allow only in limited degree. The student's leave of absence from the school should be awarded credit toward graduation.

A NEW PROGRAM[21]

Any effective educational program must keep uninterested teachers away from students and discourage unconcerned students from participating in learning programs. Where there is no motivation on the part of either teacher or student, learning certainly cannot occur. Participation in learning activities must be voluntary. There must be a careful matching of faculty interests and student interests. Instructors must be genuinely interested in the material they teach; otherwise, motivating students is impossible. Student and teacher must inquire together into matters they think fundamentally important. In order for cooperative, enthusiastic inquiry to occur, several conditions must be satisfied:

1. Teachers and learners should cooperate in inquiring only into issues about which they are both enthusiastic.
2. Involvement in inquiry activities should be voluntary.
3. The issues for inquiry learning should not be spelled out in terms of specialized disciplinary problems but rather in terms of fundamental human concerns.
4. Teachers and students should enjoy an opportunity to participate in choosing issues for inquiry learning.
5. Students should have the opportunity to participate in an orientation program that will allow them to clarify their mutual interests and promote a sense of belonging to a community of inquirers.
6. Students must be free to leave the inquiry activities at any time without penalty.
7. The inquiry experiences should be organized as flexible time modules, thus allowing the inquiry agenda of learners to be easily contracted or expanded.
8. A program of voluntary inquiry activities should be readily available throughout a person's lifetime.
9. Employers and technical institutes should assume the major responsibility for vocational training. Training is not inquiry and should not be a school responsibility.

Schools must offer incentives to teachers to collaborate with students in only those inquiry activities that deeply interest them. If certain teachers lack commitment to a study of issues that concern students, they should be assigned duties that keep them away from students, such as preparing curriculum materials, organizing field trips, and developing programed texts.

THE FORMAT OF INQUIRY

Several procedures must be followed in order to successfully match teacher and student interests:

1. Teachers and students should periodically announce the topics they are interested in, inviting others to join them in cooperative inquiry. Each individual or group expressing an interest in an inquiry activity should publicize their background and experience and the expected length of the first phase of the activity.
2. Students should be admitted to the proposed activities solely on the basis of interest. There should be no prerequisites. Students who are contemplating joining a particular interest group should provide prospective participants a capsule summary of their background and interests. Teachers should also provide a summary of their background and interests.
3. If more students apply than can be accommodated, students will be randomly selected. Those who are admitted will assess the backgrounds and interests of the other participants. They will then decide whether they wish to continue in the first phase of the inquiry activities, group formation and agenda matching. Each interest group will offer diagnostic services to help each student who desires counseling to make decisions about the group he wishes to join and the interest he wants to pursue.
4. Each interest group will offer a short-term orientation period to enable students to clarify their interests and consider possible avenues of inquiry. During this initial period of the interest group's life cycle, participants will select a general format for inquiry, for example, field experience, group discussion, or work-study. Any participant may leave the group at any time during the orientation period.
5. The school calendar should be organized in modules of time so that the length of inquiry can be adjusted to the resources, needs, and interests of the group. Thus some topics might be exhausted in a few days, whereas consideration of others might be extended over a few months. Students could leave a module system when their learning needs had been satisfied.
6. Students should have access to money to hire teachers that they believe can meet their learning needs. The teacher can be any person, with or without a credential, whom the students believe has something genuinely educational to offer. Students should also have funds to move temporarily to another location when it is not financially feasible to organize an activity locally.
7. Every citizen should have a right to a minimum number of educational vouchers to finance inquiry experiences throughout his life. This would allow the poor, the old, and the unemployed, as well as the school-age population, to enjoy and benefit from learning (see Chapter 4).

This program is one of voluntary learning through inquiry. So many students spend so much time in rows of desks in the schools with so little measurable result that a learning model that capitalizes on students' vital interests and human concerns must be rapidly substituted for the old compulsory education model. To pursue the present course of educational policy promises the continuing waste of human and financial resources, which could just as well produce a creative form of human learning when channeled through a uniquely new educational program.

A SPECTRUM OF ALTERNATIVES

A democratic society must have educational alternatives if it is to justify its claim to government of, by, and for the people and if it hopes to remain free. The recent programs furnishing a variety of alternatives reaffirm the society's democratic commitment and give expression to the multiplicity of values that characterize our heterogeneous nation.

Critics and dissidents have directed heavy fire at the American schoolhouse. They have gone on strike against the public school by founding about 1,000 alternative institutions. But their voices are not the only ones expressing discontent. The very heartland of the status quo has become uneasy with the educational system it has benignly tolerated and neglected. It has even begun to act upon its perceptions. The Ford Foundation sponsored the research project reported in Gerald Weinstein and Mario D. Fantini's *Toward Humanistic Education: A Curriculum of Affect;* the Charles F. Kettering Foundation supports I/D/E/A, an organization that seeks educational and social change; the federal government is supporting experimentation in such change-producing reforms as vouchers; and the Carnegie Foundation funded Charles Silberman's research into the state of the public schools as reported in the best-seller *Crisis in the Classroom.*

That many alternative educational programs and abundant criticism have developed is a measure of our cultural strength—not an indicator of a decline of consensus. The only meaningful consensus, as far as education is concerned, is the universal devotion to diversity, alternatives, and openness. Antiestablishment groups have acted upon this value and alternative educational systems have proliferated. They include Edvance Combined Motivation Education Systems (6300 River Road, Rosemont, Illinois 60018); The Teacher Paper (280 North Pacific Avenue, Monmouth, Oregon 97361); The

Teachers Drop-Out Center (School of Education, University of Massachusetts, Amherst, Massachusetts 01002); The Bay Area Radical Teachers Organizing Committee (1445 Stockton Street, San Francisco, California 94133); The New Schools Exchange (301 East Perdido, Santa Barbara, California 93101); and Vocations for Social Change (Canyon, California 94516).[22]

The existence of private alternative schools and the continuing criticism compel a response by the public school establishment. As we have seen in this chapter, public schools can provide alternatives within the system. Perhaps the most encouraging aspect of this consideration of alternatives is that we can reshape our educational institutions to fit the changing times. School programs and teachers can change the old patterns of authority. They can renew themselves.

NOTES

[1] Mario D. Fantini, "Participation, Decentralization, Community Control, and Quality Education," *Teachers College Record*, 71, no. 1 (September 1969), 96.

[2] Donald W. Robinson, "Alternative Schools: Is the Old Order Really Changing?," *Educational Leadership*, 28, no. 6 (March 1971), 605.

[3] Joshua L. Smith, "Free Schools: Pandora's Box?," *Educational Leadership*, 28, no. 5 (February 1971), 465.

[4] *Ibid.*, p. 466.

[5] Herbert Kohl, "Options," *Grade Teacher*, 88, no. 6 (February 1971), 50–51, 59.

[6] *Ibid.*, p. 51.

[7] "Open Education: Can British School Reforms Work Here?," *Nation's Schools*, 87, no. 5 (May 1971), 47–51.

[8] *Ibid.*, pp. 48–49.

[9] I. Ezra Staples, "The 'Open-Space' Plan in Education," *Educational Leadership*, 28, no. 5 (February 1971), 458–463.

[10] "Open Education," *op. cit.*, p. 49.

[11] "Open Education," *op. cit.*, pp. 49–50.

[12] "Open Education," *op. cit.*, pp. 50–51.

[13] "Open Education," *op. cit.*, p. 51. The section on Criticisms And Rebuttals is based on this source.

[14] Staples, *op. cit.*, pp. 460–462.

[15] Kay E. Aylor, "Peephole into the World of Work," *American Education*, 7, no. 2 (March 1971), 29–30.

[16] Luvern L. Cunningham, "Educational Reform and the Principal," *The Bulletin of the National Association of Secondary School Principals*, 59, no. 349 (November 1970), 10–11.

[17] Cunningham, *op. cit.*, pp. 12–14.

[18] Wayne E. Williamson, "A New Learning Center Thrives in New York," *The Clearing House, 45*, no. 1 (September 1970), 26–28.

[19] Cunningham, *op cit.*, p. 16; and Ivan Illich, "Why We Must Abolish Schooling," *The New York Review of Books*, 2 July 1970, pp. 9–15 and "The False Ideology of Schooling," *Saturday Review*, 17 October 1970, pp. 56–58, 68–72.

[20] Cunningham, *op. cit.*, p. 21.

[21] This section is adapted from Professor David C. Epperson's inquiry model for higher education contexts. See David C. Epperson, Center for Urban Affairs, Northwestern University, "An Alternative To Anesthetic Learning Climates," 10 pp., Draft 11/4/70 (mimeographed).

[22] Robinson, *op. cit.*, p. 605. The section A Spectrum Of Alternatives is based on this source.

6
Student rebellion

High school students and, to a minor degree, elementary school students have challenged the authority of teacher and school to continue the conventional forms of education. They want changes now. Their zealous demands have included a redefinition of the curriculum and student rights. When student demands and school authority have collided, disruption has often resulted, threatening the teacher's and school's capacity to discharge their responsibilities. The schools must find ways to creatively respond to students' challenges to traditional forms of authority, devising new educational responsibilities to satisfy legitimate grievances. If the school's positive approaches fail and students rebel, the schools must have at hand intelligent procedures to efficiently restore order and the school's full teaching function without violating students' civil rights. The school should be impressionable to purposeful reform but firm against mindless disruption.

RESPONDING CREATIVELY[1]

The school can pursue several courses of action to divert student discontent into constructive channels. If students can be involved in established structures, they will work within the system rather than feel compelled to attack it. The following six-point program should achieve this goal:

1. *Schools should open up channels of communication and publicize them.* Most administrators are willing to listen to students but students frequently are unaware of their concern. This deficiency can easily be corrected by regular opportunities for dialogue among students, teachers, and administrators.
2. *Schools should establish their own programs of student involvement.* This reform should mean more than resurrecting old forms of student government. Students can participate in teaching teams, departmental meetings, and faculty government. They can help to evaluate student progress, initiate regular faculty-administration-student dialogue, and develop "minicourses." Students can be valuable colleagues in the educational process (see Chapter 5, section on A New Program).
3. *The schools should base the curriculum, rules and regulations, and instructional methods on sound educational principles that educators and the public can endorse.* This policy insures that the school system will be oriented not toward controlling but toward educating students. When students, especially dissidents, perceive that the logic of a school is to manipulate rather than educate, they can easily criticize it and find others to support their cause. However, if the school is educationally solid, students cannot trace their alienation back to the school.
4. *Schools should offer courses on institutional change and assist students with non-violent, constructive reform programs.* Few argue that the schools are perfect. The widespread student unrest indicates something is wrong. Reform is necessary. The real polemics concern the means of realizing change. Disruption and violence certainly create problems and seldom solve any. We must look to institutional renewal to solve our problems and meet the challenge of youth. We must believe enough in our schools to both reform them and offer educational alternatives (see Chapter 5). The schools must trust their students and cooperate with them in establishing new educational forms of authority and responsibility.
5. *Schools should establish a district-wide policy on student protest that includes a grievance procedure.* Teachers, students, and parents should participate in the formulation of the policy. The grievance procedure should specify what is permitted or prohibited, based on court decisions and educational principles. The important point is that a policy does exist that is legally and educationally defensible. Lacking a policy, the schools become quickly disrupted by student dissent.
6. *The schools should evaluate student demands according to what is educationally tenable, not what is politically expedient.* Some student demands may be antieducational. The school can reform radically but

it cannot abdicate its educative function. Thus, when students demand that no one should be required to take courses in basic math, the schools must stand firm upon their professional prerogatives. On other occasions, when students request courses on drugs, for example, the schools can redefine the curriculum without abdicating responsibility for the development of learners. Schools should try to balance responsiveness with responsibility.

CONSULTATIVE COUNCILS[2]

An excellent way to constructively involve students in the schools is through consultative councils. A consultative council is an elected body of five parents and community residents, five students, and five teachers who meet regularly with the principal. The council advises the principal on a wide range of matters, especially course offerings and student affairs. Although the principal is not bound to heed the advice of the council, most principals will listen, and many will act on the basis of their consultations.

Where consultative councils have been established, they have proved of great help during crises. They have functioned much as the Security Council of the United Nations; they are similarly powerless but provide an excellent way to get together and talk to keep the lid from blowing off for lack of communication channels. New York is the best example. In one case where an explosive situation had required massive police intervention, the president of the parents association and the principal called a meeting of the consultative council to discuss the critical issues with militant student leaders. The dialogue produced a student statement that cooled down the confrontation. In a similar situation in another New York school, the conflict and confrontation persisted and escalated. That school had no consultative council.

New York has attempted to maximize student involvement by establishing a city-wide council to meet with the high school superintendents and superintendent of schools to talk about the most important problems. The council includes representatives from city-wide student organizations and splinter groups of students. The other groups represented are labor, industry, local school boards, civic organizations, and city-wide parents organizations.

THE HARRIS POLL AND NEW JERSEY

A nationwide Harris poll revealed that administrators are more sympathetic to student protest than are teachers and parents. At least half of the teachers and parents sampled favor harsh measures for protestors. Far fewer students and administrators agree. They feel it is more important to seek to understand dissidents.

Most superintendents express a desire to listen to student demands. They want to work out a mutual solution with students rather than impose order. But teachers and parents view students' involvement in controversial issues differently; they feel that students should have no role in controversy, that they should do their homework and leave the world to "adults."[3]

The definition of a reasonable student demand, as opposed to an unacceptable one, has occupied many hours of state education boards' time. New Jersey has arrived at a balanced definition:

Any disruption of the schools or interference with their normal operation offends this right (of children to attend school) which is constitutional in origin, violates the law, and cannot be condoned or tolerated. The state board of education and the commissioner deplore the use of means which flout the law, and they condemn any resort to such methods to express protests or enforce demands for redress of grievances. A local board of education should adopt as a first and indispensable principle that neither violence, disruption, vandalism nor seizure of school buildings can be permitted under any circumstances. . . . At the same time, from the standpoint of justice, we must recognize that there are conditions in need of improvement and that students should have some means by which their concerns may be effectively expressed, considered and disposed of fairly.[4]

The New Jersey state board charged each school district with the task of preparing and submitting "its specific plan for dealing with student grievances, and its specific plan for coping with potential student disorder." The New Jersey policy recognizes the legitimacy of student protest "from a standpoint of justice" but condemns disruption and violence. It seeks to offer students an opportunity to express their discontent through institutionalized channels. They are trying to keep the renegade student within the system where he can be reasoned with rather than forcing him underground.

New Jersey is not the only progressive state in the realm of student rights. The Montgomery County, Maryland, board of education involves students in policy decisions concerning such matters as discipline, dress codes, grading and reporting procedures, and curriculum development. The Sequoia school district in California consults students in its selection of teachers. The California state board of education has appointed a high school junior to serve on the board, the first such student appointment. The student, a sixteen-year-old girl, screened by the State Student Council Association prior to final selection, will serve as a nonvoting member. Her involvement is a definite measure of receptivity to students, even though her participation is limited. She cannot, for example, attend closed meetings on legal problems or teacher certification.[5]

THE IOWA PRECEDENT[6]

In 1969 the U.S. Supreme Court ruled against *in loco parentis*, the legal adult control of students. The court ruled in Tinker vs. Des Moines Independent Community School District that school officials cannot wield absolute authority over students. The ruling stated that students are "persons" as referred to in the Constitution and are therefore protected by the rights set forth in the document. The state and its local school districts must respect those rights. If the state or the districts act to limit students' freedom of expression, they must give a constitutionally defensible justification.

The Tinker decision requires school authorities to respect student rights where they had previously defined the rights as they wished. Perhaps most important, if school officials interfere with the free exercise of a student's rights without constitutional justification, they may be liable to personal suit. Thus the Tinker decision has provided some very powerful machinery to guarantee students their rights.

Teachers and administrators must be aware of the implications of the Tinker decision. There are four basic points that must be observed in order to avoid legal problems:

1. Under the First Amendment, a student may dress as he wishes (subject to final approval in the courts). He will be able to dissent in any form the courts find acceptable.
2. The school board must recognize that the Constitution protects all of the contestants—teachers, administrators, community residents, and students—in a dispute.
3. The school board must observe due process in any disciplinary action against a student. The charges against him must be specified and he must be given reasonable notification for a personal appearance at a hearing.
4. The school board cannot establish "arbitrary" and "unreasonable" classifications or rules discriminating against students. Equal protection of the law prohibits such forms of authoritarianism.

THE ADMINISTRATIVE VIEW[7]

A 1971 poll revealed that school superintendents believe that the worst of student disruptions in the high schools have run their course. Of the superintendents sampled, 64 percent did not anticipate an increase in disruptions. Of the 34 percent who believe disturbances will grow, some feel that open lines of communication will help to solve the problems. Others insist on stringent disciplinary measures.

Only 11 percent of the nation's high schools have experienced student protest, which has been largely an urban phenomenon. The percentage of metropolitan schools that have been disrupted is undoubtedly considerably higher.

The unrest has *not* focused primarily upon national political issues such as Vietnam, as mass media coverage might lead one to expect. Issues closer to home are more important. Racial tension, student self-governance, disciplinary procedures, and dress standards are very significant concerns. Only 30 percent of the superintendents who indicated their districts had weathered disruption thought antiwar feeling precipitated the unrest. Only 15 percent thought that students' direct action had been addressed to changes in the curriculum.

More than half of all superintendents had made plans for dealing with student disruptions. No superintendent felt that police should "never" be used. However, 53 percent thought that they should be brought in "as a last resort," whereas 47 percent wanted to call them "right away." These statistics indicate a moderating trend. In a 1968 poll, only 39 percent responded "as a last resort," whereas 61 percent responded "right away."

THE NASSP STUDY[8]

The National Association of Secondary School Principals gathered complete information in a study of student activism and conflict conducted in 1969. The study revealed that high school protest is basically an urban phenomenon. Conflicts occur more frequently in largely black schools than in basically white ones. But the most frequent disruption occurs in integrated schools having between 21 and 60 percent black students. Thus student unrest is especially linked to integrated urban schools.

Superintendents whose schools had undergone conflict during 1967–1969 were asked to describe the conditions that prevailed before and during the unrest. They reported nine basic conditions:

1. Damage to the school's physical facilities.
2. Physical confrontations involving staff and students.
3. Physical confrontations among students.
4. Protest marches or picketing.
5. Refusal to attend classes, usually in the form of a student strike.
6. Disruption of classes for at least half a day.
7. Approval of students' behavior by adults other than parents.
8. Involvement of more than half the student body.
9. Active or tacit support for the students by at least one staff member.

The NASSP survey also sought to determine the concerns of student dissidents. The study found that the protestors were concerned with nine categories of issues:

1. Dress and appearance codes (natural hair style, hair length, miniskirts, etc.).
2. Special accommodations for ethnic and minority groups (black lounges, soul food, Martin Luther King memorial, etc.).
3. National issues (poverty, inflation, unemployment, Vietnam, etc.).
4. Curriculum (Swahili; Black, Chicano, and Native American studies; sex education, etc.).
5. Instructional process (tracking, racial prejudice of teachers, irrelevant assignments, etc.).
6. Freedom of speech and press (arm bands, buttons, underground newspapers, etc.).
7. Ideology (Black Power, white racism, American imperialism, police brutality, etc.).
8. Student social relations (segregated school social events, white cheerleaders, etc.).
9. Student personnel services (guidance, detention halls, regulations for tardiness, disciplinary procedures, etc.).

The importance of a particular issue depends on the type of school. In all-white schools, the basic issue for conflict is the dress code. In integrated and all-black schools, dress and appearance are much less serious problems. Rather, the pivotal issues concern curriculum, ideology, special accommodations, student personnel services, and social relations. Surprisingly, national issues such as Vietnam are not a major concern for high school students in any type of school.

The issues that concern the dissident students are an indirect indictment of the American schools. James Coleman's research[9] on school social systems demonstrates that the highest student statuses are awarded to the most anti-intellectual roles, such as cheerleader and athlete. Add to this the facts that teachers come from the lowest intellectual rank of their graduating college classes, that they have been historically afraid of controversial issues,[10] and that school administrators are more often businessmen than educators, and one can understand why the school has frequently generated a rather childlike student approach to the real world.

In the suburbs, students protest more often about dress codes than they do about the misery of a ghetto a few miles away or the very significant American presence in Vietnam. Something is tragically and perhaps criminally wrong with a school system that teaches such an infantile mentality.

SOME RESPONSES

The schools have responded to student unrest in five principal ways. Administrators have arranged meetings for student representatives and school superintendents. They have created new channels of communication between students and staff. They have initiated small-group faculty-student discussions. They have offered new courses and modified the existing courses. And they have catalyzed dialogue between community residents and school administrators. A sixth course of action the schools have pursued, but slightly less frequently than the most important five, is to establish new school regulations and student personnel procedures. One should note that these most frequent school actions during crises are all nonpunitive, nonviolent, and constructive. Seldom is student dissent crushed. When police are called, however, it is usually to low socioeconomic, all-black, or integrated schools.

The schools have devised a number of specific programs to handle student unrest. A student ombudsman who hears student grievances has been hired in Berkeley, California. Schools in Winnetka and Northfield, Illinois, have established the position of coordinator of community services to approve and plan student community projects. Students in Miami, Florida, have been assigned as aides to the school board.

A new program designed to promote student self-discipline has been developed in Cold Spring Harbor, New York. A student may decide how he wishes to use his study period. He may study in the library or pursue an independent study project. Or he may discuss any issue or merely socialize with peers in a cooperative study room. When a student abuses his privileges by skipping his study period or exhibiting unruly behavior, he must attend a supervised study hall for a specified period of time. The Cold Spring Harbor schools have found that students choose interesting activities responsibly and learn them well.

The charge that instruction is irrelevant is a serious challenge to the stability of the school. Teachers and administrators must seek to introduce innovations to satisfy legitimate demands. The reforms that are possible include individually diagnosed instruction, modular scheduling, field work outside the school, advanced placement courses, seminars, and independent study.

Administrators in ghetto schools have sought to achieve racially integrated and balanced faculties, establish literature and history courses, and organize a human relations council.[11]

THE ASHBAUGH MODEL[12]

Carl R. Ashbaugh has surveyed the range of school responses to student activism and derived a model of nine specific actions and policies. More than one line of action may be employed, and the approaches are in no way sequential or mutually exclusive. These nine ways the schools have been able to creatively and successfully deal with unrest can serve as the guidelines for teacher and administrator:

1. *Maintaining lines of communication.* Everyone directly or indirectly affected by student conflict should be consulted and involved. They can play a crucial role in resolving conflict on a long-term basis. Since many who are influenced by or interested in the events on campus will be calling to ask questions, schools should set up a "control room" or a centralized communication center where all information can be received and checked for accuracy. The control room can disseminate periodic fact sheets to prevent the spread of inflammatory rumors. The fact sheet should be sent to every mass media organization in the area and made readily available to students and staff.

2. *Controlling influences; enforcing attendance.* Outside influences can be critical. They can enlarge a conflict that might otherwise be resolved. A school district can seek an injunction to prevent non-student agitators and sensationalist journalists from exploiting unrest. The Philadelphia and Los Angeles school districts have both secured injunctions during crises. The school should also inform students that absence during a boycott does not constitute an excused absence and that missed work cannot be completed for credit. The school should appeal to parents to encourage their children to attend school.

3. *Talking with student leaders.* Teachers and administrators should agree to talk over the pressing issues with student leaders, provided hostilities cease. Since student movements generally are unstable social units, leaders very seldom have firm control. They will usually welcome the opportunity to meet with the school staff to establish their authority. The dialogue that ensues can reduce tension and unrest and stabilize deliberations. If school and student leaders can hammer out a resolution that incorporates a spirit of accommodation and perhaps some substantive points of agreement, a cooling-off period can begin; it is hoped that such a period will produce an accord that provides the foundation for a lasting peace.

4. *Third-party mediation.* The school board is often ineffective as mediator. When an impasse occurs, a third party might be able to mediate the dispute. He should be a prestigious person with experience in settling disputes. Prominent judges and professors fall into this category. The services of a third party can make a rational settlement possible. If the school board accedes to certain student demands, the public may become irate. However, if it assents to a third party's reasoned recommendations, it cannot be charged with the major responsibility for the agreement.

5. *Identification of student demands.* The school should request student leaders to verbalize or write their demands for publication and distribution. The identification of specific demands is crucial to the mediation process. Mediation is impossible unless all parties to a dispute agree upon what is being disputed.

6. *Responding to student demands.* Once student demands have been specified, teachers and administrators can devise a response. School personnel who command the most expertise about a particular demand should formulate and present the response. The entire staff should consider the means and implications of implementing a particular response. If implementation is not feasible, even the most reasoned response to the most legitimate demand can be only an academic exercise.

7. *Hearing all viewpoints.* The issues involved in student unrest usually have ramifications throughout a school system and community. To achieve a workable solution, all constituents—all those affected by particular issues—must be heard. One way to secure a cross section of opinion and analysis is to empanel a group to operate

much as a grand jury. The panel would include school administrators, board of education members, and student leaders. The president of the board of education would preside. The panel would invite recognized experts and representatives of various groups and points of view to present and scrutinize possible lines of action and their consequences. It would collect information and consider policy proposals in order to clarify the issues. A firm deadline for completion of the panel's tasks is important; otherwise, the panel might procrastinate interminably.

8. *Selecting a course of action.* The school board must eventually make a decision. The panel may provide badly needed time for deliberation, but the board must ultimately discharge its legal responsibility to establish school policy. It should employ the seven foregoing procedures to select a course of action that will be agreeable to all and achieve a long-lasting solution.

9. *Institutionalizing student participation.* Much student unrest derives from the students' feeling excluded from the decisions that determine the quality and type of their experience in the schools. A substantial amount of the rebellion can be prevented by institutionalizing student involvement so that uncompromising confrontation need not occur. Discussion and reconciliation should be continuing processes rather than for crises only.

The conventional form of student government cannot fully meet the need for student involvement. Students must have procedures for appeal and redress. An ombudsman, a person students can go to with their complaints, must be hired. Berkeley, California, and Winnetka, Illinois, have done so with positive results.

The solution to student rebellion is thoughtful, creative change. Learners usually do not express their alienation for no reason at all. There is generally substance behind the smoke. Teachers and schools must inquire into the causes of their students' disaffection and attempt to remove the sources of alienation through reform.

NOTES

[1]Richard A. Gorton, "Militant Student Activism in the High Schools: Analysis and Recommendations," *Phi Delta Kappan,* 51, no. 10 (June 1970), 548.

[2]Jacob B. Zack, "Restless Youth—What's the Message?," *The Bulletin of the National Association of Secondary School Principals,* 54, no. 346 (May 1970), 154–155.

[3] Lesley H. Browder, Jr., "The New American Success Story Is Called Student Confrontation," *The American School Board Journal*, 157, no. 12 (June 1970), 24.

[4] *Ibid.*

[5] *Ibid.*

[6] *Ibid.*, pp. 24–25.

[7] "Worst Of Student Disorders May Be Over, Schoolmen Say," *Nation's Schools*, 87, no. 2 (February 1971), 17.

[8] "Student Activism and Conflict," *The Bulletin of the National Association of Secondary School Principals*, 54, no. 346 (May 1970), 70–89.

[9] James S. Coleman, *The Adolescent Society* (Glencoe, Ill., Free Press, 1961).

[10] Harmon Zeigler, *The Political Life of American Teachers* (Englewood Cliffs, N.J., Prentice-Hall, 1967).

[11] Raphael M. Kudela, "Facing Student Unrest," *The Clearing House*, 44, no. 9 (May 1970), 549–550.

[12] Carl R. Ashbaugh, "High School Student Activism: Nine Tested Approaches For Coping With Conflict Situations," *Nation's Schools*, 83, no. 2 (February 1969), 94–96.

7
Ecology education

The promise that the environment will collapse about us if we do not reeducate ourselves for survival compels the schools to include a consideration of ecology in the curriculum. The science of ecology encompasses a recognition that all forms of life are related. In order to study the interrelations, the schools must use an interdisciplinary approach. All knowledge is related just as all life is related. A solely disciplinary approach is insufficient. Thus ecology and interdisciplinary studies are part of the same educational package. Both are part of the new educational responsibility schools and teachers are now assuming.

THE TEACHER'S NEW ROLE

The new teacher must present more than information in teaching about ecology. The subject matter is certainly important, as we shall discuss later in this chapter, but values are the most important consideration in ecology education. The teacher must train the learner to recognize his responsibility toward the environment. He must teach students that a serious threat exists to all life and that everyone must make sacrifices in order to prevent the destruction of the environment and create aesthetic, clean surroundings conducive to a high level of human welfare.

By studying the relations between man and environment,

students will learn how important it is that we weigh the total impact of our actions upon ecological systems. If we act stupidly, we upset balances and equilibriums that are ultimately destructive to ourselves. Thus teachers must make students aware that we are all part of the environment and that what we do will determine the quality of both the environment and our lives.

THREE ECOLOGICAL THEMES[1]

The new teacher should present three basic ecological themes in the classroom. First, the state of the ecology is not a matter of fate. How we treat the environment is the basic determinant of environmental quality. We can make the environment as good or as bad as we wish. Second, the quality of our environment involves the satisfaction of human needs: The aesthetic is very important, for without some beauty in his life man goes insane. Man has a great need for a high-quality environment. Third, the state of the environment depends greatly on how much we respect property we hold in common, that is, how well we conserve public property. If we act as though maintenance and wise use are up to the other fellow, we will be unable to develop the conservationist ethic necessary for survival.

ECOLOGICAL OBJECTIVES AND PROGRAMS[2]

There are a number of objectives teachers must pursue in order to effectively carry through on the three ecological themes. They are based on involving students in both classroom and environment. Only by linking the school and the environment can teachers provide adequate ecological education. The primary objectives should be as follows:

1. Teachers must increase the environmental literacy of their students. They must teach learners to act upon the basis of facts to improve surrounding ecological systems.
2. Teachers must devise and participate in programs to train personnel in environmental science and technology.
3. Teachers must involve their students in the environment as concerned technologists, social scientists, and humanists. Students can benefit greatly by testing their book learning against the real world. In fact, it is the only way they can really learn ecology.

Experience and aesthetics are important to the ecology teacher. The teacher's operational assumption should be that experience, a direct contact with the environment, is the best method of learning ecology. The teacher's programs should be quantitative, requiring inquiry and discovery in the environment whenever possible. Even indirect experience—the use of newspapers, films, TV, and magazines—is highly desirable. The mass media are supersaturated with ecological information and the new teacher should make good use of them. Finally, aesthetics and an appreciation of the environment are almost the same thing. If the student learns to appreciate beauty, he cannot avoid a healthy respect for the environment. The teacher must work hard on the aesthetic development of the child in art and music. If students learn to appreciate pleasing sights and sounds they will not tolerate ugliness and dissonance in the environment.

The American ecology movement has arisen only recently. The schools have not had sufficient time to respond with a variety of curricula to meet ecological learning needs. However, the Science Curriculum Improvement Study (SCIS), developed at the University of California at Berkeley under a grant from the National Science Foundation, meets many needs and is readily available. The SCIS builds a comprehensive, sequential view of the environment through the elementary school grades. If the SCIS life science sequence were supplemented with social science units, the total package would provide an excellent environmental education program. The laboratory-centered units of the SCIS are as follows: First Level—Organisms, Second Level—Life Cycles, Third Level—Populations, Fourth Level—Environments, Fifth Level—Communities, Sixth Level—Ecosystems. By adding a social science unit at each of the six levels, the sequence would be highly educational ecologically. For example, in the unit on Ecosystems, the learner might experiment with substances that become pollutants when they reach sufficiently high concentrations in the environment. He soon discovers what pollution is and what the harmful effects are. He should study the economics, politics, sociology, and psychology of environmental pollution as well as the science. He might consider, for example, the political power of polluting corporations in our national life.

MIDDLE AND SECONDARY SCHOOL ENVIRONMENTAL CURRICULUMS[3]

The environmental curricula, as we have seen, must be interdisciplinary to be ecological. One can study ecology in conjunction with almost any subject. Thus environmental curricula are similar to conventional "correlated curricula." The substance, however, is totally new.

Let us consider a few ways environmental curricula can be organized in the middle and secondary schools:

1. *Humanities.* Teachers can emphasize the concern of great writers and humanists for pleasing surroundings. They should require students to read such works as Rachel Carson's *Silent Spring* and René Dubos' *So Human an Animal.* In this way the humanities can be correlated with environmental issues.
2. *Political science.* Politics and pollution are related. Teachers and students should consider how environmental abuses are perpetrated in our political system. They should also explore how the political process might be used to end pollution. For example, students might explore how citizens can work for legislation requiring exhaust-free automobiles.
3. *History.* A historical analysis of the increasing pollution of the environment will give students a time perspective. For example, a focus upon the impact of our society's growing use of technology and the environmental consequences through the past half-century will allow learners to see new relationships and make inferences about environmental quality.
4. *Biology.* Teachers can present ecological principles by using the green version of the Biological Sciences Curriculum Study (BSCS). The green version has been developed with an ecological outlook and is easily included in a classroom ecology unit.
5. *Earth science and geography.* Students can examine the impact of changing environments on all forms of life. For example, they might explore the effect of prehistoric climate changes on plants and animals. The emphasis should be on showing learners that changes in the environment can kill species and entire populations.

INVOLVEMENT
AND INTERRELATIONSHIPS[4]

Teacher and school should involve their students environmentally in many different ways. Student activities can range from outdoor camping and nature exploration to political games simulating the clash between various environmental interest groups. Teachers should help students become active in the community in such efforts as environmental education campaigns and park improvement projects. In metropolitan areas, teachers might find opportunities for students to learn in a work-study arrangement with city planners. The possibilities are virtually unlimited. Any activity that brings the student closer to his environment, either through experience or information, is a legitimate educational objective.

The young must have an opportunity to study the consequences of human behavior upon the environment. They must become aware of alternative forms of behavior that can improve their surroundings. The development of this awareness requires a social as well as a scientific approach to ecology. Today, most schools dwell on the scientific, largely ignoring the social. Teacher and school must instruct learners that environmental problems are really social problems. The way our society consumes and produces directly affects the environment. If we are all so status conscious that we want high-powered cars and will not vote for bonds for mass transit systems, then there is no hope for us or the environment. Learners must be given abundant opportunities to realize this—their future depends on it.

Genuine interdisciplinary ecological curricula are almost nonexistent. The reason is that science and social science teachers generally are not qualified to develop or teach interdisciplinary curricula. The colleges and universities where they studied did not and now seldom mix science and social science. The four-year institutions and teacher colleges must break down the disciplinary barriers and train teachers who can educate students to be aware of ecological problems. They must equip the young teacher with the skills and values necessary for a total approach to the interrelationship of man, society, and environment.

INNOVATION IN THE SCHOOLS[5]

The schools have been responding to the national ecology movement. Although adequate ecology curricula have yet to be developed, the public schools have improvised by incorporating new material into existing courses and sending youngsters directly into the environment for field work and experience. The schools are demonstrating that they can effectively innovate to meet the needs of the times.

A six-year project in South Carolina has produced eight curriculum guides for teachers, grades 1 through 12, in home economics, outdoor education, social studies, and science. The guides contain more than 400 lessons a teacher can use to teach ecological concepts.

The National Park Services' National Environmental Education

Development (NEED) program seeks to create a greater understanding of the environment by building a curriculum on five basic ecological principles. NEED has produced student materials and teacher guides for grades 3 through 8. It will eventually offer materials to include kindergarten through twelfth grade. Each NEED lesson focuses on an important ecological theme. The NEED program involves local schools in a national environmental education effort. The schools use the NEED materials in the classroom and follow classroom study with trips to National Environmental Study Areas (NESA's). The environmental areas may be cultural, historical, or natural. Most of the environmental areas will be near metropolises, offering many youngsters their first sustained encounter with the natural world. However, the NESA program considers the urban environment just as fit for study as the natural environment. The artificial surroundings of the city are, after all, the only environment for millions of Americans.

The Center for Urban Education in New York City has begun Planning for Change, an ecology action program for upper-elementary children. The children participate in a number of environmental projects. A consortium of more than sixty school districts has established the Conservation and Environmental Science Center at Brown's Mills, New Jersey. The center, funded under Title III of the Elementary and Secondary Education Act, has produced enviromental curriculum guides. It is now working on new curricula for environmental education in suburban, rural, urban, and marine contexts. The program at Brown's Mills includes week-long resident programs and one-day field study programs.

National environmental and conservation organizations sponsor numerous educational programs for the schools. The National Wildlife Federation publishes *Conservation News* and it furnishes educational materials under its "Ranger Rick" program. The Conservation Foundation produces educational films on ecology and publishes *CF Letter*, a monthly newsletter on environmental issues. The National Audubon Society runs environmental workshops for teachers. It has collaborated with the New York City Schools to develop a study series called *A Place to Live* for fourth-, fifth-, and sixth-grade students living in metropolitan environments.

OUTDOOR EDUCATION

The most appropriate setting for the study of ecology is the natural environment. However, the schools have been slow to accept school camping programs that provide opportunities for outdoor education. Youngsters who spend a week or more at a school camp enjoy great advantages in developing a knowledge of and respect for the environment. It is important that teachers become aware of the potential of outdoor education.

School-sponsored camping, now becoming known as residential outdoor education, has been primarily recreational to date. There was seldom an educational component until the dawning of the new ecological awareness. There were exceptions, particularly a few pioneering programs in Michigan and California. In these outdoor education programs, regular classes were conducted in the environment. Today, a number of school districts sponsor outdoor education that focuses on developing ecological understandings. But the active districts are only a small percentage of the total. The schools' great potential for environmental education and participation remains largely untapped.[6]

BENEFITS OF THE GREAT OUTDOORS

There are a number of reasons that education conducted in the natural environment is highly conducive to ecological learning. First, the flora, fauna, earth, and atmosphere are all there to illustrate the entire range of academic concepts and principles. In our consideration of open education (see Chapter 5) we discussed how children learn concepts by first having direct or "concrete" experiences. This same learning method applies to the very open classroom that is the environment. Second, students have sufficient time in the environment to explore thoroughly. They can learn ecology in ways that the classroom experience cannot duplicate. Since they are learning in such a direct way, they will not easily forget what they have learned. Third, learning ecology outdoors is fun. Students learn best what they enjoy. The outdoor ecology education programs may even seem a form of play. This rather ecstatic approach to knowing and understanding the environment translates into very positive attitudes toward our surroundings. That may be the ultimate payoff in taking the kids out of the classroom and into the wilderness.

The typical resident outdoor educational program lasts from three days to two weeks. The average is about five days. The student has the opportunity to know the local environment intimately. He reports his experiences and observations in group discussions with peers and teachers. This allows each student to compare his impressions with others' and see if he is interpreting his experiences correctly. If he must return to the field to check his observations, he is certainly not far away. As the camp program progresses, campers can select and pursue independent projects. Whether alone or in groups, the learners operate as young scientists, experiencing, interpreting, and drawing conclusions about how the environment works and how they might act to live harmoniously in it.[7]

EFFECTIVE STAFFING AND PROGRAMING[8]

Resident outdoor education programs are effective only to the degree they are staffed with competent personnel. The staff must be knowledgeable about the environment and committed to teaching about it. There are two basic staffing patterns. The camp may be staffed by permanent specialists whom classroom teachers assist. This is probably the most dependable arrangement because it insures that somebody will be available who knows the geographical area, ecological subject matter, and effective outdoor teaching strategies. The danger is that the outdoor curriculum will become too professionalized and insufficiently responsive to student needs and interests.

In the second staffing arrangement classroom teachers are charged with the major responsibility for outdoor instruction. Ecology professionals and volunteers assist the teachers. This pattern makes the student's transition from classroom to camp easier, but the work load for the teacher increases considerably. If the teacher does not know the area surrounding the camp, if she is a novice in ecology, and if she has never taught outdoors, she, like the vast majority of teachers, must face a bundle of homework before she can even begin to teach in a resident outdoor education program. Thus the first staffing pattern would seem preferable in most contexts.

Whatever the staffing arrangement, the camp program is not isolated. It should serve only as a laboratory for field work and direct observation. Students must study ecology in school to make the camp experience worthwhile. Students should learn data collection techniques and the methods of constructing, operating, and maintaining certain equipment prior to arriving in camp. Following their field experiences, it is essential that they examine data and draw conclusions. Unless students go through the painstaking scientific enterprise of carefully examining field data to find underlying principles, the camp program will be a mere outing.

The urban student, living in the artificial surroundings of the city, may have no opportunity to become familiar with another environment if not through the school. This is particularly true if he is poor or nonwhite. The outdoor programs enable city youngsters to learn ecological principles first hand. They become aware that the city environment is not perfect and is, in many ways, psychologically and physically unhealthy. Teachers must instruct their students that they can make a cleaner, safer environment. Students need only join together and act out their new ecological consciousness. They can campaign in support of returnable bottles and low-phosphate detergents. They can even organize politically, writing letters to congressmen and publicizing their environmental stands. The greatest significance of resident outdoor education programs is that they teach our young to survive.

ECOLOGY EDUCATION MODELS

A few schools have established environmental education programs. Some have been very successful. There are five programs in particular that illustrate different approaches. They can serve as excellent models for other schools seeking to provide effective instruction in ecology.

THE SAN BERNARDINO ECOLOGY ACTION MODEL[9]

Junior high students in San Bernardino, California, have been working with an environmental organization called the Natural Beauty Program. The Natural Beauty Program evolved from the Conservation Club of Richardson Junior High. Members of the club, and later the program, have planted trees, cleaned up San Bernardino, and sponsored campaigns to educate the public about pollution since 1958. In the fall of 1959, club members decided to work to restore a nearby area devastated by a summer fire. They cooperated with the U. S. Forest Service to restore the area by clearing stream beds, planting pine seedlings, constructing terraces, and checking dams and ponds to prevent erosion. They have continued to help in the restoration of fire-ravaged timberlands.

Disturbed by public apathy, Richardson Junior High students undertook intensive environmental research in order to build a public educational program. They visited sewage disposal and water reclamation plants and air-pollution control and experiment stations. They traveled to desert, mountain, and urban sites to inquire into ecological problems. They then organized to tell the public about their findings and impressions. The citizens of San Bernardino have become better informed about the dangers of pollution and imbalances in ecological systems. They have become more concerned about and involved in local environmental problems.

In 1965, the Natural Beauty Program was organized to expand the environmental activities of the Richardson High Conservation Club throughout San Bernardino. By 1970, the program included 2,500 students from twenty-two of the city's schools as well as members of such groups as the Campfire Girls, Girl Scouts, and Boy Scouts. The program conducted thirty-six antilitter drives in 1970. San Bernardino youth volunteers devote their Saturdays to these efforts.

The Natural Beauty Program's goal is to annually involve 4,000 students and several hundred representatives of youth groups in their activities. Such a large number is particularly useful in meeting the very critical need for volunteer help caused by summer and early fall fires in Southern California. Another major concern is environmental eyesores. Three hundred young people helped the U. S. Forest Service clean up an abandoned garbage dump that was polluting underground water and offending the aesthetic sensibilities of passers-by. Another group planted 650 trees and landscaped to improve a scenic overlook area. The young manpower the Natural Beauty Program has mobilized has improved the environment substantially.

THE DETROIT URBAN ECOLOGY MODEL[10]

A group of life-science students in Detroit has become involved in a study of environmental pollution. They conduct much of their field study in the Detroit metropolitan area. Each student research team divides into four groups to assume specific responsibilities. Some students record environmental data, such as the type of topography, the climate, and the industrial origins of pollution. Others take photographs and movies. These are used later to determine whether ecology action programs are producing positive results. Some students are assigned to collect water, soil, and air samples and animal and plant specimens such as insects and grass. A final group records the types of plant and animal life in the area under study.

In their field investigations, students develop sufficient knowledge and data to produce an ecological profile of the plant and animal communities that have survived in a polluted metropolis. They determine the impact of pollution on all forms of life, drawing revealing ecological maps of Detroit. Advanced biology students conduct controlled experiments with the water, soil, and air samples the student groups have collected. One ongoing experiment involves growing plants in contaminated air. Another project is the study of aquatic and soil samples collected in various parts of Detroit.

The life-science students have recently begun to study the human environment. They study overcrowding, disease, noise pollution, and mental health. What does a congested city do to human beings? That is their central concern. The degree to which they and their counterparts across our nation learn what makes for human happiness and survival will determine the quality of our society's future and, indeed, whether there will be a future at all.

THE TEMPLETON MODEL[11]

The sixth-graders at Templeton Elementary School, Tigard, Oregon, are studying the causes and effects of land, air, and water pollution and possible solutions. The children learned about pollution in Tigard by examining the research findings of a local environmental control agency. Each pupil was responsible for bringing news items to class to report and discuss. The clippings eventually found their way to bulletin board displays.

Through their studies, the children became alarmed about the seriousness of pollution. They decided to awaken others by developing an educational program. They participated in interest groups to produce skits and puppet shows, slide presentations, and chalkboard and picture demonstrations. They also wrote stories and addressed classes in the primary grades. They soon expanded their program to sponsor an assembly on pollution to educate the entire student body. Several students spoke at the assembly, elaborating factually on the environmental crisis. The sixth-grade ecologists later presented the same program to the school's Parent-Teacher Association.

Many pupils at Templeton have volunteered to pick up litter on school property during recesses. They have also worked weekends to clean up litter and debris in Tigard. The Templeton program demonstrates that the school can provide opportunities for children to become informed and concerned about the environment. They can learn information and values at school that are the antecedent to constructive action.

THE ELYRIA MODEL[12]

The Elyria, Ohio, City Schools have provided an environmental education program since 1966. Students in grades 3 through 6 study nature science and art at an outdoor site. Their classroom studies are correlated with their outdoor activities. The indoor program focuses on the theme "Man, Art, and the Environment." Each art teacher prepares a unit on this topic for her classes. Pupils interpret the environment artistically, creating posters, graphic prints, and paintings. Some pupils pursue projects such as studying the effects of pollution on the coloration of birds and insects. Others look at changes in coloration of buildings in various parts of the town. Social studies and science teachers also devise activities to reinforce the theme.

The basic point of the Elyria experience is that high-quality environmental education requires cooperation between art, social studies, and science teachers. Coordination of the curriculum is absolutely essential.

THE OUTDOORS FOUNDATION MODEL[13]

The School of the Outdoors Foundation sponsors an environmental education program for elementary school pupils. The Institute of Child Studies at Newark State College, New Jersey, administers the program. The Institute sends "research teams" of sixth-graders on three-day field trips for the purpose of exploring the environment and pollution. It operates on the principle that students learn best when actively involved and inquiring (see Chapter 5, especially the section entitled A New Program).

The Outdoors Foundation program is based on concepts that pupils first learn and then explore in the field. For example, in an outdoor unit on air-pollution control, students learn concepts about air and its properties and then consider the effects of air pollution on the environment. Finding the effects is basically a process of *doing*. Pupils constructed a weather station and made daily weather reports and forecasts. They soon added a pollution station, building devices to measure some of the less complex pollution components. They took pollen counts, measured particulate fallout in selected locations, and observed and analyzed the effect of the sun in producing air currents and dispersing pollutants.

The pupils constructed and tested a number of devices. They made "minigreenhouses" from flowerpots and plastic bags and grew plants in them. At various stages of growth, they subjected the plants to car exhaust fumes and observed the harmful effects. The devices the pupils built were all simple, made from readily available materials, in a standard workshop, and with tools sold in any hardware store. The program's essential supplies were simple: milk containers, an old vacuum cleaner, tin cans, bottles, balloons, laboratory glassware, aquarium tubing, and wood. The single piece of relatively complex equipment was a set of detector tubes for mine safety work. The Outdoor Foundation program is not oriented to scientific precision but toward environmental awareness. Hence easily obtainable, simple devices are sufficient.

Participants in the Outdoor Foundation program took frequent field trips. They visited pollution research centers to consult professionals. They tested air at mountain, seashore, urban, rural, and suburban sites. They ran experiments to determine the effect of polluted air on human beings. Comparisons of odor, visibility tests, and estimations of lung capacity under different circumstances using a spirometer constituted the specific experimental procedures. The pupils found that pollution adversely affected nerves, pulse rate, and endurance. Their findings had a great deal of shock value.

The program did not rely solely on direct experience. Pupils also discussed, heard lectures, read, and saw films, filmstrips, and demonstrations.

During their field work, students compiled several outdoor instructional units on ecology. An advisory committee of educational professionals and scientists reviewed the material and converted it into a form suitable for mass use. Nine classes in the middle grades of five public schools in New Jersey tried the units during 1970. An evaluation of their learning indicated favorable results. The mid-Atlantic division of the Air Pollution Control Association has shown considerable interest in the evaluation and has expressed a desire to publish the units.

THE NEA ENVIRONMENTAL SURVEY[14]

The National Education Association Research Division conducted a pilot study in 1969-1970 to determine what the public schools were doing in the realm of environmental education. The study was designed to survey programs in outdoor, environmental, and conservation education. It covered the entire range of grade levels, from kindergarten through adult education. The study sampled only school systems with enrollments in excess of 1,000 pupils. Since these systems enroll 90 per cent of all pupils, the 1,000 cutoff is justifiable. The survey concerned only those public systems that assigned the equivalent of at least a half-time staff member to an environmental program. There were 700 such systems.

The survey revealed substantial variety in environmental education programs. The major research findings provide us an image of how the schools are conceiving their new role in ecology education:

1. A majority of programs operate on a regularly scheduled basis throughout the school year.
2. The programs are intended mainly for pupils in the upper elementary grades.
3. The majority of environmental education programs are called "Outdoor Education." They are designed to provide pupils a general familiarity with the natural environment and man's relation to it.
4. Most programs use National Park Service curriculum materials, especially films and pamphlets.
5. The most frequent areas of study are biology, ecology, conservation, botany, geology, insect study, weather study, and general science.
6. Most programs are centrally administered, but a few are operated on a decentralized basis.
7. Most programs offering courses at the secondary level grant academic credit, but few give grades.
8. Most programs seek to evaluate attitudinal changes.
9. An instructional team usually determines the curriculum of a program. The needs and wishes of students are taken into account.
10. The maximum feasible distance for day trips is fifty miles one way. The distance for overnight trips is 100 miles. However, these are only averages. No school reported a restriction on travel distances.
11. The sites most frequently visited are campgrounds, wildlife natural areas, ponds, lakes, forests, and woodlands.
12. In most programs, pupils visit locations where they remain overnight. Cabins or bunkhouses, cooking and dining facilities, and an infirmary are usually available. Classrooms, an exhibit center, a swimming pool, and a crafts shop are also often available.
13. The local school board usually furnishes most, if not all, the funds for a school district's environmental program.
14. The directors of environmental programs are academically qualified, possessing a master's degree or higher, but few have been trained in environmental studies. However, most schools solved this problem by providing in-service training to their faculty.
15. The majority of programs relied on the regular school faculty to

staff the environmental programs. Resource persons, such as biochemists and conservationists, assisted. A regular faculty member is seldom assigned full-time to a program. It is usually a part-time responsibility.
16. Most districts expressed a need for greater financial help and increased assistance with in-service training programs.

The survey discovered three types of environmental programs according to grade level. Some school systems provide environmental education to elementary students only. This may be because they are elementary schools or because they have designed their programs specifically for elementary students. Other school systems offer ecology programs only in one or more of the junior or senior high grades. Another category of public systems offer environmental education at both elementary and secondary levels. This category is the most numerous, but almost as many schools provide programs solely at the elementary level. A relative few restrict their offerings to the junior-senior high grades.

Distinct differences exist among the three programs. Programs serving only elementary students are usually one-year programs for sixth-graders. They operate usually for only one-quarter of the calendar year during the regular school session. Their purpose is to teach pupils to appreciate the environment and take advantage of opportunities to enjoy the outdoors. Most elementary programs are camp programs where pupils spend a few days exploring natural surroundings.

Programs restricted to the junior-senior high grades operate almost exclusively as a part of the conventional academic curriculum. Most are two- or three-year programs for the senior grades. They generally continue throughout the school year and focus chiefly on the technical and scientific aspects of ecology. They emphasize classroom work with occasional field trips. The junior-senior high programs are much more academic than the elementary programs. The students generally receive both grades and academic credit.

Programs that operate on both elementary and secondary levels are more comprehensive than the other programs. Over half serve six or more elementary grades. A sizable percentage serve a similar number of secondary grades. The vast majority of elementary-secondary programs are directed at the middle grades, 4 through 8. Their stress is on a total approach to the study of man and his environment. A large percentage of the programs operate on a year-round basis. They cover a greater range of study areas, use more locations, and employ more personnel than do strictly elementary or junior-senior high level programs.

THE NEW RESPONSIBILITY

The public schools have responded to the national environmental movement by devising new programs. Although many changes are only experimental and hardly measurable, the schools are properly assuming the new responsibility that has been thrust upon them by a rapidly changing society. The schools have traditionally been charged with preserving our cultural heritage by transmitting it. Now they are charged with saving it by teaching not only the old values but also new ones. The new role of the teacher and school is to help save our culture and environment by teaching the young to think and act respectfully toward both natural and social worlds.

NOTES

[1] Edythe Margolin, "Ecology in the Primary Grades," *Social Education*, 35, no. 1 (January 1971), 63–66.

[2] Arthur D. Roberts and Odvard Egil Dyrli, "Environmental Education," *The Clearing House*, 45, no. 8 (April 1971), 451–455.

[3] *Ibid.*, p. 453.

[4] *Ibid.*, pp. 454–455.

[5] The Council on Environmental Quality, "Environmental Education," *American Education*, 6, no. 8 (October 1970), 23–24.

[6] Robert L. Dwyer, "School Camping Programs: Ecology in the Outdoor Classroom," *Social Education*, 35, no. 1 (January 1971), 75.

[7] *Ibid.*, pp. 75–76.

[8] *Ibid.*, pp. 76–77.

[9] "What Secondary Schools Are Doing," *Today's Education*, December 1970, p. 22.

[10] *Ibid.*, pp. 22–23.

[11] "What Elementary Schools Are Doing," *Today's Education*, December 1970, p. 25.

[12] *Ibid.*

[13] *Ibid.*, pp. 25–26.

[14] "A Survey of School Environmental Programs," *Today's Education*, December 1970, pp. 28–29.

8
Sensitivity education

The emphasis in the public schools has been on the cognitive development of the child, but a new emphasis has recently emerged. Humanistic psychologists and educators argue that the educational experiences the schools have provided have been too exclusively intellectual, that they have not creatively harnessed children's emotional energy for learning. The schools have begun to respond to the criticisms and new perceptions. They have begun to establish sensitivity training programs, largely for teachers. This response, if acted upon fully, can enrich the curriculum so that it is not nearly as monolithic and mechanical as it is now. There can be much more individualization of instruction, pluralism, participation, and even ecstasy.

What is sensitivity training? It is also called sensitivity education, the encounter group, the T-group, and has many other names. Beyond the names, it is a group process by which people attempt to know one another better. The focus is on feelings. Group participants attempt to be as honest as possible in expressing their real feelings. They seek to examine and deal with them. The teachers' inner and social lives become objects of study. Teachers examine values critically, inquiring into their origin and usefulness for living humanistically. They explore how they might, as a group and as individuals, move toward genuine happiness and full humanness. The accent is on the here and now:

How might I achieve happiness and enjoy improved human relations today?

The immediate human concerns of the learner are the subject matter of the sensitivity training sessions. The moment rather than the future is paramount. Immediacy replaces deferred gratification so that urgent emotional needs can be satisfied now rather than being left unattended to cause serious injury later.[1]

SENSITIVITY GROUP ACTIVITIES[2]

There are a number of sensitivity group activities that teachers might try with their colleagues. By using them, communication and the general socio-psychological climate of the school can be improved. Let us look at some of the possible preliminary group activities:

1. Everyone should obtain a copy of William Schutz's *Joy*, published by Grove Press. It is perhaps the best single source on sensitivity groups. The book describes the substance and purpose of numerous activities. It is a good volume to keep near at hand.
2. The group should arrange a convenient locale and time for meetings. The room used should have a carpet so the group can lounge on the floor. Everyone should dress casually. The atmosphere should be relaxed and informal, as nonthreatening as possible.
3. Everyone should seriously attempt to be direct, open, and honest at all times. Everyone who participates in the sensitivity sessions should do so voluntarily.
4. The group should begin its encounter with everyone sitting in a circle facing the center as he wishes.

At this point, the group can proceed with any of the activities described in *Joy*. For example, one activity that promotes intensive interaction is *blind milling*. The leader tells the group to form a cluster in the center of the circle. He emphasizes that everyone should be very aware of the immediate moment, the "right now." He tells participants to close their eyes and explore the space around them with their hands. Participants bodily contact one another. The physical contact and resulting sense of group intimacy release inhibitions and stimulate group cohesion.

After a brief period of blind milling in the circle, group members move about the room, eyes still closed, doing what they wish. This goes on until everyone has had a chance to interact with others. This generally lasts three to five minutes. The leader, who has been watching the milling, then instructs the participants to slowly open their eyes and become aware of their position. He asks, "How do you feel right now?"

The group members then return to the circle and discuss their feelings openly. Members consider the benefits of blind milling. Most groups recognize three positive outcomes:

1. Milling causes participants to reveal whether they are the type who get involved in the heavy traffic in the middle, retreat to the sidelines, or uncertainly feel their way about. The character traits of individuals become identifiable.
2. In milling about, the group becomes aware of our taboos against touching. In subsequent discussion, they release their anxieties about physical encounter. Participants become less inhibited and more relaxed.
3. The body contact and closed eyes involved in blind milling increase the solidarity and intimacy of the group.

If the group includes more than eight members, the leader should ask members to form smaller groups of from four to eight. The leader should allow the members to select their own groups or assign members on the basis of some random procedure. He should never decide which group any particular member should join.

The subgroups should participate in activities that promote honest personal interaction and self-awareness. They can use one or more of the following activities:

1. *Indian wrestling.* This is an excellent way to release hostilities and explore aggressive feelings. Each person should Indian wrestle with every other participant.
2. *Nonverbal communication in dyads.* A dyad is an interaction involving two people. Each person communicates through gestures and contact such as pantomiming, touching, and embracing. This sort of simple interaction diminishes adult inhibitions. Some participants even enjoy a certain childlike ecstasy and joy during the activity. In this activity, as in wrestling, each member should pair off with every other member.
3. *Imitation.* One participant in each dyad imitates his partner's behavior. The partners then reverse roles. This process of participating in the other person's experience creates mutual understandings that facilitate group dialogue.

The group members might briefly discuss their participation in these activities, but it is best not to become too psychoanalytic, looking for motives that do not exist. Each person's interpretation should be accepted as his honest and personal way of viewing the group process. The group must operate on the assumption of mutual trust or else it will not function at all.

The mutual trust that makes possible an effective group can be buttressed by an activity that Schutz refers to as "roll and rock." The subgroup members stand in a circle. They choose a member they feel is insecure or mistrustful to stand in the middle, shut his eyes, and fall. The others catch him and pass him around the circle. Everyone takes their turn putting their complete trust in the group by dropping toward the floor. No one talks. Discussion is postponed until everyone has undergone roll and rock.

Participants reveal their personalities through the various group activities. Some will demonstrate that they feel excluded and neglected. The subgroups should form a circle, everyone facing outward, and require each "excluded" person, one at a time, to force his way into the center. Some persons will become very aggressive in their efforts to get in, demonstrating their great desire to be an integral part of the group. Once a person has broken through, much tension is released and group interaction is facilitated. It may be that members feel closer because they have, in a sense, survived a crisis as a group.

Following the nonverbal activities, there are two verbal activities the group can pursue. These activities are proven methods of increasing group cohesion and dialogue:

1. *Group Fantasy.* The subgroups gather once again. Participants should lie on the floor with their heads toward the center, or they may sit in a circle. The group leader begins a story and anybody can continue it until an ending is reached. Teachers can imagine any conceivable school-related plot they wish. Or they can fantasize about the outside world. Fantasy is an excellent means of sharing feelings and experiences. Through fantasy, teachers can say things about themselves that they might not wish to say directly. The consequence is that the level of group cooperation and solidarity in the school increases.

2. *Recounting Peak Experiences.* Each group member relates his most significant personal experience. Humanistic psychologist Abraham Maslow calls such an experience a "peak experience." Through these accounts, teachers express the most important and meaningful dimensions of their inner lives.

The activities described constitute a basic sensitivity training session that requires one to three hours depending on group size and the speed with which activities are completed. If the group functions well, a number of important results should follow:

- Increased awareness of each other's presence and significance.
- A decrease of tension and anxiety and more open dialogue.
- Insights into individual values and actions.
- Greater empathy, trust, and solidarity in the group.

The basic sensitivity session described here can be expanded by adding activities that William Schutz presents in *Joy*. If a group of teachers want a full-fledged sensitivity program in their school, they should settle for nothing less than a professional group leader. He is trained to guide all the activities Schutz relates to successful conclusion rather than an intergroup disaster in the school.

BRAINSTORMING AND ROLE PLAYING[3]

As teachers do their jobs, friction and conflicts with colleagues inevitably develop. This state of affairs is the natural consequence of associating with others in a complex organization. However, the new teacher should seek to convert stress and tension into opportunities for growth and the harmonization of school social relations. Gossip, arguments, and discussion often produce more animosity than relief. Two excellent methods, brainstorming and role playing, are available to enhance the sociological climate of a school. They are usable at sensitivity sessions, faculty meetings, and informal rap sessions.

The technique of brainstorming was developed in industry by businessmen who sought solutions to problems of personnel, production, or the marketplace. The idea is to think of any new solution to a given problem, no matter how far-fetched. Feasibility can be considered later. Highly innovative and successful solutions have emerged from this process. The abandonment of intellectual discipline frees the subconscious to function fully, so that teachers who use this technique will articulate solutions to a problem—say the inadequacies of a faculty grievance procedure—that are beyond their awareness. Later, they can explore what they have said. It is wise in brainstorming sessions to run a tape recorder.

Role playing can be employed by teachers to explore problems in teaching, gain insight into self, and work through family problems. The procedure is to initially state the problem and how it developed. A "cast" is then selected from sensitivity group members. Selection can be made according to physical resemblance or intuition. There is no one "right" method. After establishing the context of the problem, improvisation begins. Whatever "audience" there may be can participate in a reactive, not a participatory, fashion.

ROLE REVERSAL AND ALTER-EGO[4]

In sensitizing themselves and building a positive school social climate, teachers can use role reversal and alter-ego, two role-playing techniques of the "psychodrama," J. L. Moreno's psychotherapeutic version of theater.

In *role reversal* teachers switch roles at crucial points in the psychodrama. The objective is to help teachers see the events they are acting out from several perspectives. The reversal of roles promotes understanding of both the conflict situation depicted in the psychodrama and the points of view portrayed by the various participants.

To employ the *alter-ego* technique a teacher stands behind an actor and verbalizes the thoughts he believes should accompany the action. This procedure opens up to the actor new ways of reacting and clarifies motives of both the alter-ego and the actor.

Teachers can use this technique to solve the most routine human problems. The alter-ego method can help a teacher develop insights into a disliked student or colleague and handle serious discipline problems. A teacher can also assist the parties to a dispute in reasoning together by having the dispute acted out before them. He might also do a little role playing to prepare for his encounters with parents and the PTA.

Teachers, like everyone else, do not listen to each other well enough. Thus tensions develop that must be relieved. The feedback that reversing roles and the alter-ego technique provide can produce what humanist psychologist Carl Rogers terms "clarification of feelings." This simply means that teachers will learn to know the real feelings of their colleagues and thereby work and socialize with them on a high level of efficiency and satisfaction.

SENSITIVITY AND CURRICULUM

The teacher should not be the sole beneficiary of sensitivity education. He should use sensitivity techniques with students so they can improve the quality of their human relations. The best place to introduce sensitivity education is in the classroom, as an integral part of the subject matter. For example, if a teacher wishes to sensitize students to democratic as opposed to authoritarian human relations, she should do so in the government class where she can take advantage of the immediacy and relevance of the learning experience.

The research literature indicates that sensitivity education can be successfully combined with course work. Dr. George I. Brown experimented with activities in the "affective domain" in 1967-1968 in a project sponsored by the Fund for the Advancement of Education. Experienced elementary and secondary teachers employed many different sensitivity approaches with their classes as a component of course content. The evaluation of results was largely clinical, relying on teacher observations rather than statistical analysis of data. The conclusion was that sensitivity techniques could be used fruitfully in the classroom.

The Human Relations Education Project of Western New York, funded under Title III of ESEA, seeks "to improve the teaching of human understanding by developing in teachers a greater awareness and sensitivity to the human relations approach. This approach stresses respect for the dignity of every individual and the development of more effective interpersonal relations." Teachers trained in the use of sensitivity techniques work through in-service programs with the entire faculty of a participating school. They give demonstration lessons and advise how sensitivity education can be included in classwork. The Human Relations Education Project staff reported a significant change in attitudes of participating teachers. The evaluative instrument was a semantic differential pretest and post-test.[5]

A number of organizations work to bring sensitivity training programs to the schools. The National Training Laboratories (NTL) of the National Education Association are very important in this effort. NTL offers training opportunities and program development for schools on a nationwide basis. The Institute for the Development of Educational Activities (IDEA), the Center for the Advanced Study of Educational Administration (CASEA), the Western Behavioral Sciences Institute (WBSI), and many other private and federally funded groups are involved in studies and applications of sensitivity training techniques.[6]

THE HIDDEN CURRICULUM

The hidden curriculum is the affective curriculum. Its subject matter is human relations and emotion. Although these are difficult to see and specify in the school program—that is, they are hidden—they are just as legitimate a concern as learners' cognitive growth. Anyone who has read the chapter on ecology in this book and has breathed in deeply on a smoggy day should be aware of the need for more humane learning.

Most schools' efforts to contribute to the emotional growth of students have been supplementary to the regular program. They include techniques for developing self-respect, methods of examining values, group development techniques, and processes for handling one's feelings. For example, the Human Development Training Institute in San Diego has worked with the hidden curriculum. In the elementary program, children sit in a "magic circle" and the teacher leads discussions on such questions as "What makes us happy?" The group attempts to explore particular happy experiences they have had.[7]

One activity in the hidden curriculum of Philadelphia's Affective Education Project demonstrates how the new teacher works for the emotional development of learners. The teacher, Terry Borton, seeks to integrate affective, cognitive, and psychomotor learning activities:

Students interlock fingers of the right hand with thumbs free, and are told to imagine that they are their thumbs expressing their personalities. They are to meet their partners and write poems about the experience. . . .

Experiment with new ways of meeting the same person's thumb. See how many ways you can develop. Change partners. Do you enjoy any of these other patterns of behavior? Pick one (your original if you like) and try shaking hands the same way. Try talking the same way.

After class, try acting the same way for a few minutes. If you like this new way of relating, practice it and live it.[8]

MARATHONS AND CONFRONTATIONS

Two types of sensitivity training, marathon labs and confrontation sessions, warrant special attention. Marathons differ from sensitivity training sessions in degree of intensity. Marathon sessions are operated on a nonstop basis in an attempt to break through participants' normal defense mechanisms. It is hoped that participants cannot keep their defense mechanisms in place during intense, intimate, and prolonged encounter. The goal is to enable group members to behave more genuinely and openly.

The confrontation session is especially used to bring blacks and whites together to examine the character of their conscious or unconscious prejudices in order to open up lines of communication, even if rather hot ones. The confrontation gives participants an opportunity to examine the origins and consequences of their attitudes and consider ways of reducing racial tensions.[9]

RACE AND SENSITIVITY[10]

One of the main uses of sensitivity training is the improvement of human relations between teachers and students in recently integrated schools. In schools bringing the races together for the first time on more than a mere token basis, there is considerable anxiety on the part of all groups. To allay the fear, it is essential that teachers meet in groups to examine their attitudes and uncertainties, preferably with students included.

Sensitivity education can be offered as an in-service program in the integrating school. The school has a vested interest in preparing teachers for handling interracial classrooms successfully from the very beginning. If it provides an in-service sensitivity program, teachers can become more skilled and confident before even teaching their first integrated class. This state of affairs could make unnecessary a lot of disastrous trial-and-error learning.

THE EVANSTON PROGRAM

An in-service sensitivity program in the Evanston, Illinois, elementary schools is providing experiences for teachers that help them successfully meet the unique learning and social needs of black children. The Evanston program is typical of other schools' efforts to enhance race relations by sensitizing teachers to the black life style and experience in American society.

The Evanston program features summer institutes, which attempt to achieve several objectives by sensitizing the school staff. The institutes have the following goals:

1. To familiarize teachers with the multicultural deficiencies in standard curriculum guides and texts.
2. To help teachers recognize their own racial biases and stereotypes and deal rationally with them.
3. To assist teachers in developing a better understanding of their new roles in the integrated classroom.

The institutes have been successful, but it soon became apparent that Evanston needed an in-service program during the school year. Race relations were much too important to be considered just in summertime. Thus the summer institutes developed materials on ten critical issues for an ongoing in-service program:

1. Grouping students in integrated schools.
2. The relationship of family background and educational achievement.
3. Problems of discipline.
4. The prejudices of blacks and whites toward one another.
5. The Black Power movement and its impact on race relations in schools.
6. The black's role in American history.
7. The black self-concept.
8. Sensitivity to interracial social relations.
9. The relationship, if any, of race and intelligence.
10. Interracial social relations among students.

The institutes developed a teacher and student manual and a thirty-five-minute film for each of the ten issues. Every Evanston elementary teacher studied one issue a week. For example, teachers view a film on the black self-concept. A school's teachers then break up into groups to discuss the film and any ideas and information they may have about the black self-concept. They discuss how material about the black self-concept can be incorporated into the curriculum. This form of sensitivity training has proved very helpful to teachers suffering racial prejudice. The factual information presented in the in-service units has helped biased teachers overcome much of their anxiety.

The Evanston public schools have sponsored weekend sensitivity training sessions for principals, assistant principals, and the superintendent's council as well as teachers. The weekend retreat is a complete sensitivity session rather than a component of an in-service program. Each retreat begins on a Friday evening and continues until noon Sunday. A competent trainer conducts each session in a secluded locale such as a state park lodge or YMCA camp. The sessions operate with all the opennness and dangers we have discussed. They have produced positive results that please the Evanston school administrators. Evanston is now expanding its sensitivity program to include the entire district.

SOME APPLICATIONS[11]

Sensitivity training has been incorporated into educational systems throughout the country. For example, Bristol Township, north of Philadelphia, Pennsylvania, offered its staff of 700 teachers and administrators two- and five-day workshops on leadership and race relations. The workshops substantially changed the relationship of teachers and administrators to one another and to the minority community.

Sensitivity methods have been a very important part of the Talent Awareness Training programs conducted in seven states with more than 20,000 elementary school teachers. The Institute of Psychoanalysis in Chicago is very much on the frontier in developing sensitivity training techniques and programs for teachers. Weekend retreats have proved a vital component of the Teacher Corps training program at the University of Oklahoma. Boston University, Case Western, MIT, the State University of New York at Buffalo, UCLA, the University of Rhode Island, Harvard, and the University of Michigan offer graduate programs that include sensitivity training.

Educators are largely undecided about sensitivity education. A national survey revealed that only 3 percent of the public schools offer intensive programs. About half the educators surveyed had suspended judgment about using sensitivity training in the schools. The major reasons they cited were inadequate and contradictory information about the benefits of sensitivity education and uncertainty about group leaders.

DANGERS[12]

The sensitivity training experience can be harmful to participants if the group leaders are not well trained. Many quasi-professionals discover that they can catalyze initial interaction among participants, but they are unable to effectively guide a group's growth thereafter. They mistakenly feel that a few easily learned skills or T-group experiences qualify them as trainers. They are unable to manage the sensitivity experience in order to obtain positive results and protect individuals who might be harmed by improperly conducted sessions. Only professionals concerned with the genuine growth and psychological integrity of participants should lead sensitivity training sessions.

Sensitivity training can increase the tension between teachers and residents of the community. Poorly handled confrontations between school officials and minority group members can be particularly explosive. If a confrontation becomes uncontrollable, anxiety and conflict increase until dialogue is no longer possible. In this case, alienation between minority citizens and teachers intensifies. We discussed some of the results of this alienation in Chapters 1 and 3.

The new teacher, seeking to merge the school and community, cannot afford the setback of acrimonious confrontation. He and the minority member need an encounter that will allow for mutual understanding and the development of values that both can share.

Sensitivity training sessions are oriented to breaking down participants' defenses. But this orientation ignores the fact that defenses serve critical functions. They may serve as survival devices, protecting the individual from threats, real or imagined, that he might not otherwise be able to handle. They are the ways he integrates his personality and maintains equilibrium. The defenses are really the participants' values. Any indiscriminate destruction of such defenses or values could prove very harmful. Values that cannot withstand group criticism may still be worthwhile. Even though an individual's values can be crumbled, they are still the only way he has of making sense of the world and maintaining stability. If defense barriers must be removed, it is imperative that a trained professional, not an inexperienced novice, do so. This procedure would prevent most of the personal disasters that are now occurring in sensitivity groups.

The sensitivity groups often do not attempt to individualize treatment or even determine whether a person's participation in a group is appropriate. The blanket assumption is that all people can benefit from decreased defensiveness. However, involvement may actually be the opposite of what is needed for a particular individual. That person may be a teacher for whom complete openness, the publicization of personal problems, could prove very maladjustive. Such problems might be better handled by a clinical psychologist or psychiatrist or in the privacy of an aunt or uncle's living room. Defenses help the individual seeking self-actualization. Some individuals also base a delicate equilibrium on them and should never participate in sensitivity groups.

Some observers argue that students should not be involved in sensitivity groups. They claim that students cannot benefit from sensitivity techniques. Teen-agers are deeply caught up in the conflicts of building their own value systems. They have not yet developed the stability and established a set of beliefs that can make encounter among adults a psychologically productive experience.

Without relatively fixed values, the teen-ager is defenseless against the group's criticism. This situation is particularly dangerous when novices lead groups. What happens is that the dominant adults in the group impose their values on the teen-agers if the group is mixed, or aggressive, status-conscious teen-agers impose values they imitate and think are their own upon their peers in homogeneous groups. In any event, sensitivity groups are not healthy experiences for teenagers. Teen-agers in sensitivity groups form values artificially; according to the critics, this is the equivalent of a neurosis.

VALUE FORMATION[13]

Values serve important purposes. They give an individual a sense of identity and allow him to participate successfully in social relations. In the early phases of value formation, criticism by sensitivity group members tends to disintegrate developing values related to friends, family, religion, and so on. Criticism may disrupt the development of identity and social relations. We have discussed some of the dangers. Whether disruption is good depends on one's perspective. The opportunity to break down the conventional growing-up patterns that lead to conformity in the name of adjustment is perhaps worth the risk of an identity crisis. The dropout rates, rebellion, and violence in the schools indicate that something is drastically wrong. These phenomena perhaps reflect the societal pattern where divorce, crime, drugs, and other forms of deviance are common. Perhaps the American single-standard value system and common life style are not as satisfying as they may seem and should be disrupted.

The dangers of sensitivity training are certainly great, but the present tragedy of our society's human relations poses an even greater threat. Students and teachers must be given a way to critically examine each other and themselves. That seems the only legitimate sort of educational format in a pluralistic society that prides itself on differences.

GOING SLOW, BEING CAREFUL[14]

Sensitivity education is controversial. Some teachers and administrators do not like such a radical departure from the traditional cognitive approach to learning. The change threatens them. It is therefore necessary to develop a sensitivity program slowly and carefully so that those who do not initially care for it do not kill it. The best strategies for establishing a program are as follows:

1. Only volunteers should participate. If individuals threatened by sensitivity experiences are required to participate, they may undercut a program's effectiveness.
2. The organization of a program should begin at the top, with the administrator. If his support is not forthcoming, it is almost impossible to establish a fully effective program.
3. Follow-up programs should be provided because a considerable washout effect takes place six months after the sensitivity experience.
4. Building a workable sensitivity program is difficult; there will be no spectacular results. Program developers should allow six weeks during the summer for the first effort.
5. A school should be cautious in its selection of consultants and trainers. A trainer who promises miracles is always suspect. He may be a charlatan who will cause more harm than good. The school should look for a trainer who is willing to cooperate in achieving its organizational objectives.
6. Teachers should be advised to use training exercises carefully in their classes. Some exercises are beyond the competence of teachers or are simply inappropriate.
7. The introduction of sensitivity education into a school inevitably produces some conflict and criticism. Program planners should be aware of their innovative role and be prepared to defend it.
8. The school should provide extended training for sensitivity group personnel. This means follow-up sessions for continuing personnel and intensive training for new staff.
9. The program developers should avoid giving the impression that there is something mystical about sensitivity education. Creating a cult of mysticism produces problems because participants begin to expect magical results.
10. Sensitivity education helps to create mutual respect and confidence among staff members. Although teachers become very aware of the consequences of their behavior on the group's welfare, the psychological benefits do not include teachers' learning to solve problems. More direct methods must be used to develop specific competencies. For example, teachers do not learn to teach the new math in sensitivity sessions despite the fact they may become exemplary human beings.
11. As many members of a school staff should be involved as possible. If everyone participates, all the better. The more teachers who learn to open up and encounter each other, the better will be the school's human relations and teaching. If too few join the training

sessions, communication barriers may develop between those who are sensitized and those who are not.

12. Program developers should recognize that everyone must proceed at his own pace. Some change rapidly, some slowly, and some not at all. The objective should never be uniform progress.

13. It is essential to inform the board of education and the community of all sensitivity education activities, and an attempt should be made to involve these groups. The controversial nature of sensitivity education requires that the program developers pay careful attention to relations with the school board and community.

14. Sufficient time should be allowed for adequate planning and staffing. This phase requires a minimum of six months.

15. Program objectives should be limited realistically.

STREAMLINING[15]

Sensitivity education programs can be improved greatly. Anxieties can be allayed and the diffuse character of group goals eliminated. The term "sensitivity training" should be replaced by the term "human relations training." "Sensitivity" has become such an emotion-laden term that a new word would clear the air, at least temporarily.

Sensitivity education should move from relative amorphousness to a structure that promotes the achievement of well-defined objectives. The undisciplined use of sensitivity training has often produced more ill effects than good ones.

Much more research should be undertaken to evaluate sensitivity education so that improvements can be made. Some research should be directed toward making successful, direct applications in the classroom. Professional certification standards for trainers should be established to guarantee that interested schools will receive high-quality group leadership. Reliable evaluation techniques should be devised to determine the outcomes of sensitivity experiences.

THE BENEFIT AND THE RESPONSIBILITY

The ultimate goal of the sensitivity experience is not the development of more effective teachers. It is rather the development of more effective learners. The proficiency that teachers develop in the art of being human inevitably influences the classroom. Education is a set of human relations; in fact, as indicated in Chapter 4, the human relations in the school are *the* basic determinants of achievement and motivation. Therefore, what could be more important than giving teachers training in the affective domain? Absolutely nothing is more significant. Since the benefits are so great—more and better learning and more and better social relations—the responsibility to provide teachers affective learning experiences is equally great.

NOTES

[1] Harold C. Wells, "To Get Beyond the Words . . .," *Educational Leadership*, 28, no. 3 (December 1970), 241.

[2] Victor L. Schermer, "Encountering Other Teachers," *The Grade Teacher*, 88, no. 3 (November 1970), 71–74.

[3] *Ibid.*, p. 75.

[4] *Ibid.*, pp. 78, 82.

[5] Gene Stanford, "Sensitivity Education and the Curriculum," *Educational Leadership*, 28, no. 3 (December 1970), 246–247.

[6] Thomas W. Wiggins, "Sensitivity Training: Salvation or Conspiracy?," *Educational Leadership*, 28, no. 3 (December 1970), 254.

[7] Wells, *op. cit.*, p. 243.

[8] Terry Borton, *Reach, Touch, and Teach* (New York, McGraw-Hill, 1970), pp. 100–101.

[9] Clifford H. Edwards, "Sensitivity Training and Education: A Critique," *Educational Leadership*, 28, no. 3 (December 1970), 258.

[10] Laval S. Wilson, "Inservice Training: Lifeline For Integration," *Nation's Schools*, 84, no. 4 (October 1969), 70–71, 76. The section titled The Evanston Program is based on this source.

[11] Wiggins, *op. cit.*, pp. 256–257.

[12] Edwards, *op. cit.*, pp. 259–260.

[13] *Ibid.*, p. 261.

[14] James A. Kimple, "Sensitivity: A Superintendent's View," *Educational Leadership*, 28, no. 3 (December 1970), 269.

[15] Wiggins, *op. cit.*, p. 257.

9
Sex education

A new role has been thrust upon the American teacher, that of sex educator. The traditional image of the schoolhouse absolutely excluded considerations of sex. That was strictly a family matter. But as the American family became less close-knit and the old forms of supervision of boy-girl relations were abolished, the school became a logical agency to assume the authority for sex education.

Since the family has abdicated this function or is inadequate to teach about sex, the school has suddenly been thrust into the role of sex educator. Schools have been and are now attempting to redefine their role to both justify a sex education program and genuinely educate students.

THE OPINION CLIMATE

There has been both substantial opposition and substantial support for sex education. Opposition has come primarily from extremist right-wing groups such as the John Birch Society and the Christian Crusade. These groups have managed to secure the support of some moderate citizens who were raised in an era when sex was not talked about and cannot now fathom why sex education is needed in the schools. The Birchers and other fundamentalist extremists believe that sex education is a Communist plot or at least a conspiracy.[1] Dr. Gordon Drake, former Christian Crusade education director, and author of the infamous *Is the Schoolhouse the Proper Place to Teach Raw Sex?*, has written:

> *Several prominent individuals and some of the largest U. S. corporations, as well as the United Nations, were involved in the sex education plot.*[2]

The sex education opponents have organized numerous local groups to prevent the Communists and conspirators from taking over. These groups include ACRE (Associate Citizens for Responsible Education), POPE (Parents for Orthodoxy in Parochial Education), MOMS (Mothers for Moral Stability), MOTOREDE (Movement to Restore Decency; sponsored by the John Birch Society), POSSE (Parents Opposed to Sex and Sensitivity Education), CHIDE (Committee to Halt Indoctrination and Demoralization in Education), PAUSE (People Against Unconstitutional Sex Education), and SOS (Sanity on Sex).[3] Such groups are active in forty-one states. They have convinced legislatures to consider bills prohibiting sex education or restricting the curriculum in at least nineteen states.[4] Perhaps their greatest harm has been to so polarize public opinion that a rational discussion of the real issues involved in sex education becomes impossible; the major issues are not even identified, let alone understood.

Despite the thunder on the right, there is great support for sex education. A June 1969 Gallup poll indicated that 71 percent of the nation's adults approve of sex education. Moreover, 55 percent favor a discussion of birth control devices.[5] The overall climate of national opinion is definitely predisposed to sex education.

THE DANGER OF NONEDUCATION

The critics have argued that sex education produces sexual delinquency. However, nothing promotes erotic obsession more than ignorance, hypocrisy, and semisecrecy.[6] If we do not provide our youth professional sex education, they will learn sex as they can. If the schools abdicate on their new responsibility, reverting to the puritanic image of their authority, they will compel students to learn what they can from sordid sex films and erotic paperback novels, in remotely parked cars, at unchaperoned parties, and in front of TV sets. The school and society cannot leave youth so defenseless. We have abolished the old protective rules and the era of the chaperone.

The family does not exert the influence it once did. The only way to fill the dangerous vacuum adequately is through education.

One country where sex education is accepted without question is Sweden.[7] The Swedes' foremost concern is the human use of human beings. Swedish values and laws, oriented toward allowing mature individuals to select their own forms of sexual behavior, are reflected in their education. The only qualification is that people do not infringe upon the rights of others. The vast majority of Swedes feel that openness and knowledge are the best guarantees of morality, whereas a vociferous and reactionary minority of Americans believe that the only way to virtuous living is through ignorance and silence. This vocal minority has often successfully intimidated the 71 percent of Americans who approve of sex education and cautious school administrators who would prefer to avoid a major controversy. Hence, although sex education is no focus of polemics in Sweden, in the United States it is a major issue.

TWO PLANS

One major way to organize a sex education program is to involve the entire community, including ministers, nurses, doctors, psychologists, and parents, in a drive to win community support for a program. Calderone, the first to propose this approach, would have teachers invite physicians, ministers, and psychiatrists into the classroom to lead discussions about human sexual behavior. However, students might conclude that sexual behavior and human reproduction pose such large problems that only specialists can meet the educational needs, and that the teacher is inadequate to even present routine, objective information.[8]

The other major way to offer sex education is as an important but regular part of the curriculum. In this approach, suggested by Hinrichs and Kaplan, the sexes would not be segregated for special lectures and specialists would not be used. The teacher would handle the entire program. Community support would, of course, have to be mobilized first.[9]

SCHOOL AND COMMUNICATION[10]

Students often find it easier to talk with an outsider than with their parents. The teacher possesses an advantage here because he is less emotionally involved than parents. He is more capable of initiating and sustaining an open dialogue. He might be able to communicate about sensitive matters where an attempt by parents to communicate about the same concerns might only break down.

It is possible that the best person to discuss sex with students who have questions may be a total stranger. The teacher may certainly serve more effectively than a parent, but the teacher still encounters the student either occasionally or daily. When a student knows a teacher is familiar with his most intimate concerns, the routine teacher-student relation may become strained.

The school might eliminate such an educationally injurious situation by hiring sex education counselors, who would circulate among a district's schools hearing and discussing student concerns. This approach might guarantee the identity and informational protection that is necessary for communication on sensitive, even taboo, questions. In fact, the student could even speak anonymously through a partition so that there would be a minimum of barriers to communication. For example, a student suffering a venereal disease might not seek any help if such guarantees were not offered. If the school is to accommodate the "sexual revolution," it must initiate a revolution within its own walls, radically changing old practices and patterns of authority.

THE TEACHER'S VIEW[11]

A substantial majority of public school teachers believe the schools should offer sex education programs. Almost three in four approve of sex education, whereas one in eight is opposed and one in seven is uncertain. More than four-fifths of the secondary teachers and two-thirds of the elementary teachers support sex education.

Opinions are not nearly as uniform regarding which grade level sex education should begin. Almost half the teachers feel that sex education should begin as early as the first grade, kindergarten, or even prekindergarten. A greater percentage of elementary than secondary teachers prefer the early introduction of sex education. Of the elementary teachers, 31 percent believe sex education should begin by grade 1, whereas only 28 percent of the secondary teachers believe so. Conversely, only 4 percent of the elementary teachers think sex education should not begin until grade 7 or later, whereas 18 percent of the secondary teachers think so.

CHANGING TEACHER FOR VD EDUCATION[12]

American youth have contracted venereal disease in virtually epidemic numbers. The U. S. Public Health Service estimates that almost

½ million adolescents contract VD annually. These same adolescents are usually unaware of the symptoms. They have not been informed at all, are ill informed, or are only partially enlightened. Parents generally avoid any discussion of VD. The responsibility is thus passed to the schools. But the teacher has much the same problem as parents. He is reluctant to discuss venereal disease with students. Building a successful VD education program depends on reeducating and reorienting the public school teacher. Only then can he effectively teach about VD.

The teacher is inhibited in presenting VD information because diseases linked to sex are taboo topics. A survey of California high schools demonstrated that only a handful of schools offered any VD education. The combination of a high rate of adolescent sexual activity and sexual ignorance makes a venereal disease epidemic inevitable. The epidemic is now with us. To successfully handle the crisis, the teacher's inhibitions to teach about VD must be broken down through proper in-service, pre-service, and teacher training. Education is the only solution to the VD problem, unless an immunization formula is soon discovered.

Every school faces stiff opposition when it attempts to redefine its authority for learning experiences to include sex education. The antagonistic influences to be overcome are several. Opposition by parents, school boards and administrators, teachers, and community leaders seems universal. Teachers often assume a posture of middle-class superiority, viewing VD as exclusively the problem of the poor, the minorities, and juvenile delinquents. Anyone who gets VD is guilty of sexual sin. Therefore, since sin deserves only retribution, one need not deal with the VD problem. Reeducation is urgently needed before a sex education program will be possible in the schools.

The teacher can explore his fears about sex education in sensitivity training groups and human relations workshops. Teachers together can inquire into attitudes that block effective sex education. They will also discover that they share much the same inhibitions. The alter-ego method, described in Chapter 8, might well be used in group exploration. Teachers must learn that they must change their attitudes about VD for the schools to have successful sex education. They must abandon their middle-class myths about VD through confrontation with each other and professional sensitivity leaders.

A VD education program should involve the entire faculty. If ever there was a sensitive area where each individual needed group support to proceed effectively, it is in the realm of VD education. Through cooperative planning and group discussion, teachers can redefine the school's values in the direction of accepting sex education. This effort requires mobilizing the support of parents, community, and the local health department. For example, the health department can offer lectures and seminars to administrators, teachers, and parents and provide appropriate educational materials. Such projects can produce a sociological climate of positive values and expectations that can help the individual faculty member proceed confidently.

School and community must work together in any VD education program. The school should sponsor workshops and forums on VD in cooperation with the PTA, civic and youth organizations, and the health department. When groups throughout the community collaborate with the school, positive results will be forthcoming. Only with support outside the school, as well as within, will the majority of teachers be able to overcome their reluctance to teach about VD.

RURAL SEX EDUCATION[13]

Sex education in rural areas presents special problems. Small communities often lack the resources necessary for an adequate sex education program. Where sex education cannot be implemented locally, a county-wide effort can be very effective. This type of effort was successfully employed in Hillsdale County, Michigan.

Hillsdale County established a county sex education committee to assist local schools to implement sex education curricula. A number of volunteer professionals served on the committee. The final composition included two school counselors, a physician, a county health nurse, a psychiatric social worker, a school superintendent, a minister, and citizens. The committee requested assistance from the state health department. The department provided a sex education specialist and educational materials.

The county-wide committee proceeded to develop sex education programs by first mobilizing community support and then providing services:

1. The county committee notified all local communities about its program.
2. The committee encouraged each community to establish a sex education committee, suggesting that parents, teachers, ministers, and students be included.
3. Leadership workshops were sponsored by the county committee for the local communities. The programs consisted of speakers, films, and discussions. A representative of each community was present at every workshop.

4. Each community conducted two meetings. In the first, a panel of county committee members or county resource people presented information and answered questions. The community committee conducted the second meeting. The purpose of this meeting was to determine whether the residents wanted sex education and, if so, what type of program they preferred.
5. County committee members and resource people paved the way for informed local community meetings. They spoke before social and service clubs and wrote articles for the local newspapers. The county committee also advised community committees to use available audio-visual materials, read the research literature, and discuss contemplated programs with students and teachers.
6. Communities that elected to introduce sex education requested county members and resource personnel to assist with program development. The county experts do not stress any particular program but only attempt to professionally meet the expressed needs of a community.

Most communities elected to begin sex education programs. The county-wide approach proved very successful because it involved both professional and citizen. The citizens participated in building their sex education program from the ground up, relying only on county professionals to supply them with advice. This type of community planning guarantees an effective, enduring sex education program.

THE SKOKIE PROGRAM[14]

A model sex education program called "The Study of People" was introduced at the first-grade level at the Jane Stenson Elementary School in Skokie, Illinois, in 1965. The program was enlarged to include all first-, second-, and third-grade learners in the district after the pilot program was received enthusiastically by parents, community, and children. The program will soon be expanded to include fourth- and fifth-graders, too. No parents have excluded their child from The Study of People curriculum, although school policy allows them to do so.

The basic assumption of The Study of People program is that the elementary child has fundamental questions about his origin, development, and role as a male or female within a family context in American society. Another program assumption is that sex education is a pressing social concern that must be considered in a program touching upon all aspects of human growth.

The Study of People program is concerned with five major objectives:

1. To enable a consideration of sexual information in an open, natural manner.
2. To provide a social climate that encourages children to discuss all aspects of human behavior.
3. To assist a child to interpret his role as a male or female in American society.
4. To foster a positive, healthy attitude within the child toward human sexuality.
5. To evaluate each child's level of sexual understanding and remove deficiencies and misconceptions by presenting appropriate information.

Teachers trained by a Northwestern University child psychologist conduct The Study of People program. They serve as discussion leaders, dividing classes into groups that include both boys and girls. The average group size is seven. Many children do not benefit fully from large group discussion. The intimacy of a small group facilitates open expression, which is certainly educational and can be enjoyable. What the learners wish to talk about becomes the daily curriculum. Thus the program is purely Deweyan: the children translate their most fundamental concerns into educational experiences. The discussion leaders attempt to provide a free, nonthreatening learning climate. The children are encouraged to give unrestrained expression to their feelings, thoughts, and questions.

Most of the questions asked by first- and second-grade children concern the development and birth of the fetus and pregnancy. Third graders' questions focus on conception and sex itself. The questions are direct and genuine. The Study of People program is an excellent model for teachers seeking to fulfill their new roles as sex educators.

ATTITUDES IN TEXAS[15]

Little systematic research has been done on attitudes toward sex education. A major Texas study does, however, provide insights into the total community situation that educators who plan sex education programs face. The study questioned a sample of Texas public school superintendents about a wide range of concerns. The basic conclusions are probably, in varying degrees, applicable to all regions of the country:

1. Most superintendents of Texas school districts believe that the public schools are now responsible for sex education.
2. Sex education in Texas is usually confined to grades 7 through 12. Few elementary schools include it in their curriculum.
3. Few qualified sex education teachers are available in Texas. The superintendents did not offer in-service training to prepare their faculty for sex education instruction. They wanted colleges of education to provide such training.
4. Citizens do not generally request that the schools offer sex education curricula. Only residents in larger districts express any demand for sex education programs.
5. Specific topics considered in sex education programs include dating, petting, divorce, sex roles, marriage and family, human reproduction, and venereal disease.
6. The superintendents maintain that the planning and implementation of a sex education program should involve citizens, ministers, administrators, teachers, and students.
7. Most Texas superintendents believe that sex education classes should not be coeducational.
8. The main reasons schools seek to avoid sex education are inadequate teacher preparation and public opposition and apathy.
9. A deep division of opinion exists among Texas superintendents regarding the consideration of controversial issues such as premarital intercourse.

NEW VALUES

The schools must be aware of and act upon the new morality in sexual relations. They cannot legitimately avoid a consideration of Women's Liberation[16] and homosexuality. They must indicate in the curriculum that the marriage institution has been criticized, that women increasingly want equal status with men and careers of their own. Children and homemaking are not the woman's only way to a meaningful life. Some want more liberty and dignity than the domestic scene allows. Some men avoid marriage, opting to found their identities upon careers and nonmarital personal relations.

Personal relations also may be homosexual or lesbian. These alternatives, which defy our core social values, should not be ignored by the schools. They should be discussed intelligently so that learners can know that the sexual life styles outside the school are not as single-standard and happy as the schools would now have them believe. The level of adolescent nervous breakdown and rebellion and the divorce rate in the general population demonstrate that students are not made aware of alternatives to the dating and marriage relationships. One way to promote a realistic consideration of sexual alternatives might be to follow a non-discriminatory policy of hiring lesbians, homosexuals, and feminists to assure an ideologically sexually balanced staff. The classroom has always been too feminized, motherhood has always been too glorified, and the school has always oversimplified the real world of sexual and human relations.

THE NEW AUTHORITY

Human sexual activity relates to many aspects of society. Divorce and homosexuality, for example, have not been systematically and realistically touched upon in the schools to date, yet they are very much realities and do not disappear because of this omission. Students must become aware of both the sexual mechanisms of our society and the human body. They must be able to relate sexual behavior and social behavior, sexual problems and social problems. The authority for sex education has been passed to the school. How well the teacher discharges the new responsibility will determine whether that authority is justified or should be delegated to another agency in our society.

NOTES

[1] Loren L. Hoch, "Current Views On Sex Education," *The Science Teacher*, 37, no. 8 (November 1970), 42.
[2] Gere B. Fulton, "Sex Education: Some Issues And Answers," *The Journal of School Health*, 40, no. 5 (May 1970), 263.
[3] Hoch, *op. cit.*
[4] Fulton, *op. cit.*
[5] Hoch, *op. cit.*, p. 41.
[6] Eberhard Kronhausen and Phyllis Kronhausen, "Sex Education—More Avoided than Neglected?," *Teachers College Record*, 64 (January 1963), 325.
[7] L. A. Kirkendall, Preface to *Sex and Society in Sweden* (New York: Pantheon Books, 1967); Birgitta Linner, *Sex and Society in Sweden* (New York: Pantheon Books, 1967).
[8] M. S. Calderone, "Planning for Sex Education," *NEA Journal*, 56 (January 1967), 26–29.
[9] M. A. Hinrichs and R. Kaplan, "The Home, the School, and Sex Education," *Today's Health*, 44 (February 1966), 16.
[10] Hoch, *op. cit.*, p. 43.

[11] "Teacher Opinion Poll, Sex Education," *Today's Education*, 60, no. 1 (January 1971), 60.

[12] Florence B. Benell, "Overcoming Teacher Reluctancy Toward VD Education," *The Journal of School Health*, 40, no. 9 (November 1970), 483–486.

[13] Linda M. Kesling, "Sex Education: A County-Wide Approach," *The Journal of School Health*, 40, no. 10 (December 1970), 544–545.

[14] Arlene S. Uslander, "Study of People in Skokie," *Instructor*, 80, no. 3 (November 1970), 78–79.

[15] J. David Holcomb, Arthur E. Garner, and Harper F. Beaty, "Sex Education In Texas Public Schools," *The Journal of School Health*, 40, no. 10 (December 1970), 565–566.

[16] Nancy Frazier and Myra Sadker, *Sexism in School and Society* (New York: Harper and Row, 1973).

10
Drug education

Drug education is a new responsibility of the American schools. Since the drug problem is a recent one, the schools have had relatively little time to define their authority for drug educational experiences. Their major effort to date has been to build programs and change attitudes in response to the magnitude of the problem and the need of the society.

SCOPE OF THE PROBLEM[1]

The drug problem has reached a significant scale in the high schools and in some elementary schools. More than 43,000 of 162,000 persons arrested for narcotics violations in 1968 were under age eighteen. This constitutes an increase of 322 percent since 1960. In some high schools, a large proportion of the student body has used or is using drugs. Only a few elementary schools have encountered a significant drug problem.

In 1966, thirty teen-agers in New York City died from an overdose of heroin. In 1969, 224 teen-agers in New York City died from an acute reaction to heroin. There has been a very rapid increase in the deaths attributable to heroin; indeed, heroin addiction is now the greatest single cause of death for persons aged fifteen to thirty-five in New York City.

A recent survey found that only a small minority of students approved of drugs. Most students think drugs, particularly LSD and heroin, have deleterious effects. Only 5 percent would advise others to use marijuana. Less than 1 percent would advise the use of LSD or heroin. About 33 percent thought that students should decide for themselves whether to use marijuana. Only 9 percent felt students should make a decision about LSD and heroin. Boys opposed drug use most often on the basis that it harmed careers. Girls were most concerned about the physiological dependence drugs caused.

The survey determined that students do not trust teachers on the issue of drugs. They go for help to peers, and second to parents, rather than teachers. Students feel that teachers are not seriously attempting to understand student attitudes toward drugs. Most students think that the average teacher cannot detect a student drug user.

THE FEDERAL RESPONSE

Congress responded to the drug crisis by passing the Drug Abuse Education Act in 1970. The act provides $58 million for a three-year classroom drug education program. Teachers and counselors are trained to provide an adequate professional program.[2]

In 1970 the U. S. Office of Education awarded $3 million, through the Education Professions Development Act, to train teachers and community personnel in drug education. All fifty states have received money to improve drug education programs. Puerto Rico, the Virgin Islands, the District of Columbia, Guam, and American Samoa have also been awarded grants. The grants range from $33,360 to $180,140 depending upon how many children in each state are in the five- to seventeen-year age range.

More than forty states are using part of their grant money to send teachers to four national drug education training centers administered by the U. S. Office of Education. The centers are located at the Universities of Texas and Wisconsin, San Francisco State College, and Adelphi University in New York. When teachers return home they conduct workshops throughout their states for other teachers, administrators, students, and community leaders. The Office of Education estimates that the teachers trained at the four centers will be able to provide drug education for about 150,000 teachers and 75,000 students and concerned citizens.[3]

IN-SERVICE PROGRAMS[4]

The schools cannot educate students about drugs before they compensate for teachers' deficiencies in this area. Federal programs will certainly help to bring adequate drug education to the schools, but the schools must also undertake to provide high-quality in-service programs. Few teachers have received drug education in college; many graduated before there was a significant drug problem. The schools must require every teacher to be familiar with the most common drugs and be able to detect drug abuse. They must establish a continuing in-service program.

Every teacher in a school should be involved in the drug education in-service program. If the courses offered interfere with the regular school day, substitute teachers or teacher aides must assume responsibility for classes. If some teachers cannot possibly attend the drug sessions and workshops, the sessions should be taped for their later use. Adequate drug education can be provided only if all teachers know the facts and cooperate to counsel and inform students. Other school personnel and community leaders should also participate, because drug education can be successful only as a joint effort of school and community.

The in-service program must be well planned. Any program must use reliable materials. The federal government and appropriate private groups can supply adequate references; especially useful are *Drugs of Abuse* and *Fact Sheets*.[5] The school board, superintendent, and teachers should decide together what will be taught at particular grade levels. They can develop a very thorough program by selecting from American Medical Association and Bureau of Narcotics and Dangerous Drugs materials.

THE ROOSEVELT DRUG PROGRAM[6]

Roosevelt High School in East Los Angeles is dealing realistically with its drug problem. Ninety-four of its 3,300 students were arrested on narcotics charges between February 1968 and June 1969. The Red Cross Medics, a school health club, decided to attack the problem. It mobilized the support of community, faculty, staff, and the board of education, who jointly produced "Drug Expo '70." The program sought to achieve three objectives:

1. Assisting students addicted to drugs to secure immediate help.
2. Involvement of all school personnel in the drug program. Participation must be as complete as possible for drug education to be effective.
3. Counseling student drug users to stop usage and nonusers to never experiment.

The implementation of these objectives was achieved not by sensationalism and guilt but through factual presentations. Adolescents read adult hypocrisy too well (adult consumption of alcohol, cigarettes, tranquilizers, etc.) for any drug program to rely successfully on authoritative pronouncements and commands. The Roosevelt staff realized the most success with the following techniques:

1. Pamphlets, literature, films, booths, and displays designed to provide facts, leaving the affective response up to the learner.
2. Free-wheeling discussions on drugs organized as sensitivity groups (see Chapter 8).
3. Use of former narcotic addicts as resource personnel. The former addicts explore with students the impact addictive drugs had on their lives. Students are more likely to believe one who has experienced drugs than an "uptight" representative of the Establishment.

Roosevelt High prepared its teachers with drug-awareness sessions a week before Drug Expo '70 began. The faculty was given an orientation lecture and a packet of literature. Los Angeles Police Department officers and a former narcotic addict spoke. Discussion sessions were provided for the airing of teachers' questions.

The daily Drug Expo '70 schedule offered a variety of informational activities. Former narcotic addicts, probation officers, and representatives of community agencies participated in the week-long program. Each former addict was assigned to a home room for a day; here he talked with students about the dangers of drug use. Booths and displays providing information on drugs, tobacco, and alcohol were open during the students' lunch hour. Different booths and displays were added daily to sustain learner interest. A new film was shown daily.

Of the Roosevelt students 92 percent liked Drug Expo '70 and felt other schools should offer similar programs. Moreover, 71 percent felt they had learned something new about drugs during the program and 65 percent maintained that the week's events had turned them against drugs.

Addicts and films seemed to be the students' most popular learning resources. A large minority of Roosevelt students suggested that former narcotic addicts be hired permanently to assist counselors in group sessions involving student drug users. Some also pointed to the need for a drug abuse center near campus to which student referrals could be made. Virtually all students felt that the films that they viewed were the most effective deterrent to drug abuse.

Before Drug Expo '70, 31 percent of the Roosevelt students had experimented with narcotics. An average 59 percent, 55 percent of the boys and 66 percent of the girls, felt they were less inclined to take drugs following the program. This figure is only slightly less than the 65 percent figure for the entire student body. Some self-identified users claimed they had dropped their habits permanently.

LEAVING NICOTINE[7]

Few schools have offered adequate education programs on tobacco abuse, although the schools are full of nicotine addicts. Bentley High School in Livonia, Michigan, is one of the exceptions. It has conducted week-long, smoking-withdrawal clinics during school hours for those who wish to participate. The original impetus for the program developed when a survey of the school's 2,000 students revealed that 435 were smokers.

The Michigan Cancer Foundation helped Bentley High schedule a clinic for the first hour daily of an entire school week. Physicians from the Veterans Administration Hospital near Dearborn, Michigan, conducted the program. They sought to provide students up-to-date, scientific information on smoking and its health hazards. They discussed the effects of tobacco use with students, showed films, and gave demonstrations with authentic cancerous brain and lung tissues. Students who were attempting to give up smoking were given suggestions during the clinic.

The smoking education program involved as many as 289 students. Of the 108 who responded to a questionnaire six months later, eighteen indicated they had quit their habit completely. Others claimed they had either cut down on their consumption or viewed their addiction negatively. These results demonstrate that a smoking informational program can be effective.

POLICY AND FACT[8]

The school should formally state its policy concerning drug abuse. It is better to set forth explicitly an unpopular policy than rely on separate decisions and procedures for each case. A no-policy policy can result in the total breakdown of student trust of teachers and administrators on the issue of drugs.

The policy should be written and it should specify how the school will respond to detected drug abuse. A clearly detailed plan can guide the teacher in referring a child suspected of drug use to the school nurse, who, in turn, decides whether hospitalization or the care of a family physician would be appropriate. Some school plans require that school officials be notified each time a student is detected under the influence of illegal drugs. Most plans stipulate that administrators must inform parents. The police are usually not involved. However, if an ambulance must be called to transport a student for immediate hospitalization, the police learn about it because they monitor all ambulance calls. Furthermore, if a student is discovered selling or possessing illegal drugs on school property, school officials inform police as well as parents.

Whatever the substance of a plan, the main concern is to clearly spell out procedures that will help a child. Any policy should be oriented to correction rather than punishment. For the policy to elicit the confidence of students, it is best to involve law enforcement agencies only when absolutely necessary.

A few high schools and junior highs have experimented with organizing teachers selected by students into a "Drug Cadre." Students select the teachers who have established good rapport with them. The teachers then participate in an in-service program on drugs and addiction. The Drug Cadre, usually about five teachers, can provide the small-group support and intimacy that many students seem to accept as a condition for discussing problems and learning the facts. The students who consult with the Drug Cadre can subsequently counsel elementary school sixth-graders.

Teachers and students must not only have a policy and procedures to live by but they must also have the facts. Medical facts are very important. Heroin and other narcotics cause central nervous system depression. The user develops a tolerance so that he requires increasing doses. This is addiction. When an addict attempts to quit his habit, the withdrawal symptoms are generally severe. Death may occur due to an inadvertent overdose.

Stimulants such as the amphetamines are also addictive and create withdrawal symptoms. They may eventually cause psychosis. Hallucinogens such as LSD, taken regularly, cause mental regression and may precipitate psychosis.

Marijuana is not addictive and does not cause any of the side effects associated with heroin, stimulants, and hallucinogens. But there is no complete scientific evidence yet to indicate it is medically safe.

Epidemiological and demographical facts include the drug use patterns in the community. Teachers should know that about 20 million persons in the United States have used heroin and that 250 million people worldwide have taken the drug. Estimates for heroin use in the United States range between 40,000 and 100,000. These users are concentrated in ghettos, especially in New York City.

Teachers should learn the laws relating to drug use in their states and communities. Laws vary considerably among states, as do judicial practices. For example, some communities allow students apprehended while possessing marijuana, a felony, to plead guilty to possession of amphetamines, a misdemeanor. Some juvenile courts use strictly penal procedures, whereas others rely heavily on group therapy and counseling programs.

THE HOPE HOUSE MODEL[9]

Vincentian High School in Albany, New York, has conducted a drug treatment and prevention program in cooperation with Hope House. The results and structure of the Hope House program provide instructive guidelines for schools seeking to deal with the drug problem.

Hope House, accredited by the New York State Narcotics Addiction Control Commission, is private and nonprofit. It was founded in spring 1967 to treat Albany heroin addicts. Today the program deals with all types of addiction.

Hope House operates a therapeutic community much like Synanon House, a nationwide organization that has enjoyed remarkable success in rehabilitating addicts. Addicts in groups help one another. Each knows the others' problem and they can force one another to confront it. Those who have successfully left drugs play a very helpful role in such groups. They can serve as an example that life can go on without drugs. Open, frank human relations constitute the therapy. The addict can express his feelings among peers capable of understanding him. He will accept criticism and analysis from other addicts that he would refuse from anyone else.

The constant direction and counsel of the group helps the individual accept his condition and consider the path back to normalcy. The addict is able to release his feelings of guilt and develop a new, positive self-image that helps him deal constructively with his situation. He learns to act deliberately, to meet responsible objectives, rather than acting compulsively. He learns to examine the source of his addiction, which he cannot eradicate but can accept and expose to critical analysis. Thus he learns to live in a new way, to solve his problems through personal growth rather than gradual self-destruction.

About 300 addicts received help at Hope House its first two years of operation. Most were inner-city black heroin addicts, aged twenty-five to forty. Many had criminal records including rape and homicide. They were referred from jails, courts, and probation departments. A few came voluntarily in absolute desperation.

By 1969 the type of drug abuse, source of referrals, and social background of those seeking treatment had changed. Correctional and penal institutions no longer supplied most of the referrals; schools and parents did. The problem drugs were the psychedelics—barbiturates, LSD, and amphetamines. The new referrals were not poor nonwhites but white, middle-class adolescents. Hope House expanded its group therapy program to include sessions exclusively for teen-agers and young adults on psychedelic drugs. Regular attendance was required to stabilize the group and make group therapy effective. Nonetheless, the program lost about 75 percent of its young clients before they completed the program, usually a six-month process. Some found the sessions boring, threatening, and excessively structured. Others were arrested. Still others sought private psychiatric help. These losses greatly impaired the effectiveness of the program. A student needs six weeks to two months to benefit from the therapeutic aspects of group processes. Therefore schools, parents, and health agencies must stress the importance of consistent attendance, insisting upon it when necessary.

A SYMPTOMS APPROACH[10]

Much of the student drug problem goes unnoticed because teachers, parents, and counselors are often uninformed and naive, believing that their students or children would never use drugs. This head-in-the-sand approach only serves to intensify the problem. The situation can be easily corrected. When genuine understanding of drugs is lacking, school personnel and parents who wish to help might at least look carefully for the symptoms of abuse. Competent professionals can then deal with the causes. The symptoms are:

1. *A pronounced personality change.* Drugs alter behavior and perceptions, and large doses or addiction can transform an individual's basic personality structure.
2. *Marked decrease in motivation, interests, and achievement.* Drug abuse impairs a student's scholastic achievement and upsets his normal pattern of motivation and interests.
3. *Deviousness.* The user may lie and steal to conceal his habit and obtain money to buy drugs. This behavior should cause friends, relatives, and teachers to be suspicious.

4. *New friends.* Once a student becomes a member of the drug subculture, he leaves his old friends, unless they also take up drugs, in order to avoid detection and enjoy the peer support of other users. The young convert to drugs also begins to show up at new places and keep different hours. His whole life style is affected, if not restructured.

5. *Physical cues.* The most common signs of drug abuse are dilated pupils, loss of weight and appetite, drowsiness, sleeplessness, and extended periods of daydreaming. These symptoms vary among adolescents, depending on the individual's emotional and physical constitution and the quantity and frequency of use.

These symptoms, singly or as an aggregate, do not mean that a particular student definitely uses drugs. In fact, some of the symptoms can simply be a part of normal adolescent development. Thus the symptoms should be used only as clues to help find students who may be in need of help. A teacher may have a forthright discussion with a student and perhaps refer him for physical examination. The responsible concern of teachers can prevent many of the tragedies that now eventuate in school dismissals and legal penalty. A professional awareness of the adolescent drug problem and the capacity to act knowledgeably and sensitively will do much to prevent the injury that drugs now bring to our youth.

Students are often moved to take drugs initially because of alienation from their parents. Thus a school will find it advantageous to involve parents in drug orientation programs. Parents can gain a knowledge of the drug subculture and how they might resolve the intergenerational conflict that partially precipitated the new adolescent society.

A DRUG CURRICULUM[11]

David C. Lewis, assistant professor of medicine at the Harvard Medical School, developed ten practical guidelines for building a drug curriculum. They are designed to establish the credibility of drug programs and involve students:

1. *Estimate the students' knowledge about drugs.* In order to build an appropriate curriculum, one must determine the present state of students' drug knowledge. To neglect this groundwork is to very probably overestimate or underestimate students' understanding. Overestimation means teachers will ignore areas about which their students know little or nothing. Underestimation involves the risk of insulting students' intelligence, boring the students, and undermining the teacher's authority.

2. *Ask students to participate in planning the drug program.* Students must be involved in planning so that they can identify with the drug program, feeling it is in part theirs. Their suggestions can be invaluable in curriculum building. Above all, their participation is critical to establishing the program's credibility; without it, the program becomes an instrument of the enemy, the Establishment.

3. *Incorporate experimental data into the drug curriculum.* An extensive body of data has been collected about drugs. Students should be given the opportunity to draw their own conclusions. They can only conclude from the facts that drugs can be very harmful. But they must have the facts and decide for themselves. Authoritative pronouncements by teachers are totally inadequate. Today's student is much too cynical for that. If he weren't, he wouldn't be taking drugs.

4. *Avoid sensationalizing.* No attempt should be made to terrorize students into not taking drugs by detailing tragic case histories. This approach strikes the present generation of critical students as a form of intimidation. Sensationalism may well backfire, inducing students to try drugs to see if the dire consequences that have been described will actually result.

5. *Include drug education as a part of the classroom experience.* Drug education should be an integral part of the classroom scene. It certainly should not be restricted to special workshops and school assemblies addressed by experts and former addicts. Drug experts and experienced users must certainly play a role in building curricula. However, the teacher need only learn how to effectively teach the new materials. A great part of this new teaching role will involve developing the skill to discuss drugs knowledgeably and sensibly in the classroom. Properly trained and equipped with materials, the new teacher can meet the drug education needs of his students.

6. *Compare and contrast drug use and abuse.* The teacher should distinguish carefully between the indiscriminate taking of a drug and drug use prescribed by a physician. A drug that can help heal when professionally administered can injure and kill when used for nontherapeutic purposes. For example, barbiturate sedatives and amphetamine stimulants can do either great good or great harm. The outcome depends on how the drugs are used.

7. *Be sure to discuss tobacco and alcohol.* A major component of the drug education program should concern alcohol and cigarette consumption. Teachers should stress that there are great health hazards related to these drugs, that alcohol disrupts the lives of millions, and that half the traffic fatalities in the United States are attributable to living under the influence of alcohol, including a large number of deaths of teen-agers. Arrests for public drunkenness number many more than arrests for the illegal possession and sale of drugs. Chronic smoking causes more premature deaths than the total of drug abuse. These facts must be presented or the students will not find the drug program credible. They know their parents suffer the effects of cigarettes, tranquilizers, and alcohol. They simply will not believe that drugs can hurt them if no mention is made of the most commonly abused "Establishment drugs."

8. *Allow students who have experienced drugs to become involved in the educational program.* Students impute a great deal of credibility to what their peers say. They will listen to other students and young people who have experimented with drugs. Direct encounter is preferable, but tapes and movies can be used. They can catalyze discussion between students and teachers. Directly or indirectly, students should be exposed to those of their peers who have used drugs.

9. *Explore students' motivations to try drugs.* The teacher should explore with students the social and personal motivations for drug use. Group pressure, boredom, the pursuit of an aesthetic experience, enjoyment, and rejection of adult authority are among the motivations for drug use. A drug education program should also inquire into why some students use drugs only once and others use them regularly.

10. *Discuss the social and psychological forces that inhibit the use of drugs.* Many students are motivated not to take drugs. They may wish to abide by the law or follow their parents' admonitions. They may not wish to chance physical and psychological injury. Their friends may disapprove of drugs and, in this case, peer pressure would predispose a student against experimentation.

These ten guidelines can be used to develop drug curricula. They can also be used to evaluate proposals for programs submitted by teachers, students, or community residents. They can help the teacher and school build programs to deal with drug abuse before it even begins. To teach students to deal rationally with the world about them, a world that includes drugs, is, after all, the ultimate objective of the schools.

THE CHALLENGE

The teacher cannot ignore drug abuse. He must employ the best available knowledge to deal realistically with the situation. By participating in innovative programs, as described in this chapter, he can be an agent of change when the problem is the school or teacher and diagnose and treat the student when the student is the problem.

NOTES

[1] Joseph P. Zima and Gene A. Smith, "High School Students, Drugs, and Teachers," *School & Society, 99,* no. 2333 (April 1971), 250–252.

[2] William W. Brickman, "Drug Addiction and the Schools," *School & Society, 99,* no. 2332 (March 1971), 147.

[3] "Strengthening Drug Education," *School & Society, 98,* no. 2328 (November 1970), 400.

[4] Phyllis C. Barrins, "How To Face Up To Drug Abuse in Your Schools and Your Community," *The American School Board Journal, 158,* no. 2 (August 1970), 18.

[5] *Drugs of Abuse* (GPO 1968-0-312-959) and *Fact Sheets* (GPO 1969-0-350-436) may be ordered from the Superintendent of Documents, U.S. Government Printing Office, Washington, D.C. 20402.

[6] Herbert Blavat and William Flocco, "A Survey of a Workable Drug Abuse Program," *Phi Delta Kappan, 62,* no. 9 (May 1971), 532–533.

[7] Albert A. Zack, "Smoking Withdrawal," *Nation's Schools, 87,* no. 2 (February 1971), 56.

[8] Frank M. Ochberg, "Drug Problems and the High School Principal," *The Bulletin of the National Association of Secondary School Principals, 54,* no. 346 (May 1970), 54–56, 58.

[9] The Rev. Howard Hubbard, "Drug Treatment and Prevention," *The Bulletin of the National Association of Secondary School Principals, 54,* no. 349 (November 1970), 96–98, 100–101.

[10] *Ibid.,* pp. 103–104.

[11] David C. Lewis, "How the Schools Can Prevent Drug Abuse," *The Bulletin of the National Association of Secondary School Principals, 54,* no. 346 (May 1970), 45–49.

11
New media

The new teacher must use the same media that the learner encounters regularly—television, radio, and motion pictures. He must also expose the learner to new media to expand his cognitive and affective capacities. There are many more ways in this world for human beings to interact than through speaking and written and printed words.

The media have enveloped our society, and the school and the teacher now must employ the most up-to-date, efficient means of communicating and teaching, using all media. If the school does not adopt the new sounds, celluloid, and techniques, it will effectively turn over much of a child's learning activities to an unregulated, unsupervised consumption of the mass media. It is far better that the schools adopt the new media and construct educationally justifiable multimedia learning environments that are suitable for a space age. In this context the teacher becomes more than a teacher. She becomes a teaching engineer who devises sophisticated learning experiences through the manipulation of media toward the achievement of specified instructional objectives. Research demonstrates that lessons can be made more effective by using more than one media.[1] One medium is no longer adequate for teaching ideas and information to learners who are accustomed to many media.

THE MEDIA LABORATORY[2]

Multimedia instruction is the skillful integration of two or more communications media into a classroom presentation. Adequate facilities and services are necessary to create multimedia learning environments. A properly equipped and professionally staffed media laboratory is needed. The basic purpose of the laboratory is to provide teachers and learners every media technology and service that can facilitate the effective communication of information and concepts in the instructional process.

The media laboratory's objectives should reinforce the instructional objectives of the school it serves. The basic general objectives of a laboratory are:

1. To provide experience for learners in every communications medium that contributes to achieving the school's instructional objectives.
2. To counsel teachers and learners in the intelligent use of media.
3. To provide a centrally located set of instructional materials in all communications media.
4. To plan with public librarians and civic leaders the educational use of community resources.
5. To establish an in-service program in media for teachers.
6. To aid teachers in selecting, producing, integrating, and evaluating instructional materials.

Media laboratories have generally been organized on an individual school basis or on a district-wide basis. For example, Gary, Indiana, has employed a decentralized approach by providing each school in the district a self-sufficient media laboratory. Torrance, California, has selected centralization, establishing a single large media laboratory. Teachers visit the laboratory and select materials for use at their own schools.

Districts often choose the centralized media laboratory for reasons of economy. However, the research demonstrates that if materials and equipment are stored in on-the-site school buildings, 80 to 90 percent of the faculty will use the available media, whereas only 15 to 20 percent will take advantage of centralized media laboratories. Thus an excellent case can be made for establishing a media laboratory at every school.

Perhaps the best way to organize a media laboratory is to combine both centralized and decentralized patterns. A central media laboratory could be established to loan the most expensive equipment to individual schools in a district. A decentralized laboratory could be set up at each school to handle the most frequently used, less expensive equipment. This dual approach guarantees maximum use of media facilities and equipment and the development of a district-wide media service program.

THE MEDIA SPECIALIST

Only well-trained professionals can operate a media laboratory successfully over the long term. If the laboratory serves a small number of teachers and learners, the media specialist who is employed should be familiar with both librarianship and instructional materials. If the clientele is large, a suitable number of media professionals should be employed whose specialties complement one another.

A media specialist must perform many duties. His major responsibilities are:

1. Assisting with the preparation of instructional materials.
2. Encouraging teachers to use recent media innovations.
3. Assisting teachers in finding appropriate instructional resources.
4. Helping students effectively use the media laboratory.
5. Establishing and operating a program to train teachers and students in the case of technical hardware and equipment.
6. Organizing and administering an in-service program for teachers that focuses on the selection and use of instructional materials.
7. Supervising the distribution and circulation of equipment and instructional materials.
8. Assuming responsibility for the procurement of equipment and materials.
9. Assisting curriculum committees and teachers to effectively use curriculum guides and syllabi in conjunction with media.
10. Assisting school personnel in evaluating the contribution of the media laboratory to the achievement of a school's instructional objectives.
11. Coordinating district-wide media services with individual school media programs.

The media specialist can help teachers most in the selection of appropriate media for realizing instructional objectives, the preparation of instructional materials, and the integration of media into the classroom instructional process.

MEDIA LABORATORY SERVICES

The media laboratory is designed to furnish full media equipment, information, and services for teachers and learners. The laboratory personnel must plan in awareness of school size, faculty and student needs and interests, and the wishes of the community. The school must provide the following basic services to discharge its responsibility for keeping the school current in the realm of media:

1. A continuing program for keeping faculty, learners, and the community informed of available services and materials.
2. Provision for learners and teachers to use every type of instructional resource.
3. A program enabling learners to become sufficiently skilled to identify and locate appropriate instructional materials.
4. Full reference services for students, teachers, and community.
5. Counsel and encouragement for teachers to construct instructional aids and study new media methods.
6. Effective, efficient distribution and maintenance of materials.
7. Provision of independent study and research activities.
8. An inventory of media resources available in the community.
9. Materials should be made available for different intellectual ability levels.

SELECTION OF MATERIALS

A critical concern is the selection of the specific items to be used in the media laboratory. The basic thrust of any selection process should be the procurement of a well-balanced collection of all varieties of instructional materials. Selection can be made intelligently only in terms of a school's instructional objectives. Many objectives are specified in detail as behavioral, so materials should be chosen to contribute to the achievement of those objectives.

Materials should be selected not for their contribution to teaching but to learning. Attainment of desirable changes in the learner should be the foremost consideration. Thus any selection procedure must incorporate the following elements:

1. A precise statement of instructional objectives.
2. A selection of media that contribute to the achievement of the objectives.
3. The selection of a diversity of materials to assure that different means of communication will be used to advantage.

Some attention should be devoted to the evaluation of technical quality. Format, workmanship, and color quality, for example, are important. The instructional message must be an absolutely clear medium. It must also be sufficiently appealing to engage the attention of learners.

Selection of media laboratory materials is very important. It warrants the careful formulation of school policy and the involvement of curriculum committees, teachers, administrators, and media professionals.

MEDIA RESOURCES

A well-balanced assortment of resources is necessary. The teacher must have enough media from which to intelligently make selections. Basic media that should be included as a part of any effective media laboratory are:

1. Models or mockups, which are imitations of real things such as a globe or diorama.
2. Printed materials including periodicals, newspapers, pamphlets, and books.
3. Realia or real things; for example, rock specimens and Indian baskets.
4. Motion pictorial, which are single-concept films, 8-mm films.
5. Graphic symbols such as maps, diagrams, and charts.
6. Nonprojected still pictures, including study prints and flat pictures.
7. Teaching machines such as programed tapes, programed textbooks, and programed computer systems.
8. Still-pictorial-projected; for instance, opaque projection materials, transparencies, and filmstrips.
9. Auditory media, including radio programs, tapes, and records.
10. Instructional kits such as science and mathematics kits.
11. Television, especially educational TV programs and videotapes.

MEDIA LABORATORY FACILITIES

Building a sophisticated laboratory requires cooperative planning by both technical experts and educational professionals. The laboratory should certainly be located for convenient access. A first-floor location with an outside entrance will facilitate evening use.

If laboratory services and units cannot be conveniently situated, they should be well coordinated. The laboratory's physical facilities should accommodate the school's educational program and objectives. They should provide for the coordination of printed and audiovisual materials.

The plant of the media laboratory should include at least four functional areas in order to furnish basic media services:

1. *Utility area.* This area supports media activities such as radio and television reception, teacher-pupil conferences, still projection, small group interaction, and motion picture viewing.
2. *General use area.* Media laboratory clients use this area for such activities as viewing, reading, and listening. Materials are also stored and exhibited here.
3. *Materials production area.* This area is utilized for the preparation of instructional materials. The available equipment includes thermal copy equipment, typewriter, dry mount press, tracing table, duplicating equipment, and lettering equipment.
4. *Work-storage service area.* This area is used for receiving, unpacking, and inspecting new equipment and materials. It is also employed for labeling, cataloging, and classifying materials.

DIAL ACCESS

Dial Access is an automated system that enables students to obtain visual and audio materials immediately by dialing a code number on a device similar to a telephone dial. A teacher can assign a project and supply learners with an inventory of all appropriate materials in a media laboratory. Learners may select materials at their carrels by dialing the code numbers for a particular instructional item. For example, a learner might select and request a filmstrip on a specified topic.

Dial Access is a very advantageous innovation. First, the student can select the medium in which he learns best. Second, the teacher can assign study projects on different ability levels at one time. Third, students can progress at their own rate since Dial Access allows them to play a film, tape, or record as often as they wish. And fourth, students using a Dial Access system can be geographically separate; they need not be present at a single media laboratory. Thus Dial Access offers easy use of different media, at different ability levels, different rates of learning, and different locations.

Dial Access is a piece of educational modernization that is right in step with the "media revolution." Ultimately, learners will be able to dial into a centralized system from their homes or neighborhood media centers. The network of media that envelopes our nation will become the classroom. A learner in Maine will never see his counterpart in Arizona, but they will be classmates. They both can obtain any type of information instantly through a Dial Access system that hooks up with television and computer networks.

COMPUTER-ASSISTED INSTRUCTION[3]

Computer-assisted instruction (CAI) promises to provide some of the improvement that other innovations have failed to produce. CAI has the flexibility necessary for individualizing the educational process. It can meet specific learner needs in a way that is impossible in face-to-face student-teacher interaction.

CAI has two basic characteristics that make it potentially the advance educators have been hoping for. First, the computer can evaluate a learner's responses instantly and provide an indication that the response is correct or state exactly what the correct response should be. Every student is involved. In a conventional classroom situation only the most intelligent, self-assertive students respond to questions and benefit from teacher feedback as many as four times per period. Less motivated and bright students regress even further relative to the better students because they receive feedback only two or three times weekly. But the computer involves the student anywhere from once per four seconds to once every thirty-second interval. Consequently, each student responds and receives feedback from forty to six hundred times during every forty-minute session in a CAI situation.

Second, the computer can individualize instruction in any number of specified ways. The greatest use would be to individualize instruction according to differential aptitude, achievement, and interest. The computer can chart a learner's performance and progress and modify his program according to an evaluation of his ongoing achievement and need. The instant responsiveness and flexibility of the computer make it a tool that can revolutionize, or at least greatly modify, the way teachers instruct students.

TYPES OF COMPUTER-ASSISTED INSTRUCTION

There are four basic ways to apply the computer to instruction.[4] The first is to use the computer as a *laboratory computing device*, probably its most frequent educational application. A single terminal, usually a teletype or electric typewriter, is placed in a classroom to provide direct access to an externally located computer. Students can develop their own computer programs to correlate with their classroom assignments, as students in physics, chemistry, and mathematics frequently do. About 500 secondary schools in the United States provide the necessary computer facilities.

The second application involves the utilization of the computer as a *record keeper* and *retriever*. In this case, teachers and administrators program the computer basically for batch processing of data concerning learners and instruction. For example, the computer might handle such tasks as printing report cards, storing and retrieving test results, and scheduling classes.

The third application is *simulation*. Inputs are fed into the computer to develop models of structure and process. To date, the public schools have not used simulations. (This is not the same as simulations wherein students act out the roles, say of a legislature or army.) Eventually this application will probably be used frequently. Medical schools now use computers to construct lifelike models of the human body to demonstrate clearly to students vital processes. There is no reason that biology and life science instructors in the public schools cannot also use such simulations for instructional purposes.

The fourth form of CAI employs the computer as a *tutor*. The most simple form of tutoring is that of providing drill and practice problems to students at a computer terminal. The most sophisticated type of tutoring is sequential exposition wherein a computer presents a complete course to a learner.

WHAT THE RESEARCH SAYS

The research has demonstrated that students taught with CAI achieve at least equally and often superior to students functioning in conventional learning environments.[5] Suppes found that experimental classes in McComb, Mississippi, drilled 10 to 15 minutes daily at a computer terminal, progressed 1.10 to 2.03 years in mathematics achievement compared to a range of 0.26 to 1.26 years in control classes.[6] Butler reported similar research results in a study of fourth- and fifth-grade classes in 1968 and 1969.[7] It is important to note that these impressive educational outcomes were produced with only ten to fifteen minutes of daily drill and practice at a computer teletype terminal. The main point is that students learned more mathematics with CAI than through conventional instruction and did so in substantially less time. By using more complex computer applications to instructional situations for longer time periods, even more favorable outcomes would probably result.

THE COST OF CAI

The cost of computer-assisted instruction is not prohibitive. For example, the cost of conventional public education in New York state ranges from $400 to $4,000 per pupil year. The cost per pupil hour ranges from $0.33 to $3.33.[8] By way of contrast, cost-effectiveness analysis has demonstrated that a computer instructional system costs about $3.00 per pupil hour. And D. L. Bitzer is developing a system he estimates will cost only $0.27 per hour.[9]

Since conventional school costs are rising and the cost of computer technology is decreasing, the price tag on CAI is far from intimidating; it is, in fact, very appealing. Thus cost is not a significant factor in considering the possible adoption of CAI.

ADOPTING CAI[10]

The NEA Research Division sponsored a survey of public school teachers in the spring of 1970 to determine to what extent the nation's schools had adopted CAI. Only 7.7 percent of the teachers sampled indicated that their district was using CAI. However, almost 20 percent did not know whether their system was utilizing it. More high school teachers (10.8 percent) than elementary teachers (4.9 percent) replied that their school was making computer applications. CAI was also more frequently used in the Northeast and Middle states than in the West and Southeast.

Teachers reported computer applications to instruction in large school systems (3,000 students or more) more often than in small systems. However, the "Don't know" responses were most frequent in the large systems. Suburban and urban teachers reported computer instruction more frequently than rural faculty members. Thus computers are primarily a metropolitan, large-school phenomenon.

The teachers surveyed reported most often that computers were used for teaching mathematics in the schools. CAI was also used for English, reading, foreign language, science, business education, and social studies. Few teachers, less than 1 percent, were directly involved in computer-assisted instruction. CAI is apparently still only at an early developmental stage.

TELEVISION

Television is a very important aspect of American life. Over 95 percent of the 60 million households in the country have TV sets. More than 25 percent have more than two sets. In the average household, the set is on for almost six hours daily. By the first grade, 90 percent of all children in the United States view TV regularly. Preschoolers watch as much as seven or eight hours daily. The average American child watches TV 22,000 hours before he turns eighteen.[11] Unfortunately, very little programing is educationally committed to children's needs and interests. This deficiency is particularly telling upon the 12 million three- to five-year-old children who are not in school. Research indicates that half the potential intellectual growth of a child may occur by age four.[12] The major exception is "Sesame Street" which could be the beginning of an era of learning-oriented programing.

The preschool child has not learned that work is not fun. "Sesame Street" capitalizes on this innocence by presenting educationally valuable programs that are full of engaging characters who pun, tell jokes, and laugh. The very young child, especially the ghetto child for whom "Sesame Street" is targeted, learns rudimentary information, skills, and important values as he is ecstatically involved with the fascinating "Sesame Street" medium. He learns nutrition, language skills, rhythms, music, and humor. And he learns socially essential values such as fairness, kindness, self-respect, and friendliness. The primary educational objectives of "Sesame Street" include several categories: reasoning, problem solving, and perception; mathematics and numerical skills, language and reading skills; and affective, social, and moral development.[13] The realization of those objectives flows naturally and uninhibitedly from preschoolers' enthusiasm for "Sesame Street." Such learning is an excellent preparation for the formal school experience.

TELEVISION IN NEW TRIER[14]

A substantial number of school systems are adopting TV as an instructional medium. New Trier Township, Illinois, is utilizing TV in an exemplary manner in one high school and six elementary school districts. The school system schedules regular programs on any one of four channels as many as eight times weekly. A teacher may ask for a program for later use if he cannot fit a regularly scheduled program in. He may also request the transmission of any videotape in the Telecourse Catalog or the Cooperative Film Library Catalog.

New Trier enjoys great flexibility because it has a 2500-megahertz Instructional Television Fixed Service (ITFS) system. This system broadcasts a microwave signal that is picked up by special receivers in participating schools. When set up in November 1966, New Trier's ITFS was the first such system operational in the country. Today, the system is administered and maintained by five professionals and twenty-five high school student staff employees. The staff secures regular and special programs from every source, especially teachers, resource personnel, the public, and the commercial mass media. The staff goes wherever feasible to videotape material of educational utility. A questionnaire study has determined that the New Trier faculty believes TV is a highly helpful educational medium. They wish to expand the program.

SOCIAL IMPLICATIONS[15]

The educational community cannot reasonably assume that an unregulated application of technology to instruction will result in positive results in every instance. Educators are as responsible for their actions as are other citizens. Some argue that physical scientists abdicated the responsibility for their own behavior in the prelude to Nagasaki and Hiroshima; educational professionals should take steps to insure that contributing to a different but comparably tragic holocaust is not their moral fate.

The potential for the control of human learning and living that the new knowledge of behavioral scientists and the new media and technology presents is truly great. That potential can be directed either to 1984 or to utopia. Professional educators must study the possible social consequences of the various technologies they now use or might use. They should then work for national policies that guarantee that educational hardware will be utilized only in socially beneficial ways. To begin, everyone who teaches in a school could urge the President and Congress to establish a National Advisory Commission on Educational Technology and Society. This commission would be an interdisciplinary group of physical and social scientists, humanists, and technicians.

THE NEW DIMENSION

The media revolution has transformed American society into an information-saturated social system. The computer and television have stimulated a quantum jump that has converted the society into a highly charged learning environment. The school has had to respond to this implicit challenge to its authority by renewing its own learning environment. This response has included, as we have discussed in this brief chapter, the computer, television, and the media laboratory. By applying technology, the school has streamlined the instructional process, making it more effective and efficient. In doing so, it has reestablished its right to define learners' educational experiences.

NOTES

[1] John P. DiSanto, "The Media Laboratory," *Education*, 90, no. 4 (April-May 1970), 339–347. The discussion of the media laboratory, media specialist, selection of resources, media laboratory services and facilities, and dial access are based on this source.

[2] *Ibid.*

[3] Keith A. Hall, "Computer-Assisted Instruction: Problems And Performance," *Phi Delta Kappan*, 52, no. 10 (June 1971), 628.

[4] See H. E. Mitzel and G. L. Brandon, *Experimentation with Computer-Assisted Instruction in Technical Education*, University Park, Pennsylvania State University Computer Assisted Instruction Laboratory, Semi-Annual Progress Report No. R-9, 31 December 1967.

[5] See A. E. Hickey and J. M. Newton, *Computer-Assisted Instruction: A Survey of the Literature*, 2nd ed., Newburyport, Mass., Entelek, Inc., 1967; D. N. Hansen, *Learning Outcomes of a Computer Based Multimedia Introductory Physics Course*, Tallahassee, Florida State University CAI Center, Semi-Annual Progress Report, 1967, p. 95; H. E. Mitzel et al., *The Development and Presentation of Four College Courses by Computer Teleprocessing*, University Park, Pennsylvania State University Computer Assisted Instruction Laboratory, Final Report No. R-7, June 1967.

[6] Patrick Suppes, "The Use of Computers in Education," *Scientific American*, September 1966, pp. 207–220.

[7] C. F. Butler, "CAI in New York City—Report on the First Year's Operation," *Educational Technology* (October 1969), 84–87.

[8] Hall, *op. cit.*, p. 360.

[9] D. L. Bitzer, "Economically Viable Large-Scale Computer-Based System," *Computer-Assisted Instruction and the Teaching of Mathematics*, Proceedings: National Conference on Computer-Assisted Instruction, Pennsylvania State University, 24–26 September 1968.

[10] "Report of a Survey: The Use of Computers for Instruction," *NEA Research Bulletin*, 49 (March 1971), 3–4.

[11] Nicholas Johnson, "Beyond Sesame Street," *The National Elementary Principal*, 50, no. 5 (April 1971), 7–13.

[12]David D. Connell and Edward L. Palmer, "Sesame Street: A Lot of Off-Beat Education?," *The National Elementary Principal*, 50, no. 5 (April 1971), 14.

[13]*Ibid.*, p. 16.

[14]"Joining the Revolution," *Instructor*, 80, no. 6 (February 1971), 53–55.

[15]Mark Everet Siegel, "The Random Dumping of Educational Technology," *Educational Technology*, 10, no. 6 (June 1970), 31–32.

12
Minorities

Indian, Mexican-American, and black citizens have experienced the worst of the American social order and its schools. First the blacks, then the Mexican-Americans and Indians mobilized civil rights movements to contest the authority of school and society. They knew well that their children were treated less than equally in the classroom just as in the society. The Red, Brown, and Black Power movements have demanded that the school redefine its relation to them and cease what they regard as the destruction of their culture and children or, more pejoratively, "mental genocide," a term regularly used by prominent Indian leader Lehman Brightman.

MENTAL GENOCIDE

The 1966 Coleman report demonstrated that the school is not an instrument of educational equality and pluralism. The studies of the Harvard Center for Law and Education (publisher of *Inequality in Education*) have documented this in much detail. The school and teacher are biased against red, brown, and black learners. They abuse the authority the state delegates to them to teach minority learners. They teach the minorities to hate themselves and track them into low-status programs, making them feel they are not meant for a white man's success.

This country was founded on an attempted genocide of the Indian, enslavement of the African, and discrimination against the Mexican. This intent is translated in the schools as "mental genocide." The educational endeavor to extinguish cultural and racial identity or, simply, pride is an extension of the doctrine of Manifest Destiny, the doctrine that proclaims that the white race is destined to dominate black, red, and brown citizens. The schools educationally reinforce and act out this value orientation. Culturally myopic teachers, often unconscious of the extent and depth of their racism, actually cause black, Indian, and Mexican-American learners to fail. The curriculum they teach and the way they teach it so thoroughly contradict and deny the American minorities' cultures, life styles, and aspirations that the minorities simply cannot learn from such a foreign set of educational experiences. They are precluded from learning and eventual success due to the fact that they were born, in the eyes of the school, the wrong color.

The destruction of the nonwhite's mind and culture is inconsistent with the formal egalitarian and democratic goals of the American school. But numerous factual analyses of the school indicate that it is far from democratic and egalitarian. It acts in a very indifferent, authoritarian, and monolithic way toward nonwhite American children to depress both their hope and their achievement. The minorities, however, have recently contested this state of affairs.

MINORITIES AND EDUCATIONAL REFORM

The Indians, blacks, and Chicanos have been applying political pressure to the schools. The schools have responded at least to the extent of acknowledging criticism. A few schools have even begun to reform, reshaping the conventional forms of authority to satisfy legitimate minority needs and aspirations. We shall next consider the educational condition of red, black, and brown learners and a number of the most significant educational reforms and developments.

THE INDIAN

The Indian learner confronts a number of serious problems in obtaining an adequate education. The problems stem largely from the fact that the values and practices of the school are so widely disparate from the values and practices of the Indian community. The Indian learner has six basic problems.[1]

1. English is generally a second language for him. All the Indian languages are so structurally different that a curriculum taught in English presents a major obstacle. Indian words that translate into English may have different connotations, which a direct translation cannot capture. The many subtleties of English are lost on the Indian learner, just as the nonverbal communications among Indian learners are lost on the teacher.

2. The Indian child is raised to cooperate rather than compete. Hence the competitive culture of the classroom baffles him. He cannot comprehend why he must exceed the achievement of a friend in order to rank higher on a "normal curve." He usually views school as a place for learning rather than competing. He is not concerned whether another pupil learns more over a designated time span than he. Pitting one Indian learner against others is not a useful device for the teacher in motivating students.

3. Indians usually suffer a negative self-concept. Virtually every experience the Indian learner has outside the tribal community indicates to him that he is inferior. The fact that white discrimination and domestic imperialism have relegated the Indian to the bottom of the socioeconomic ladder reinforces the stigma. The average Indian family has an annual income of only $1,500, the Indian unemployment level is ten times the national average, and the average Indian life span is forty-four years. This dismal condition reinforces substantially the Indian learner's self-hatred.

4. Indian students do not have successful academic role models. Few Indians have graduated from college and become teachers. A mere 1 percent of the teachers of Indian pupils are tribal Americans. Lacking role models, the Indian learner often concludes that academic success for him is impossible. When he seldom or never sees an Indian in a position of authority, the fatalism that flows from social prejudice and discrimination is reinforced.

5. The Indian learner detects a basic conflict between the school's value system and the tribal value system. The white teacher often assumes the universal validity of his values and ethics. Those who deviate from the norm are something less for it. But the Indian regards the work ethic and the WASP arrogation of self-worth as a manifestation of a sick society. He resents being compelled to adhere to a value system that is not his own.

6. Indian learners often lack incentives for academic performance. Indians value learning but not the school's way of administering it. The Indian child is enthusiastic when he enters the white man's school, at first learning well. But the value orientation of the teacher

and school soon becomes apparent. White culture is superior to Indian culture. The Indian child detects this ethnocentrism early and begins to regress rapidly relative to white learners. Since his home environment and peer group can give him no advice or cues as to how to handle an indifferent, even hostile, learning climate, the Indian learner soon becomes demoralized. A situation develops where teachers expect no expressions of intelligence from Indian pupils, and the Indian children, acting out the self-fulfilling prophecy, retire to quiet hopelessness in the back of the classroom.

THE LATENT ASSUMPTIONS

The white man has historically assumed that when the Indian saw the superiority of white culture, he would be immediately converted to the white man's life style. When the Indian did not soon adopt the new culture, the white man concluded he was too primitive for civilization. When the Indian did not change after prolonged contact with whites, the white man resorted to coercion to transform the Indian identity. Today, the attitude of the schools toward the Indian learner is to assimilate him, to force him into the mainstream of culture, training him so that he can leave the communal life of the reservation for the city.

There is no attribution of value to the Indian life, culture, and mode of education. White schools simply do not regard being an Indian as a legitimate identity. Thus most schools that instruct Indian youngsters have subverted and desecrated the authority of the Indian life style. In short, the assumption is that there is something wrong with being Indian, and the learner must be educated toward something else, notably the competitive and materialistic white culture.

THE HAVIGHURST STUDY[2]

Professor Robert J. Havighurst of the University of Chicago directed the U. S. Office of Education's project, "The National Study of American Indian Education." The study surveyed thirty-nine public, private, and Bureau of Indian Affairs school systems located in fourteen states. The summary report recommended that Indians be increasingly given the authority and control for their education. The long-term objective is to enable Indians to function adequately in both white and tribal societies while still maintaining a healthy respect for Indian culture. The Havighurst report recommended the incorporation of Indian art, history, and culture into all schools, not only Indian schools, to enhance the social image of the red man and enlarge an understanding of his problematic socioeconomic and political situation. Job counseling should be available to Indians in the high schools. Financial assistance is also necessary.

The tribal community should be vitally involved in educational decision making. Indians should seek election to school boards and tribal education committees should make their influence felt in public and federal schools. To date, the school has proved a very hostile institution largely because the Indian has not participated in it. If Indians participated substantially in their schools, the high Indian dropout rate and dismal achievement record would be a thing of the past.

About 15 percent of Indian children in the five to seventeen age bracket attend government boarding schools, especially on the Navajo reservation. The criticism of these schools has been intense and abundant. But the report stresses that no immediate feasible alternatives exist for children whose families live inordinate distances from public schools or lead a migratory life.

The life of the Indian has been changing rapidly. There has been a large-scale migration to the metropolis, particularly in the Southwest and West. Of all American Indians, 38 percent, or 280,000, now dwell in cities such as San Francisco, Minneapolis, Los Angeles, Phoenix, and Tulsa. The 16,000 school-age Indians in the cities will increase to 75,000 by 1980. The Havighurst report recommended an input of $7 million from state and federal funds into special school programs to accommodate this growth.

The report recommends that the Bureau of Indian Affairs recruit more Indian college graduates as teachers for Indian schools. Only 260 of 1,772 teachers in the BIA schools are now Indian, but this figure is expected to increase about 1000 by 1980. The report also recommended enlisting the support of the community by hiring Indian adults as teacher aides.

RED POWER AT ROUGH ROCK[3]

The Navajos have established control of their own educational program at the Rough Rock Demonstration School in Chinle, Arizona. The seven school board members are all Navajos, some with very little formal education. But they govern a successful school, relevant to the Navajos' spiritual and occupational needs, which has attracted international attention and over 12,000 visitors annually.

Rough Rock is by every indicator a thoroughly Navajo school.

Navajo culture, history, and language contribute the major components to the core curriculum. Sixty-two of eighty-two full-time employees are Navajo. The school's Cultural Identification Center provides facilities for Navajo artists and writers. Recordings of Navajo music and rituals are played regularly in the dormitories. Teachers encourage children to express themselves aesthetically and culturally as Navajos. They periodically visit pupils' homes to counsel with parents concerning their children. Parents even live in the dormitories for eight-week periods, serving as paid dormitory aides. They comfort children tormented by nightmares and tell others bedtime Navajo folk stories. The children can travel home on weekends. If necessary, the school provides transportation.

The Rough Rock experiment substantiates that the involvement of the Indian is requisite to a truly Indian educational experience, that the authority for the Indian's educational experience should be vested in the Indian community. White professionals may play a role, but the Indian community must make the major decisions regarding curriculum content and methods of instruction.

THE CHALLENGE[4]

The Indian student represents the supreme challenge to the authority of the American education system. Most black students want admittance into the mainstream, although some, frustrated at not getting in, no longer try. Black culture does not constitute an inversion of the prevailing social values. The black challenge is not one of the conflict of cultures but a demand for social justice and equality. But the Indian, unbusinesslike and intent upon interpersonal harmony, has never wanted white culture; in fact, his values contradict the work ethic of collecting material wealth as a measure of success. He not only rejects the authority of the schools but the authority of the entire society. The Indian is not a status-seeker or entrepreneur, so he fares badly in terms of the meritocratic criteria of the contemporary school. The Indian is a failure in the Anglo-controlled schools by virtue of the very fact he was born an Indian. To transform the school into an instrument of equal opportunity for the tiny and weak Indian minority that dissents from our values is the supreme challenge to our schools and culture.

The Rough Rock experiment demonstrates most clearly that the challenge is not unreasonable. In fact, Indian communities can meet it themselves by administering their own educational systems. The white majority need only suspend its bigoted prejudgments. Everything we know about motivation and achievement indicates that Indian involvement in decision-making would produce quality American Indian education within the larger framework of American public education. Only when authority is shared with the Indian will the Indian genuinely learn.

THE FUTURE[5]

The Bureau of Indian Affairs should no longer discharge the federal responsibility for Indian education. A new federal commission, composed of nationally recognized Indian leaders and Indian authorities, should administer the reservation schools until they can be completely entrusted to the Indian peoples. The withdrawal should be accomplished swiftly. However, the government must fulfill its treaty obligations to guarantee Indian rights and provide essential services. The appropriate federal departments, such as HEW, Interior, and Justice, can execute the commitments, but they should act only at the behest of the tribal councils. Thus each tribe will enjoy sufficient financial resources and legal safeguards to govern its own educational affairs and sustain its communal life. Perhaps the Indian thus can develop enough political and economic power so that he need not depend primarily on enlightened policy.

THE SCHOOL AND THE TEACHER

Few schools have satisfactorily educated Indian children. "Effective" schools are those where the student dropout rate is less than the teacher dropout rate. Departing teachers express feelings of inadequacy in authentically dealing with the Indian learner and his culture. They claim their training did not prepare them for teaching youngsters of another culture, especially a culture that reverses many mainstream values. The college of education programs embody the white middle-class experience. Students generally do their practice teaching in white middle-class schools. With such a drastic discontinuity between the professional training program and the realities of teaching Indian learners, it is no surprise that the teacher is ill prepared to instruct Indian learners.[6]

The teacher must recognize the value of Indian culture, that it need not be justified in terms of the white man's experience. Only then will he seek to teach the Indian child as an Indian rather than attempt to assimilate him. (The traditional term has been "civilize.") The American teacher must not only espouse the rhetoric of pluralism;

he must practice it in the classroom. Cultural and linguistic differences present unique learning opportunities. Pupils not only learn from the teacher, but they can teach each other about themselves. White children should learn Indian culture and at least some Indian language, and Indian children should learn white culture and English. Recent events have demonstrated that the Indian never melted into the "melting pot" and never will.

The teacher should capitalize on the educational potential of the Indian's culture and language in the classroom. The American credo that all types of children should learn together under the same roof compels this response. The principal reality of the American schools should be that more than one moral system, more than one form of authority, is operative and that these are reflected in a creative, aesthetic, and pluralistic school environment. The Indian cannot survive in the absence of this reality.

BLACKS[7]

Large urban school systems are vertical bureaucracies: authority flows from the superintendent all the way into the classroom. The community has little to say about what happens there. Bureaucratic ossification and self-interested teacher professionalism guarantee this result. Recently, black communities have become intensely aware of their powerlessness,[8] and school-community relations have become accordingly very tense. The communities have launched campaigns for community control of their schools or they have attempted to establish black independent schools. They are unrelentingly seeking to fashion a genuine educational pluralism.

Blacks might not challenge the schools if the schools were, in fact, successful in educating their children or, on the other hand, if the schools were not critically important for their children's success. If the schools of East St. Louis, Harlem, and Watts were highly successful in teaching reading, mathematics, and science so that black children scored at or above grade level on standard achievement tests, the question of the community control of schools and the founding of independent schools would never be raised.[9] The authority of the public school system would never be challenged. Governance becomes a salient issue only when the professionals fail. And, to be sure, if schooling had no impact on out-of-school success, ghetto parents would not really care, in any case, if the schools failed. But American society exacts educational achievement as the crucial ingredient for success. Consequently, the failure of the ghetto school and black parents' hope for a better life for their children collide, producing, not surprisingly, major conflict.

The educational system has the capacity and intent to track students into various levels of success.[10] Since the schools do so poorly in behalf of the poor, impoverished statuses are perpetuated while the socioeconomically privileged enjoy a quality education that enhances their enviable condition.[11] The pernicious effects of tracking can be seen clearly in the statistics of students in New York City's academic high schools. For example, in the Bronx High School of Science and Brooklyn Technical High School, elite institutions that admit only students with superior examination scores, nonwhites total only 7 and 12 percent of the students, respectively. City-wide, a majority of blacks and Puerto Ricans fill lower tracks, leading them to general rather than academic diplomas. Only 18 percent of academic high school graduates are black or Puerto Rican, although they constitute 36 percent of the academic student population. And, until the recent advent of open admissions in the City University of New York system,[12] a reform that has produced indeterminate results to date, only one-fifth of that 18 percent entered college, as compared with 63 percent of the whites who graduated. Thus only 7 percent of the graduates of New York's academic high schools who went on to college have been black or Puerto Rican.[13] It is apparent that the schools function as valves for the occupational structure, diverting black students from depressed socioeconomic backgrounds into "tracks" that terminate in inferior status and employment.

The inner-city schools have elaborated greatly upon failure; indeed they have often given up entirely on their disadvantaged charges. Their program has been characterized by hallway patrols and plainclothes police, the rudimentary paraphernalia of an educational "preventive detention" system. The schools' paranoid fear of the "clientele" (professional bureaucratese for "students") and their preoccupation with the bureaucratic devices that enforce conformity preclude even diligent, committed teachers from equipping black students with the intellectual equipment for mobility (the black's prerequisite for equality in a society of polarities and strata).

The prospects for black learners seem exceedingly dim in our technocratic society when one considers the U. S. Department of Labor's 1967 data demonstrating that the average twelfth-grade black commands a mathematical proficiency somewhere between the seventh- and eighth-grade levels and a reading proficiency only slightly higher.[14] The situation is actually more depressing than the statistics indicate because the data apply only to high school graduates and do not include dropouts. The image that evolves highlights blacks learning far less than what they need to get and hold a good job and a fearful group of teachers, often predominantly white (in attitude, if not in color), managing the repressive process in rigid bureaucracies.[15]

If one extrapolates the incredible inferiority of ghetto education to only 1975, when skill requirements will be even higher than now, one is not reassured. The Department of Labor estimates that one-quarter (26.6 percent) of the workers aged twenty-five to thirty-four will be without a high school diploma then.[16] A heavily disproportionate number of these will be black. Experts from the Senate Manpower Subcommittee to the President's Automation Commission estimate that one now needs two years beyond high school training to become a successful member of the working class.[17] The inevitable inference is that, lacking a rapid transformation of the central-city schools, we may soon witness, on an unprecedented scale, the explosions of "social dynamite" James Conant warned about.[18] Massive rioting would invite hysterical, unthinking military occupations of the ghetto that could become long term.

Because the schools chronically fail, one of the few options open to the undereducated black is the military. Many have enlisted, but many more have been drafted in numbers disproportionate to the black population. This "blackening" of the military is a more significant index of the black's dearth of opportunity than it may seem; for it to occur, many more blacks than those that finally enter the services must be "processed" simply because the examining stations find that a sizable percentage are functionally illiterate and that a much higher percentage cannot pass the Selective Service achievement tests. The blackening will become even more pronounced if the country ever achieves a totally volunteer army.

The consequences of ghettoization of the army could become extreme. A study of the attitudes of black GI's in Vietnam detected voluminous anger and militancy.[19] If the schools continue to fail, whether through ineptitude or apathy, leaving the army as perhaps the black's major viable alternative; the ghettoization of the military will proceed apace, and frustration and bitterness will intensify. The Black Hessian will become an institution; he will be unable to walk away from his martial role when he discards the khakis for the mufti. For example, only 37.8 percent of the black enlisted men agree that weapons have *no* place in the struggle for their rights in the United States. Nearly 50 percent responded they would use weapons, while 13 percent said they would organize guerilla military units.

The vast majority of black soldiers believe that America will experience even more and worse racial violence of the sort that marred the nation the past decade. Most interviewees indicated they would join renewed rioting if they felt there was no other way to focus attention on their grievances.[20] An educational system that effectively tracks blacks into the military reinforces this pattern of alienation and violence. The process will become even more pronounced as the occupational structure becomes increasingly technocratic and efficient. In a society of growing expertise, the deficiencies of the school, even if held constant, produce a snowballing effect: an unstable sociological climate of distrust, frustration, and desperation develops and finally the psychic turbulence escalates into direct confrontation and violence. It is neither merely academic nor romantic to speculate that, if the inner-city schools continue to fail, channeling blacks into Hessian statuses or "cooling them out"[21] entirely, the black GI's will bring home to the ghetto military skills rather than those skills they were entitled to learn in excellent schools.

The schools must justify their authority by producing superior learning results. The alternative is that the schools will no longer possess any authority in the view of the blacks. When this process, which has already begun, is complete, the authority of school and society will have been seriously eroded. Our social institutions will then be constrained to rely increasingly on manipulation and coercion to insure their survival. Unfortunately, at that point, they will be something less than democratic. And the blacks will be something more than nonviolent.

Good schools for blacks are, of course, not enough. A well-educated black without a job is an especially bitter man. Many blacks who have managed to overcome the barriers of educational inequality have suffered terribly in the society's racially psychotic defense mechanisms. The destructiveness of the national racism is illustrated by the data demonstrating the overqualification of many blacks for their jobs. For example, 35 percent of the nonwhites over eighteen years of age had completed four years of high school in 1965 and 7 percent had finished college, but only 17 percent were in professional, technical, managerial, clerical, and sales positions, a much smaller proportion than that of whites with comparable education.[22] Good schools can only be effective within the context of genuine equal employment opportunity.

One hastens to point out that, although blacks are not securing employment equally with whites of the same educational attainment, they are winning more quality jobs than at any previous time. This development has made the school critical. The school has, in fact, become a crucial institution because the civil rights movement has opened opportunities for black Americans. Historically, no matter how good or bad a black's education, there were no occupational opportunities. Today, a limited number of jobs are accessible, particularly in public service agencies. The modest changes brought by the civil rights movement have imbued the school's credentials and degrees with an immediate relevance. The situation unfolds as one in which millions of blacks, caught up in the international revolution of rising expectations, are pursuing a relatively small number of jobs.[23] To seriously compete for openings, they need a credible education. Their intense ardor for good jobs converts into profound disgust with the schools and a demand to control them or establish their own. The black flood tide of uncontrollable expectations has washed the ghetto school of much of its authority. The ghetto and its schools will never be the same. Not even the tragedy of repression and police violence in the inner-city can extinguish this historical process.

Let us assume for the moment that a substantial number of blacks do succeed in controlling or founding their own schools as an alternative to the inferior inner-city public schools. The type of curriculum they select instantly becomes decisive to their redefinition of role in the social order. If they decide to train for jobs in the present socioeconomic structure, their schools will probably succeed, because they are meeting white society's needs. American business, hungry for expertise and the black dollar, can become remarkably color-blind if business requires that.

But if the blacks insist on a genuine pluralism—a rejection of the Liberal Establishment ideology of the "melting pot" in favor of a nationalistic assertion of subcultural and racial identity in the educational setting,[24] defiantly shunning the formula that equates an increment of education with an increment of status and income (that is, confronting the managerial ethic)—the inflammation of tension and the prolongation of poverty will ensue. If the black refuses to enlist in the achieving society, which has historically been his aspiration, if he constructs an education that focuses, in more than mere token flourishes, upon the definition of the black self and social change—a bold curriculum of participatory pluralism—the society, in the name of protecting its "standards," will increasingly reject the graduates of the black independent schools and may, in fact, shut down the schools altogether in a crisis, forcibly integrating blacks (that is to say, tracking them in the same school system that whites attend).

The professed goal of such forced integration would be to achieve a shared culture, the prerequisite for a cohesive and believable social system according to liberal, universalist ideology; but the real objective would be solely order, not a social contract. It is indeed uncertain that a guilt-laden and paranoiacally racist society can function without major violence, or even endure, if the black demand for racially actualizing education were to materialize in the form of militant, parochial, black schools.

A value challenge to the vaunted American national character, the sacred image of the "melting pot," is difficult, if not impossible, to accommodate for a society that denies the educative utility of conflict. The society prefers a veneer of sparkling consumer products, a sort of artificial pluralism, to give the impression of choice while actually repressing the expression of basic value differences. The essential issue becomes: Is America mature enough for a fully developed pluralism, where different identities contribute handsomely to the educational process rather than being ignored in favor of the narcotizing blandness of a WASPish, suburbanite, Dick-and-Jane reader? Are we sufficiently sophisticated for more than one standard of success? Or will we tolerate blacks running their own schools only if they choose the kind of education whites have always thought best? More specifically and pointedly, are we confident enough to refrain from smashing an embryonic Black Panther curriculum?

The emergence of a meaningful pluralism, characterized by real alternatives, would require a renaissance in American education.[25] The monstrous inequities in per-pupil expenditures within states must be ruled unconstitutional (see Chapter 4). Tax funds for tuition payments, not taxation for public schools, would contribute greatly to a credible racial and ethnic pluralism. Independent schools, committed to black identity, culture, and learning, would proliferate, offering meaningful choices. America has, of course, not been without educational choices, but they have been exercised only by the affluent. The majority of students, notably ghetto blacks, have enjoyed no choice. They have attended, as a rule, the school in their neighborhood, and it has failed them.

Not only must there be choices in the society as a whole, but each individual, irrespective of background, should have access, as a constitutional right, to a choice. Only within the framework of significant choices can the distinctive American subcultural groups, especially the blacks, define themselves authentically and build their own communities within the larger societal value system. The paradox is that the universalistic American value system of justice and equality needs pluralism as blood requires oxygen; particular identities must enrich the "melting pot" if the democratic ethic is to work.

The quest for community control has floundered in the quagmire of dissension that followed attempts to introduce pluralism into the public educational system. Bureaucratic reform, relying on decentralization, may be insufficient for significant change. Financial reform, an alternate method of allocating public monies, is more promising. The most frequently mentioned scheme is one of vouchers, wherein the central government distributes revenue equally among individual learners, who themselves decide how they will use their equal educational resource. The learner thereby enjoys enlarged freedom to define his own education. Black independent schools could become a reality within such a system of the just sharing of public educational monies.

Independent black schools would not necessarily provide a "better education" as traditionally defined in terms of eventual job, income, and prestige, but they would offer an alternative to the cumbersome, mechanical educational system that seeks to impose a single, majoritarian image of what education is upon the culturally unique black community. They would forge a liberating educational pluralism that recognizes that learning is a very personal, even existential, statement about whom one is and hopes to be and that differences are the value source of serious education. (Any educational program that insists upon conformity cannot, in truth, be termed "education.")

Free from public monolithic standards and bureaucracy, the black independent school will enjoy the freedom necessary for innovation. It could fashion a genuinely black curriculum, unfettered by state-enforced standards (except those that focus on basics such as reading and writing), that would articulate honestly with black identity. Smaller size would mean less bureaucratic encrustation and financial burden and an increase in responsiveness to individual students and parents.[26] And responsiveness or, more precisely, accountability is absolutely essential if the curriculum is to meet real black learning needs rather than artificial, imagined ones.

Independent black schools, established through the opportunities afforded by vouchers, would effectively subvert the dominance of white cultural values over the curriculum. Black students would not experience disconcerting challenges to their identity in the form of attempts to make them adjust or be better citizens. They would not have to tolerate the compensatory educational programs that assume they will be "culturally enriched" by being bussed to white symphonies and plays. In the independent school, the black would be free to rely on his own wealth of cultural resources, and creatively extend his heritage into the future.

Blacks, rising up angrily, are vociferously telling us that there are different but equally valid educational models, and that differences should not be dismissed or suppressed. A curriculum of black history and culture need not be justified by any universalistic standard: it need only satisfy the need of the learner who is inquiring within an educational milieu to achieve a workable accommodation with his own reality and fashion an authentic black identity and life style.[27] Only when American society recants the myth of bland homogeneity, affirming that there is more than one standard of success and more than one way to learn, will we move toward genuine educational pluralism for blacks and effectively subvert the authority of the present school system that so thoroughly fails blacks.

THE MEXICAN-AMERICAN

A 1970 U.S. Civil Rights Commission study of Southwestern and California school districts fully documents that the Mexican-American, or Chicano, child is abused in the public schools.[28] The commission report indicates that "a substantial number" of schools are still "suppressing use of the students' native language." Until recently, Colorado, Arizona, and Texas allowed instruction only in English. In Texas the ban "was often interpreted . . . to prohibit the use of Spanish anywhere on school grounds subject to penalty. . . . Principals and teachers instituted a variety of punishments, including spanking, to discourage the speaking of Spanish." The commission reported that "almost 50 percent of all Mexican Americans in first grade do not speak English as well as the average Anglo first-grader. . . . Few efforts (are) made to aid the transition from the child's other tongue. The result is academic failure and unfavorable psychological consequences." Most districts have now abolished their "no Spanish" rules. Only 3 percent have a written policy discouraging Spanish. However "15 percent of the schools which responded stated that they discouraged the speaking of Spanish in the classroom."

The major findings of the commission's study include the following:

1. In the area studied, 45.5 percent of the Mexican-American pupils attend predominantly (50 percent or more) Mexican-American schools.

2. The schools seldom teach English as a second language or establish bilingual education programs.
3. Of twelfth-grade Mexican-American learners, 63 percent read below grade level. This figure is twice the rate for Anglo students.
4. Of the Mexican-American pupils in the Southwest, 18 percent leave school by the fourth grade, 23 percent have left by the eighth grade, and 55 percent by the twelfth grade.
5. The segregation of Mexican-American teachers exceeds that of Mexican-American pupils. Of almost 12,000 Mexican-American teachers, 55 percent are employed in predominantly (50 percent or more) Mexican-American schools.
6. The most extreme segregation is found in Texas, where 40 percent of the Mexican-American children attend schools that are 80 to 100 percent Mexican-American.

The commission concluded that the situation was dismal. Most efforts to help the Mexican-American learner were directed toward alleviating problems rather than attacking root causes. The philosophy seems to be that of compensating for the Mexican-American child not being white rather than letting him learn in a pluralistic school environment on his own terms.

BETWEEN TWO CULTURES[29]

The miserable performance of Mexican-American students is not due to the home environment. James Anderson and Dwight Johnson found in 1968 that "there appears to be little difference between Mexican-American families and other families with respect to the amount of emphasis on education that the child experiences in his home." In fact, "these children experience the same high degree of encouragement and assistance at home as do their classmates." The Mexican-American child is motivated, willing, and prepared to learn. The unavoidable conclusion is that the schools have failed the Mexican-American learner.

The Mexican-American child is often reluctant to use the English he knows, or he knows little or no English. Yet the school provides instruction only in English, a tremendous handicap for a largely Spanish-speaking child. The teachers are not bilingual. They cannot help the Mexican-American child even in the rare instances when they might wish to do so. Consequently, from the very beginning of his school experience, the Mexican-American child is traumatized and stigmatized with an alien language and curriculum. This insures that he will fall increasingly rapidly behind his Anglo counterparts. In the public schools, he submits to what amounts to compulsory miseducation.

The compensatory education approach seems to be little better than doing nothing. The assumption of such projects as Head Start and Follow Through is that the Spanish-speaking preschooler can learn enough in a summer or six months' time to grapple successfully with the conventional Anglo curriculum. This approach focuses on symptoms rather than the problem. And the problem is that the school is not germane to the Mexican-American's culture, life style, and language. Schools have attempted to fit the brown pupil to the curriculum rather than the curriculum to the child. This destroys motivation so thoroughly that Spanish-speaking children are often erroneously placed in classes for the mentally retarded. Where schools equate linguistic differences with cultural deprivation, the percentage of Mexican-American children categorized as having inferior IQ's is over twice their proportion in the general population. In California, for example, Mexican-American children constitute over 40 percent of the pupils in classes for the mentally retarded. The truth is, however, that the "retardation" resides most often in the curriculum and teacher, not the learner.

Educational critics have recently disputed the authority of IQ tests such as Otis, SCAT, and Stanford-Binet as valid measures of the intellectual potential of Spanish-speaking children. They claim the standard IQ tests depress the Mexican-American child's performance because they are given only in English and their content is geared to the middle-class, white, suburban background. In 1968, the California State Board of Education established a special committee to investigate charges levied by the Mexican-American community that IQ tests discriminate against Chicano children. The committee found that Mexican-American children, classified as mentally retarded on IQ tests administered in English, improved dramatically on tests given in Spanish. The average increase was 13 IQ points, from 70 to 83. The highest individual improvement was 28 points. The special California inquiry committee concluded that Mexican-American children are placed in special or remedial classes "solely on their ability to function in what is a foreign language."

The Mexican-American community, increasingly politically active, has challenged the authority of the school to remain monolingual and monocultural. It has rejected the validity of assimilation, calling for genuinely culturally expressive education. It wants a bilingual-bicultural school that will enable Chicano children to compete on equal terms with Anglo children. It is disgusted with the school's persistent ignorance of Chicano life and culture. Thus it not only wants a relevant bilingual curriculum but a say in the decision-making process. The demand for participation and relevance is the Chicano's challenge to the traditional single-standard, middle-class conception of the authority of school and teacher.

BILINGUAL EDUCATION[30]

Congress passed the Bilingual Education Act in 1968 to provide for the language needs of pupils whose first language is not English. Spanish-speaking children, especially Mexican-Americans and Puerto Ricans, have been the primary beneficiaries of this legislation. The act provides for teacher aides, counselors, pre-service training for teachers, early childhood education, reinstatement and retention programs for dropouts, and vocational training programs. The programs and services are oriented to instructing the non-English-speaking (or limited-English-speaking) youngster in his first language while introducing him to English as a foreign language. The instruction in English is gradually increased until English becomes the language of instruction. Spanish continues, however, to be spoken.

The Bilingual Education Act is also concerned with the culture and history of the Mexican-American's language. For example, the Mexican-American child studies Mexican history and culture in order to understand his people's ancestral culture. He also studies the role of the Spanish-speaking in the American Southwest. These studies enhance the development of group pride and a positive self-identity. The Mexican-American child benefits greatly from studying characters that are believable and a history that relates directly to him in the language he understands best.

The rhetoric and professed goals of bilingual-bicultural education unfortunately seldom are converted into substance in day-to-day programs. For example, the Education Professions Development Act provides for the training of teachers in bilingual-bicultural education, but few Mexican-American teachers have been selected. Projects such as Head Start are still premised upon the preparation of learners for an English curriculum. The token number of programs with a genuine bilingual component often use curricula that make more sense to the suburban white than the disadvantaged Chicano. The standard practice is to utilize Anglo-American materials translated directly into Spanish.

Chicano militants feel that the professionals cannot meet their needs. They have seen too much failure and hypocrisy to believe in the present educational system. They want to create and administer their own programs, such as Mexican-American studies programs. They have founded such programs in many schools in Texas, Colorado, New Mexico, California, and Arizona. The main force behind these programs has been Mexican-American political activism, or Brown Power. For example, the National Council for Chicano Studies and the National Council for Mexican-American Education are two major organizations that have focused on improving the educational condition of the Mexican-American community.

Teachers must learn to collaborate with the Chicano community if they are to play any role at all in the Mexican-American educational renaissance. The Chicanos will no longer tolerate the teacher enjoying the exclusive prerogative to define their education, but they are not so bitter and uncompromising that they cannot or will not cooperate with professional efforts that respect their culture and language.

MEETING THE CHICANO HALFWAY[31]

The new teacher must begin to fully appreciate that the truly educated person speaks more than one language. He is also bicultural or multicultural. In these respects, the Mexican-American learner is particularly advantaged. He, like the educated strata of Europe who speak French, English, and German, is a product of more than one culture, a Spanish-speaking and an English-speaking one. Some Chicanos are also heavily influenced by Indian culture. Certainly, the Mexican-American's command of his languages is often imperfect, but he is an important precedent for a genuine bilingualism and biculturalism in American society. The creative teacher can involve Chicano children in the curriculum to induce monolingual English-speaking children to learn Spanish. And, of course, the best way to do this is to require assignments and instruct learners in both languages.

Teachers and administrators serving in schools with substantial Mexican-American enrollments should be able to speak Spanish. A second-best alternative is to employ aides who can converse with pupils and parents. Communications intended for parents, such as report cards and bulletins, should be printed in both English and Spanish. The Parent-Teacher Association should direct someone to translate for Mexican-American parents during meetings or organize a Spanish-speaking subsection. The PTA meetings may even serve as a means for parents to become bilingual.

Every effort should be made to create genuinely bilingual schools. This means that parents should be bilingual in order to prepare their children properly before the formal school experience and that both Spanish and English should be taught at the elementary level. The most important change, however, should be a value transformation in the schools. The new ethos should be that the Chicano's culture and language are legitimate and worthwhile in and of themselves.

THE MIGRANT [32]

A substantial number of Chicano and black, and a few Indian youngsters are children of migrant parents who travel the country harvesting crops. These youngsters are especially disadvantaged because they are mobile, a situation that presents very serious educational problems. Their mobility precludes even the semblance of equality of educational opportunity. They usually reside with their parents in a state such as Texas, California, or Florida about six months of the year. During the harvest season they accompany the family to such states as New York, Washington, Oregon, Tennessee, and Michigan. Large states such as New York and Washington may employ as many as 60,000 workers during a harvest. The Department of Labor estimates the migrant agricultural work force at over 1.5 million. This estimate does not include, however, the children less than sixteen years of age who work in the harvests.

The school must plan its program for the migrant child on the basis of a maximum six-month period involving late entries and early withdrawals. This interval usually extends from mid-October through April. The school can also establish special summer programs to provide instruction for children who are too young to work in the fields.

About three-fourths of the migrant work force is composed of Mexican-Americans. The primary states of residence for these laborers are New Mexico, Arizona, California, and Texas. Recently, however, an increasing number of Mexican-American migrant workers have been locating in Arkansas, Alabama, Colorado, and Florida. The other major category of migrants is the American Negro whose residence is most often in the South. Both the blacks and Mexican-Americans follow distinctive migratory patterns throughout the United States, harvesting crops in various regions as they ripen.

The states singly cannot deal adequately with the problems of the migrant child. Only a national approach is sufficient to deal adequately with the educational dislocations caused by interstate mobility. The states must coordinate their programs for the migrant, and this coordination has begun. A common records transfer form has been developed for migrant children. A computerized Uniform Migrant Student Record Transfer System is now being established on a national scale. Title I of the Elementary and Secondary Education Act was amended in November 1966 (Public Law 89-750) to include the children of migrant laborers. Most eligible states have submitted proposals for migrant education programs. Forty-four states have been involved in program development to date. All fifty states are using a common record form and are building teletype installations to expedite the transfer of critical data relating to migrant children. The central data bank is located in Little Rock, Arkansas, and specific information can be dispatched to an authorized school official within hours. A complete written record is forwarded by mail within twenty-four hours. Texas has even initiated interstate cooperation by exchanging teachers with states that receive Texas-based migrant children. Other states are now following suit.

A NEW ERA[33]

The Indians, the blacks, and the Chicanos have all challenged our society's social institutions. The institution they know best, and that is most crucial for them, is the school. The civil rights movement, moving from black to brown to red defiance of the school's authority, has compelled a reconsideration of the old ways and values and stimulated reform movements. The degree to which the school eventually reforms will be a measure of the vitality and equality of our educational institutions and culture. The teacher, caught up in the historical currents, must not only adapt; he must catalyze changes that make the school a more culturally expressive, aesthetic, and just enterprise. In so doing, he will help renew the school in a society that desperately needs to examine its own values, recognizing alternate values and forms of learning. The alternatives must encompass Indian, black, and Chicano cultures, languages, and life styles.

NOTES

[1]Wilfred C. Wasson, "Hindrances to Indian Education," *Educational Leadership*, 28, no. 3 (December 1970), 278–280.

[2]Susan Boyer, "Blazing a New Trail," *Saturday Review*, 16 January 1971, p. 53.

[3]G. Louis Heath, "The Life and Education of the American Indian," *Illinois Quarterly*, 33, no. 3 (February 1971), 31–32. (Published in edited

form by permission.) See also G. Louis Heath, "No Rock Is An Island," *Phi Delta Kappan* (March 1971); " 'Red Power' and Indian Education" and "Toward Culturally-Expressive Education For Indians," *Interracial Review* (Spring 1971).

[4] Heath, "Life and Education," p. 32.
[5] *Ibid.*, pp. 33–34.
[6] Wasson, *op. cit.*, p. 280.
[7] This section has been adapted from G. Louis Heath, "Toward Educational Pluralism For Blacks," *Interracial Review* (Winter 1971-72). (Published by permission.)
[8] Paulo Freire has coined the term "conscientization" to refer to the process of becoming aware of the limiting, coercive elements in one's social condition. He concludes that "The fundamental role of those committed to cultural action for conscientization is not properly speaking to fabricate the liberating idea, but to invite the people to grasp with their minds the truth of their reality." Paulo Freire, "Cultural Action and Conscientization," *Harvard Educational Review*, 40, no. 3 (August 1970), 473.
[9] Thomas Green argues that the community control debate is a logical product of the fact that the schools are both crucial for a black child's success and an incredible failure at educating the child. See Thomas F. Green, "Schools and Communities: A Look Forward," *Harvard Educational Review*, 39, no. 2 (Spring 1969), 221–252, esp. p. 230.
[10] See Aaron V. Cicourel and John I. Kitsuse, *The Educational Decision-Makers* (Indianapolis: Bobbs-Merrill, 1963).
[11] See, for example, Patricia Cayo Sexton, *The American School* (Englewood Cliffs, N.J.: Prentice-Hall, 1967), p. 51: "There is, in fact, an absence of evidence that the most able in performance of jobs or other real-life tasks are selected or produced by the standards set and training offered by higher education. Employers often hire from among the degree elite because of the prestige rather than the superior training or job performance skill attached to the degree."
[12] See Timothy S. Healy, "The Challenge of Open Admissions: Will Everyman Destroy the University?," *Saturday Review*, 20 December 1969, pp. 54–56, 67–69.
[13] The entire set of data on the New York schools presented here was seized in April 1968 by the Columbia University Students for a Democratic Society from the records of the New York City Board of Education through the office of the Reverend Milton Galamison, at the time a member of the board.
[14] Michael Harrington, *Toward a Democratic Left* (New York: Penguin Books, 1969), pp. 58–59.
[15] See Larry Cuban, "Teacher and Community," *Harvard Educational Review*, 39, no. 2 (Spring 1969), 253–272. Cuban argues that the teacher, in order to be confident and effective, must participate in the community. In fact, the community and the public school system should share the responsibility for the training of educational professionals with the university.

[16]*Ibid.*, p. 61.

[17]*Ibid.*, p. 59.

[18]James B. Conant, *Slums and Suburbs*, New York, McGraw-Hill, 1961.

[19]Wallace Terry II, "Black GIs—Bringing the War Home," *San Francisco Chronicle*, 30 June 1972, p. 13.

[20]Wallace Terry II spent more than two years in Vietnam as a correspondent for *Time* magazine. He interviewed 833 black and white servicemen regarding their racial attitudes as part of a private survey. He administered a 109-item inventory schedule to each serviceman. Terry's conclusions are based on 2500 scientifically comprised tables derived from the serviceman's replies by the Harvard Computer Center.

[21]Burton R. Clark, "The 'Cooling-Out' Function in Higher Education," *American Journal of Sociology*, 65 (May 1960), p. 576: "In summary, the cooling-out process in higher education is one whereby systematic discrepancy between aspiration and avenue is covered over and stress between the individual and the system is minimized. The provision of readily available alternative achievements in itself is an important device for alleviating the stress consequent on failure and so preventing anomic and deviant behavior. The general result of cooling-out processes is that society can continue to encourage maximum effort without major disturbance from unfulfilled promises and expectations. . . ."

[22]Harrington, *op. cit.*, pp. 70–71.

[23]For a discussion of blacks' participation in the international revolution of expectations in specific contexts, see G. Louis Heath, "Corrupt East St. Louis: Laboratory For Black Revolution," *The Progressive*, October 1970, pp. 24–27, and "Ghost Town Vigilantes: The Racial Pallor of Cairo," *The Nation*, 22 December 1969, pp. 692–695.

[24]See Leonard J. Fein, "The Limits of Liberalism," *Saturday Review*, 20 June 1970, pp. 83–85, 95–96. Fein discusses how the movement toward community control is a rejection of the "melting pot," the liberals' crucible for the assimilation of all groups into a basically secular, homogeneous, centralized society.

[25]Ivan Illich offers a radical proposal for the "de-schooling" of society in favor of self-educating, self-authenticating inquiry into problems of vital concern to learners. See his "Why We Must Abolish Schooling," *The New York Review of Books*, 15, no. 1 (July 2, 1970), 9–15, "The False Ideology of Schooling," *Saturday Review*, 17 October 1970, pp. 56–58, 68–72, and *Deschooling Society*, New York, Harper and Row, 1970. For a free copy of *Alternatives in Education*, the program Mr. Illich proposes, write CIDOC, APDO 479, Cuernavaca, Mor, Mexico.

[26]See Eliezer Krumbein, "Why Independent Schools?," Chicago Circle, University of Illinois, 1970. (8 pp., mimeo.)

[27]See David C. Epperson, "University Faculty And Cultural Pluralism: An Alternative To Traditional Myth-Making Rituals," Northwestern University, Center for Urban Affairs. (Draft 11/11/70, 20 pp., mimeo.) Epperson has developed a paradigm for inquiry-oriented learning expe-

riences within a system predicated on equal educational credits (vouchers). His scheme financially liberates learners to select their own learning experiences on the basis of interest alone, contracting with other learners to participate in cooperative inquiry. The learners, including the "master learners" (previously known as "teachers" in the Epperson model), coordinate the learning agenda as partners and evaluate it according to the quality of the total experience, not individual performance. The authority for the educational process resides in the learner.

[28]"Study Points To 'Isolation' For Mexican-Americans," *Nation's Schools*, 86, no. 3 (September 1970), 30–31.

[29]Philip D. Ortego, "Schools for Mexican-Americans: Between Two Cultures," *Saturday Review*, 17 April 1970, pp. 62–64, 80–81.

[30]*Ibid.*, pp. 80–81.

[31]Jack Forbes, "La Raza Brings Much To The School," *CTA Journal*, 65, no. 4 (October 1969), 15–17.

[32]Vidal A. Rivera, "The Forgotten Ones: Children of Migrants," *The National Elementary Principal*, 50, no. 2 (November 1970), 41–44. For another discussion of the problems of the migrant, see G. Louis Heath, "Cesar Chavez and the United Farm Workers Organizing Committee," *Interracial Review* (Summer 1971).

[33]For a thorough discussion of the new era in American race relations, see G. Louis Heath, *Red, Brown, and Black Demands for Better Education* (Philadelphia: Westminster, 1972).

Index

Accountability, 8, 60–67, 192
  charter of, 67
  conditions for, 62–63
  definition of, 59
  performance contracting, 64–67
  professional view of, 61–62
  two types, 63–64
Affective domain, 133
Affective Education Project, 134
Air Pollution Control Association, 123
Alter-ego, 132
Alcohol, 163
Allen, Dwight, 30
Alternative forms of education
  abolition of compulsory education, 92
  cooperative inquiry, 93–96
  family development center, 89–90
  free schools, 78–80
  John Dewey High model, 91–92
  open education, 82–87
  semi-residential schools, 89
  vocational counseling and work-study, 88–89
  within existing schools, 80–82
American Association of School Administrators, 46
American Federation of Teachers, 8, 23, 41, 43, 51, 54, 61
American High School Today, 40
American Medical Association, 156
Amphetamines, 159, 160, 161, 163
Ashbaugh, Carl, 107–109
Authority, 9, 15, 20, 29, 35, 38, 44, 46, 49, 56, 69, 71, 72, 76, 99, 185, 186, 189, 190, 193, 195, 196, 199

Barbiturates, 161, 163
Bay Area Radical Teachers Organizing Committee, 97
Benson, Charles S., 54

Berkeley, California, 28, 29, 80, 106, 109
Beverly Hills, 75
Bilingual Education Act, 196
Bitzer, D. L., 174
Black arts, 8
Black Hessian, 188
Black lounges, 105
Black Panther curriculum, 191
Black power, 105
Black studies, 105
Blacks, 4, 186–193
   attitudes of black GIs, 188
   authentic black education, 190–193
   community control, 186
   employment conditions, 189–190
   independent schools, 191–192
   significance of vouchers, 192–193
   tracking, 187
Blind milling, 128
Borton, Terry, 134
Boston School Committee, 79
Brainstorming, 131
Brightman, Lehman, 179
Bristol Township, Pennsylvania, 137
Bronx High School of Science, 187
Brooklyn College, 92
Brown, George I., 133
Brown Power, 197
Brown's Mills, New Jersey, 116
Bruner, Jerome, 79
Bureau of Indian Affairs, 183, 185

California Instructional Aide Act, 33–34
California State Board of Education, 30, 195
Carnegie Unit System, 91
Carson, Rachel, 114
Center for the Advanced Study of Educational Administration, 133
Center for Urban Education, 114
Charles F. Kettering Foundation, 96
Chicano studies, 105
Chicanos. *See* Mexican-Americans
Christian Crusade, 143
Clark, Kenneth B., 67
Cogen, Charles, 52
Cold Springs Harbor, New York, 106–107
Coleman Report, 9, 60, 71, 72, 106
Collective negotiation impasse procedures, 46–52
   advisory arbitration, 50
   binding arbitration, 49
   fact finding, 49
   mediation, 49
Common Cause, 7
Community control movement, 1, 5, 6, 10, 18
   clash of teachers and minorities, 4
   history of abuse, 2, 3
   politicization of schools, 6
   school councils, 6
   threat to teacher professionalism, 4, 5
Community planning, 13, 16–18
Community relations
   city as classroom, 13–18
   decentralization, 3–5, 11–12
   educational parks, 13, 16–17
   integration, 12–13
Compensatory education, 1, 4, 195

Index

Complex differentiation, 31–33
  Wayne County, Michigan, 31–32
Conant, James B., 40, 188
Confrontations, 134–135
Conservation and Environmental Science Center, 116
Conservation Foundation, 116
Contracts, 53–54
Correlated curricula, 114
Crisis in the Classroom, 96
Cross-aged learning, 21
Cross-cultural learning, 21, 83
Cunningham, Luvern, 89

Decentralization, 10
  black anti-semitism, 4
  demonstration districts, 4
  history of, 3–4
  homogeneous constituency, 11
  Intermediate School, 4, 201
  Jewish teachers, 4
  Ocean Hill-Brownsville, 4
  problems of, 4–5, 11–12
  Two Bridges, 4
  ultimate meaning of, 7–8
Demographical facts, 159
Desegregation. *See* Integration
Detroit, Michigan, 120–121
Differentiated staffing, 30–33
  career ladder, 30
  definition of, 30
  Temple City model, 30–31
Divorce, 152
Drake, Gordon, 144
Drug Abuse Education Act, 155
Drug Cadre, 159
Drug education
  curriculum, 162–164
  facts about drugs, 159–160
  Hope House model of drug treatment, 160–161
  in-service programs, 155
  Roosevelt High School drug program, 156–157
  smoking information program, 158
  symptoms of drug use, 161–162
"Drug Expo '70," 156
Drugs of Abuse, 156
Dubos, René, 114
Dyads, 129

East Palo Alto, 75
East St. Louis, 86
East Technical High School, 88
Ecology education
  benefits of, 117–118
  curricula, 113–114
  environmental survey, 123–125
  models of, 119–123
  objectives and programs, 112–113
  themes for the classroom, 112
Education Professions Development Act, 21, 27, 155, 196
Educational Development Center, 84
Educational federalism, 8, 11
Educational parks, 13, 16–17
Educational Voucher Authority, 68–69
Edvance Combined Motivation Education Systems, 96
Elementary and Secondary Education Act, 21, 27, 32, 116, 133, 199
Elyria, Ohio, 121–122
Epidemiological facts, 159
Equality of Educational Opportunity. See Coleman Report
Establishment drugs, 164

Evanston, Illinois, 135–136

Fact Sheets, 156
Fantini, Mario, 78, 96
First Amendment, 45, 50, 74, 103
Ford Foundation, 96
Fourteenth Amendment, 45, 50, 70, 75
Friedman, Milton, 64
Fund for the Advancement of Education, 133

Gary, Indiana, 167
Good-faith bargaining, 48
Goodman, Paul, 92
Greeley, Colorado, 27
Grievance procedures, 50
Group fantasy, 130

Hallucinogens, 159
Harlem, 186
Harlem Preparatory School, 80
Hartford, Connecticut, 29–30
Harvard Center for Law and Education, 179
Havighurst, Robert J., 10, 182
Head Start, 21, 31, 195–196
Heath, G. Louis, 199–202
Heroin, 154, 159
Hillsdale County, Michigan, 148
Homosexuality, 151–152
Human Development Training Institute, 134
Human Relations Education Project, 133

Illich, Ivan, 92
Imitation, 129
Imperialism, 105
Independent schools, 191–192
Indiana University psychology department, 26

Indian wrestling, 129
Indians
  Bureau of Indian Affairs, 183, 185
  challenge of educating Indian learners, 184–185
  involvement in educational decision-making, 183–184
  learning problems, 180–183
  mental genocide, 179–180
Indirect aid to schools, 74–75
Industrial Union Department, 42
Inequality in Education, 179
Inquiry House, 87
Institute for the Development of Educational Activities, 96, 133
Institute of Psychoanalysis, 137
Integration, 5–6, 12–13, 18
  busing, 12
  dispersal of low-income housing, 12–13
  open enrollment plans, 12

Jencks Commission report, 72
John Birch Society, 143
John Dewey High School, 91–92
Joy, 128

Kennard Junior High School, 88
Kohl, Herbert, 80–82

Lesbianism, 151–152
Lewis, David C., 162
Little Rock, Arkansas, 199
Los Angeles Police Department, 157
Los Angeles school district, 107
LSD, 155, 161

McLuhan, Marshall, 16–17
Marathons, 134–135

Marijuana, 155, 159–160
Martin Luther King memorial, 105
Maslow, Abraham, 130
Media
  computer-assisted instruction, 172–174
  dial access, 171–172
  media specialist, 168
  social implications, 176
  television, 175–176
Metropolitan Reading Readiness Test, 26
Mexican-Americans, 76
  bilingual education, 196–197
  culturally-irrelevant education, 194–196
  demand for bilingual-bicultural schools, 195–196
  findings of 1970 U.S. Civil Rights Commission, 193–194
  reforming the school, 197–198
Mexican history, 8
Miami, Florida, 106
Michigan Cancer Foundation, 158
Migrant children, 198–199
Mobilization for Youth, 27
Modules, 91
Moreno, J. L., 132

National Advisory Commission on Educational Technology and Society, 176
National Audubon Society, 116
National Commission on Resources for Youth, 27
National Council for Chicano Studies, 197
National Council for Mexican-American Education, 197
National Defense Education Act, 40
National Education Association, 23, 41, 43, 54, 61–62, 123
National Environmental Education Development, 115–116, 164
National Environmental Study Areas, 114
National School Boards Association, 46
National Science Foundation, 113
National Study of American Indian Education, 182
National teacher strike, 55–56
National Wildlife Federation, 116
Native American studies, 105. *See also* Indians
Natural Beauty Program, 120
Navajos, 183
New School for Children, 79
New Schools Exchange, 97
New Trier Township, Illinois, 175–176
New York Board of Education, 27, 42
New York City, 9, 51, 61, 116, 154, 160, 189
New York State Narcotics Addiction Control Commission, 160
Newton, Massachusetts, 84
Northfield, Illinois, 106

Ocean Hill-Brownsville, 61
Ohio State University, 89
Oil depletion allowance, 55
Ombudsman, 109
Open attendance rule, 18
Open Court Publishing Company, 64
Open Door project, 84
Open education, 82–87
Other Ways program, 80–82

Paraprofessionals, 25–26
Parent-Teacher Association, 21, 121, 197
Parkway Program, Philadelphia, 13–15
Pasadena, California, 75
Philadelphia school district, 86–87
Piaget, Jean, 79, 82, 85
Planning for Change, 116
Police brutality, 105
President's Automation Commission, 188
Professional negotiations, 43
Project Concern, 29–30
Psychedelics, 161
Psychodrama, 132
Psychosis, 159
Puerto Ricans, 4, 27, 155, 187, 197

Rebellion of students
 administrative view, 104
 Ashbaugh model for dealing with, 107–109
 consultative councils, 101
 findings of Harris Poll, 101–102
 Iowa court decision, 103–104
 National Association of Secondary School Principals study, 104–105
 reasonable student demand, 101–102
 six-point program for, 99–101
 types of school responses, 106–107
Recognition
 exclusive, 46
 multiple, 47–48
 proportional, 47

Red, Brown, and Black Demands for Better Education, 202
Responsibility, 11, 140–141
Rogers, Carl, 132
Role playing, 131
Role reversal, 132
"Roll and Rock," 130
Rose, Stephen T., 88
Rough Rock Demonstration School, 183

San Bernardino, California, 119
San Mateo, California, 75
Sanctions, 52
Santa Monica, California, 89
Schutz, William, 128, 130–131
Science Curriculum Improvement Study, 113
Selden, David, 8, 51–53
Semantic differential, 133
Senate Manpower Subcommittee, 188
Sensitivity education
 affective curriculum, 132–133
 applications of, 137
 classroom use, 132–134
 dangers of, 137–138
 establishing programs, 139–140
 group activities, 128–132, 134
Serrano v. *Priest*, 75–76
Sesame Street, 175
Sex education
 anti-sex education groups, 144
 attitudes of Texans, 150–151
 dangers of not offering programs, 144–145
 new sexual values, 151–152
 rural sex education, 148–149
 teacher attitudes, 146
 training teachers for VD education, 146–148

Sex education (*Continued*)
  two sex education programs, 145
  U.S. sex attitudes compared to Swedish, 145
Sexton, Patricia, 69
Silberman, Charles, 96
Silent Spring, 114
Simsbury, Connecticut, 29–30
Skokie, Illinois, 148–149
So Human an Animal, 114
Sovereignty, 44
Sputnik I, 40
Stimulants, 159
Storefront schools, 79
Street academies, 80
Strike, 5, 50–52
Study of People program, 149
Supplementary Teaching Assistance in Reading, 27
Supreme Court ruling on aid to private schools, 74
Swahili, 105
Synanon House, 160
System Development Corporation, 89

Talent Awareness Training programs, 137
Teacher aides
  benefits of, 34–35
  Berkeley, California program, 28–29
  California Instructional Aide Act, 33–34
  differentiated staffing, 30–33
  financing of, 20–21
  impact of, 26–27
  paraprofessionals, 20–21
  pre-service programs, 24–25
  recruitment, 26
  relation to community, 21–22, 28–30
  selection of, 23–24
  subprofessionals, 20–22
Teacher organizations
  alternatives to strike, 52–53
  changing patterns of power, 44–45
  collective negotiations, 46–50
  contracts, 53–54
  history of, 42–43
  impact of, 54–55
  psychological forces, 39–41
  seeking a role model, 41–42
  social and economic forces, 37–39
  strike, 50–52
Teachers Drop-Out Center, 97
Templeton Elementary School, 121
Tinker court decision, 103–104
Tobacco, 158, 163
Torrance, California, 167
Traffic fatalities, 164
Trump, Lloyd J., 31

Uniform Migrant Student Record Transfer System, 199
United Federation of Teachers, 42–43, 52
University of California at Berkeley, 81, 113
University of Chicago, 10, 64
U.S. Civil Rights Commission, 193
U.S. Forest Service, 119
U.S. Office of Education, 155

Veterans Administration Hospital, 158

Vietnam, 104–106
Vocational Information Program, 88–89
Vocations for Social Change, 97
Vouchers
  benefits of, 71–74
  California Supreme Court decision, 75–76
  dangers of, 70–71
  definition of, 59–60
  equalization of educational resources, 69–70
  legality of, 74–75
  operation of, 67–69

Wagner Act, 44
Watts, 186
Wayne County, Michigan, 27
Weber, Lillian, 84
Weinstein, Gerald, 96
Western Behavioral Sciences Institute, 133
Westminster Press, 202
White racism, 105
Williams, Rosemary, 84
Winnetka, Illinois, 106, 109
Women's Liberation, 151

Youth-Tutor-Youth Centers, 27